Does My Child Need Me to Lead or to Follow?

A Radically Simple Way to Parent Children

FROM INFANCY THROUGH AGE 6

CLAUDIA SCHWARZLMÜLLER

Translated by Elisabeth Lauffer

THE EXPERIMENT

NEW YORK

DOES MY CHILD NEED ME TO LEAD OR TO FOLLOW?: *A Radically Simple Way to Parent Children from Infancy Through Age 6*
Copyright © 2024 by Claudia Schwarzlmüller
Translation copyright © 2026 by Elisabeth Lauffer

Originally published in Germany as *Die Kinderdolmetscherin* by S. Fischer Verlag in 2024. First published in English in North America by The Experiment, LLC, in 2026.

All rights reserved. Except for brief passages quoted in newspaper, magazine, radio, television, or online reviews, no portion of this book may be reproduced, distributed, or transmitted in any form or by any means, electronic or mechanical, including photocopying, recording, or information storage or retrieval system, without the prior written permission of the publisher.

The Experiment, LLC
220 East 23rd Street, Suite 600
New York, NY 10010-4658
theexperimentpublishing.com

THE EXPERIMENT and its colophon are registered trademarks of The Experiment, LLC. Many of the designations used by manufacturers and sellers to distinguish their products are claimed as trademarks. Where those designations appear in this book and The Experiment was aware of a trademark claim, the designations have been capitalized.

Neither the author nor the publisher is engaged in rendering professional advice or services to individual readers and their children or relatives. The ideas, procedures, and suggestions in this book are not intended as a substitute for consulting a physician. All matters regarding health require medical supervision. Neither the author nor the publisher shall be liable or responsible for any loss, injury, or damage allegedly arising from any information or suggestion in this book. The opinions expressed in this book represent the personal views of the author and not of the publisher.

The Experiment's books are available at special discounts when purchased in bulk for premiums and sales promotions as well as for fundraising or educational use. For details, contact us at info@theexperimentpublishing.com.

Library of Congress Cataloging-in-Publication Data available upon request

ISBN 979-8-89303-106-5
Ebook ISBN 979-8-89303-107-2

Cover and text design by Beth Bugler
Cover photograph Lightfield Studios/Adobe Stock

Manufactured in the United States of America

First printing April 2026
10 9 8 7 6 5 4 3 2 1

The authorized representative in the EU for product safety and compliance is Easy Access System Europe, Mustamäe tee 50, 10621 Tallinn, Estonia. easproject.com | gpsr.requests@easproject.com.

Contents

Introduction   1
   Dear Reader, Meet Alex   3
   The Structure of This Book   4

Leading and Following   7
   Interaction = Parenting + Fun   7
   Moments of Following: You Follow Your Child   11
   Moments of Leading: You Lead Your Child   13
   Work-Life Balance for Babies and Toddlers   17
   Summary   18

PART 1 • Your Baby

1 Development from 0–6 Months   25
   Thinking and Play   25
   Feelings and Relationships   25
   Movement   29
   Speech   35
   Nursing   39
   Sleep   43
   At a Glance: 0–6 Months   46

2 Development from 6–12 Months   48
   Thinking and Play   48
   Feelings and Relationships   53
   Movement   58
   Speech   61

Sleep	62
At a Glance: 6–12 Months	63
What to Know in Year One	64
Moments of Leading in Babies	64
Moments of Following in Babies	70
Bonus: Sleep in Babies and Toddlers	**74**

PART 2 • Your Toddler

3 Development from 12–18 Months — 81
- Thinking and Play — 81
- Feelings and Relationships — 91
- Movement — 95
- Speech — 97
- At a Glance: 12–18 Months — 98

4 Development from 18–24 Months — 99
- Thinking and Play — 99
- Feelings and Relationships — 106
- Movement — 110
- Speech — 111
- At a Glance: 18–24 Months — 112
- What to Know About 1-Year-Olds — 113
- Moments of Leading in 1-Year-Olds — 114
- Moments of Following in 1-Year-Olds — 120

Bonus: Autonomy and Boundaries — 126

PART 3 • From Toddler to Preschooler

5 Development at Age 2 — 139
- Thinking and Play — 149
- Feelings and Relationships — 149
- Movement — 152
- Speech — 153
- At a Glance: 2-Year-Olds — 154

6 Development at Age 3 — 157
- Thinking and Play — 157

Feelings and Relationships	165
Movement	170
Speech	171
At a Glance: 3-Year-Olds	172
What to Know About 2- and 3-Year-Olds	173
Moments of Leading in 2- and 3-Year-Olds	173
Moments of Following in 2- and 3-Year-Olds	178
Bonus: Feelings and Tantrums	**182**

PART 4 • From Preschooler to Kindergartener to First Grader

7	**Development at Age 4**	195
	Thinking and Play	195
	Feelings and Relationships	203
	Movement	209
	Speech	209
	At a Glance: 4-Year-Olds	211
8	**Development at Ages 5 and 6**	212
	Thinking and Play	212
	Feelings and Relationships	224
	Competition	225
	Movement	226
	Speech	227
	At a Glance: 5- and 6-Year-Olds	228
	What to Know About 4- to 6-Year-Olds	229
	Moments of Leading in 4- to 6-Year-Olds	229
	Should I Punish My Child?	233
	Moments of Following in 4- to 6-Year-Olds	235

What to Look Forward To	241
Acknowledgments	247
References	251
Further Reading	253
Index	255
About the Author	262

Quick References

Moments of Happiness: What Does Happiness Look Like with Kids?	19
Nursing: Far More Than Food	41
Carrying: Discovering the World from a Parent's Arms	59
Play Schemas: Actively Discovering the World	86
Thinking It Through: Working Together to Find Solutions	119
Soft Skills	149
Day Care: It Takes a Village	155
Theory of Conservation: An Amount Doesn't Change Between Containers	158
Play: Harder Than It Looks	168
Lying: Acquiring the Capacity to Fib	196
Attachment Play: How Your Child Solves Problems	207
Math: Laying the Groundwork in Everyday Situations	216
No Punishment: Teach Your Child How to Find Solutions	222
Listening: Understanding from the Inside Out	238

Does My Child Need Me to Lead or to Follow?

Introduction

I was sitting in a café recently when a mother came in with her daughter, who looked to be about eighteen months old. It was clear that all Mom wanted was a quiet moment to herself for a nice cup of coffee in a cozy setting. She sank heavily into one of the comfy armchairs.

Her daughter had something different in mind. She scanned the room excitedly, taking in all the details: The colorful ice cream menu on the counter caught her eye, as did the polished tabletops, and she listened intently to the loud hissing of the espresso machine.

The toddler observed her surroundings with her own set of objectives: What new discoveries awaited? How could this environment be put to use? Sitting still was a lost opportunity for development—and at her age, this was something she simply could not afford. There were countless developmental tasks and milestones to attain before it made any sense for her to sit quietly in a café.

All my life, I have been fascinated by the different ways in which adults and small children view the world. I am grateful for my decades of experience as a child psychologist, during which I encountered many children and their families in a wide range of circumstances. My two wonderful sons are grown. Mission Mom: accomplished. Now, after years of observation and study, I would like to act as something of an interpersonal interpreter, "translating" children's behaviors at various developmental stages into a language their grown-ups can understand. My intention is to foster deeper understanding and greater ease in life together.

For that reason, I chose a different approach for this book, one that sets it apart from other parenting guides. I walk through the various phases of early childhood development from the perspective of a child named Alex. We will join Alex's everyday adventures, from just a few days after birth to the first day of school. Along the way, Alex will encounter all the usual developmental stages and snags.

You will hopefully see your child, your family, and yourself in many of these scenarios. I will equip you to understand your child better and to know exactly what you can expect or ask for—and what you can't—at any given age, from infants to school-age kids. You will learn about the development of thinking and play, feelings and relationships, movement, and speech.

I hope this will help you experience many delightful moments with your child, because when it comes down to it, seeing your child through the many stages of development is a pretty playful process. And it's easier than you might think. In addition to sharing my knowledge of children, I wish to demystify the chaos of conflicting approaches to parenting. Did you know that, in any situation with children, there is only one question you need to ask? *Does my child need me to lead or to follow?* The answer will reliably steer you in the right direction. These are the two basic elements for interacting well with children, used by parents worldwide, often intuitively, without realizing it: "leading" and "following." These words promise to make your life a whole lot easier.

> As an "interpreter" of child behavior, I'm here to:
> - outline the developmental tasks your child faces at various ages, "translating" their experience
> - clear up the many misunderstandings between parents and children, giving you greater access to what your child is experiencing
> - help you find your bearings in the parenting jungle and

- provide concrete tools in the form of leading and following
- empower you to tune out the noise of external advice and build a foundation for making your own decisions—because parenting is not a fixed state, but one that emerges anew between you and your child every day
- shed light on the miraculous development that your child is undergoing, on their own, even without perfect parents
- create greater ease in your relationship with your child, allowing you to experience far less stress.

Dear Reader, Meet Alex

Who is the child you'll be getting to know in this book? In the first chapter, Alex is a baby boy; in the second chapter, Alex is a girl; in the third, a boy; and so on. Everything is based on true stories gathered from a wide range of children.

Alex is the world's only average child, because there isn't a real child who represents the average. Truly. Not a single one. So whatever Alex does should be seen as a benchmark and not an absolute truth about your own child. Feel free to check any parental baggage, like "I feel bad because we do XYZ differently in our family," at the door. If your kiddo does things their own way, that's great.

Development varies widely. For instance, many children will develop speech first, while movement falls by the wayside, then they'll suddenly make up for the delay and start scooting around. In certain cases, your child may be up to a year and a half ahead or behind in some developmental area and still be *perfectly on track*. Some kids display extreme behaviors in certain realms, others less so—or they'll skip stages altogether.

Another important point: Faster does not mean better! Give your child space to work toward a developmental milestone and wait patiently to see if it comes up *at some point* during the year in question.

But back to Alex: Not only is Alex average, so are Alex's parents. They are a regular couple I've named John and Julia. They experience the usual fears and challenges, some of which may be familiar to you. If partnership looks different for you, or you're in a queer relationship or single or any range of other living situations, I hope you can find your way in with John and Julia. You are unequivocally included.

As an "interpreter" of child behavior, I tried hard to write from the perspective of Alex's developmental phase and internal world. This is a pretty presumptuous thing to do, since we never *really* know what someone else is thinking or feeling.

The descriptions are specifically *not* about behavioral problems, but about completely normal development. I strive to represent the latest scientific findings, but cannot guarantee the odd error didn't sneak in. From the vast field of developmental psychology, I selected what I consider to be the most important practical points for understanding and interacting with children. The tips are yours to adapt as you please—you are the best authority on your own child.

This book may not, under any circumstances, be used as a diagnostic tool for children. If you're concerned about your child, please consult your pediatrician or other professionals, like those at your child's day care or school. Libraries, community centers, and state agencies can also provide advice on available resources.

The Structure of This Book

"Leading and Following," outlines the central idea of this book. It's key to your understanding, as everything builds on it. The rest of the book describes developmental stages at different ages. In each chapter:

- First, Alex's development in various areas is presented. What do thinking and play, emotions and relationships, movement and speech look like for Alex at this age?

- Then a brief summary is given ("At a Glance"). What's important for you to know about your child at this age? How can you best support your child?
- Finally, you'll learn how to implement concrete, age-appropriate practices in leading and following.

The Quick Reference sections dive a bit deeper. These are intended for parents who would like to learn more, and for people who work with children.

I've also included "Bonus" chapters, which cover topics that apply across multiple ages.

> ### A Shortcut for When You Need to Know *Now*
>
> Feeling pressed for time and just want to understand your child's current developmental stage? All you need to do is read:
>
> - "Leading and Following," for a foundation on the complementary concepts that form the foundations of this book
> - the chapter on your child's current age.
>
> "What to Know" sections are found at the end of each part. If you're looking for concrete advice on working with two-year-olds, you'll find it at the end of the part on three-year-olds: the two ages are covered in the same part (part 3).
>
> Overarching topics like emotions, sleep, or autonomy will also be discussed, but don't worry about remembering that—I'll remind you when the time comes.

I'd like to request a small leap of faith on your part, because as a psychologist, I consider your child's development as a whole. Whereas you might be anxious to find out when your child will learn to sit still, or how to break the binkie habit, I might only mention these things in passing, if at all. Why is that?

Temporary issues often make an impression on parents, and understandably so, but that impression is as fleeting as the issues, which come and go over the course of a child's development. If you have a one-year-old, it may be hard for you to remember the challenges you faced when your baby was six months old—they simply vanished. You will encounter many of these matters over the course of Alex's story.

I emphasize enduring developmental points that extend into adulthood over passing phases. It will take time (and perhaps some doing) to wean your two-year-old off their pacifier, but then you never have to think about it again, which is why I don't discuss it here. But ensuring that your two-year-old begins to develop soft skills like empathy, cooperation, problem-solving, and individual initiative? That will make a huge difference in their life, so it deserves our attention now.

I may end up addressing questions you didn't even know to ask—but whose answers you really should know.

In the sections regarding your child, I opted for gender-neutral language. The many approaches to this question seemed too complex for a book whose primary goal is to simplify things. This book is for everyone, period. That means you too.

And now: Have fun reading, discovering, and trying things out!

Leading and Following

Interaction = Parenting + Fun

It's interesting to see how much parents enjoy interacting with their kids, especially when there's no ulterior motive. When we stop using these interactions to accomplish specific goals, we gain access to a world most of us forgot. Children's positivity—their honesty, imagination, and love of discovery—captivates and inspires us.

But when we frame interactions as "teachable moments," or instances of "parenting" or "child-rearing," they immediately feel more demanding. There's something ponderous to the term "parenting," associated as it is with tremendous responsibility, not to mention hopes, fears, and goals.

Parenting is another form of daily interaction with children, minus the fun. We're so focused on some distant, nebulous outcome for our kids that we can sometimes miss the moment we're having with them right now.

In my opinion, many parenting concepts discourage you—the parent—from enjoying the time spent with your children and from building your life together, piece by piece.

On the one hand, conceptual frameworks offer a sense of security. They help us feel like we (finally) know what we're doing. It's understandable that parents would seek this kind of support in raising their kids. On the other hand, it can be a stressful approach: First, you have to learn the concept, then stick to it. If it doesn't work in a given situation or proves ill-suited to your family's needs, then that turns into yet another source of stress and dismay.

And what's it like from a child's perspective? Children respond poorly to concepts but positively to real humans. It's easy enough to relate: Imagine that your partner treats you according to a concept I'll call "Mishmash." In your presence, your partner eagerly tells people that they've been using the Mishmash Method on you. Books on Mishmash are strewn about the house, and when conflict arises—let's say your partner wishes you would take out the trash more often—they consult those books for guidance. They look at you like a puzzle in need of solving, then apply the ten guiding principles of Mishmash in their efforts to do so. You sit down to discuss the issue, and they open the conversation by gently saying, "Honey, I know how challenging it must be for you to handle garbage—because let's face it, your childhood was kind of garbage—but it has an impact on me when . . ."

Their voice changes as they try to be something they're not. The things they're saying don't sound like them at all—they defer to Mishmash in addressing your behavior, rather than drawing on what they know of you.

How would that make you feel? Like you were the problem? Or like you were your partner's project? Might you wish that your partner would simply act like a normal human being? And that they would respect you as a fellow human being, approaching difficult conversations without bringing an outside conceptual framework into the mix?

Might that be exactly what your child wants too?

That's why this book contains much more talk of "interaction" than of "parenting." By definition, interaction is exactly what I believe ideal parenting should be: mutual influence through the act of real contact and connection. As far as I'm concerned, you need just two things to achieve this.

Good Interaction Requires Knowledge

The first thing you need is knowledge of your child's development. What can and can't your child do at a certain age?

Your adult view of the world is different—a fact that leads to many misunderstandings. There are aspects of everyday life you could do with your eyes closed, but it will take years of learning for your child to gain the same familiarity.

Take grocery shopping, for example. Grocery shopping represents a handful of conscious steps in your mind: Get a cart, fill it with the items you need, get in line at the register, wait, pay, bag. You've learned to tune out everything around you for greater efficiency in completing the errand. Do you remember the last song playing in the background at the supermarket? Maybe, if the song triggered some memory—because only then does your brain allow the information to penetrate, and you start to hum along. Generally, external factors like background music are just a distraction, as you're focused on finishing the task at hand.

Things look completely different for your child, who notices details and whose brain has not matured enough to tune things out and prioritize discrete tasks. Shopping is a thrilling adventure with a cart—on wheels!—just asking to be climbed like a jungle gym. There are countless colors, fluorescent lighting, lots of smells, warmth as you pass the hot bar and a chill in the dairy section, enticing bright packaging, music, announcements over the PA, beeping sounds at the checkout, and other people to stare at.

When you take your child to the supermarket, these two realities collide. Whereas your child is stimulated by these external factors and wants this or that, all you want is to get your stuff and go. To make matters worse, your child rarely has a set task of their own, other than to be quiet and not act up. Based on their age, what can your child do here? What can we do to make the whole ordeal easier?

This book will give you a clear idea of what you can reasonably expect from your child at any given age, allowing you to work as a team.

Good Interaction Requires Confidence

The second thing you need is more confidence in *how* you behave toward your child, because nothing gets in the way of fun like anxiety and insecurity.

Questions constantly arise while interacting with your child: Am I doing this right? Should I set rules and stick to them, or respond on a case-by-case basis? When exactly should I do what I'm supposed to do? These questions have many different answers. Ideally, the answers exist outside a conceptual framework or someone's preconceived notion, otherwise it's easy to get lost in the torrent of prescribed parenting approaches.

After many years of practical experience, I discovered that when answering a question like "How should I act toward my kid?" it's best to look at life with children at the micro level, breaking interactions down into "social atoms," in order to make sense of their foundation. What's going on down there, anyway?

What do adults who are "great with kids" do automatically? What behaviors do you observe out in public or in yourself? Decades of video analysis revealed subtle details that every "successful" adult interaction with children had in common. This method is known as Marte Meo (Latin for "by one's own power").

Life with children boils down to just two approaches, for which Marte Meo uses the terms "leading" and "following."

No one invented these approaches—they can be observed around the world, because they reflect the natural, intuitive way people behave toward their children. Interaction always follows these two patterns. Let's take a closer look.

Moments of Following: You Follow Your Child

Moments of following occur during play and discovery. Your child leads during play, and it's your job to follow. Children are fundamentally impulsive and learn to translate impulse into action when they play. This mysterious process is powered by curiosity and a love of discovery. Something will grab your child's attention, and they simply have to investigate. There's nothing they won't try out on this thing, so over the years their play grows increasingly complex. All you have to do is provide them with basic opportunities for discovery and be present during those moments or narrate the process verbally. You're just following your child's needs and ideas, because they're better acquainted than you are with their own developmental path. Your child intuits what the next step should be, and which exercise to complete next for brain development. Just get out of the way, watch, verbalize what's happening, and do whatever your child wants you to do.

Your Child Leads You

Your child, just about two years old, is sitting on the floor. You're nearby, maybe folding socks. Your child was eager to help for a while, and even managed to match a few pairs, but it was short-lived, because they can't concentrate for very long at this age. They respond to an impulse to take a red building block out of the toy box. You look over, maybe smile, and warmly say, "Yes, a red block." Your child carefully places the block atop another. You say, "You're setting it on the green block." Then they take another block, and you say cheerfully, "Oh, now comes a blue block." That's it. Maybe you continue narrating what your child is doing or, if they become engrossed in play, you might stop talking and simply sit there, quiet but present.

So what happened here?

For several minutes, you showed your child that you're aware of them and that they are someone who has good ideas. They can hear it in your voice and see it in your friendly expression. This motivates them to develop more good ideas. You warmly and casually showed your child the "developmental direction" by calling out the things that were going well. This is much wiser than not saying anything during constructive play and only responding when they do something you don't want, like throwing the blocks around. You lovingly reinforced what they *should* be doing, and not what they *shouldn't* be doing. Very wise of you—it makes everything so much easier. And what a gift for your child, for you to acknowledge what they're doing, rather than their having to fight for your attention.

While you were at it, you promoted other skills as well, giving your child the words for what they were doing—something they'll need for self-awareness and language development. Your child now knows they're someone who can build something. In a brief span of time, they repeatedly heard the word "block," along with various colors, which came at the perfect moment, as their focus on the colorful blocks allowed them to absorb the information easily.

Your child shared a moment with you, in which you followed their impulses. You acknowledged them as a person. Wonderful! During these fleeting moments of following, you fostered self-confidence, personal initiative, language, creativity, and bonding—all in the time it took to fold the socks. Your child doesn't want any more than that. Yes, it is truly that simple.

This is a natural behavior, so you might discover you've been doing it throughout the day. That's the good news—you're already encouraging so much in your child and don't need to do anything else. It looks a little different with bigger kids, but we'll get to that later.

Moments of Leading: You Lead Your Child

Moments of leading occur in situations that have both a goal and an order of operations. You know the steps required to reach the goal, but your child still needs to learn them. These are things like getting dressed, personal hygiene, cooking, shopping, household chores—anything that needs to be done in a particular order or it wouldn't make sense. It's hard to put your shoes on first, then your pants—this needs to be done in the correct order.

The grocery shopping described earlier is an example of a situation with a goal: We need food, and it needs to get from the store to our refrigerator. How do we do that? Everyone needs to follow a clear order of operations for it to work. Paying first and then loading up your cart doesn't work—and if you've ever played at "going to the store" with a toddler, you know that it takes a long time for them to internalize the process. Your child needs you to lead here. The question is not which parenting style to channel (authoritarian, authoritative, needs-based) or which "tricks" to use. Instead, the question should always be: *What does your child need from you in order to work well together?*

Again, your child notices details but might not take in the big picture yet. Far too many intermediate steps are involved in grocery shopping for small children to grasp a single statement like "We're going shopping now."

It's your job to verbally break down the situation into bite-size morsels, so your child can participate. You say and model what should be done at that moment. You only go as far as naming the next step. As your child grows, you will intuitively expand the individual steps in response to their improved understanding.

You're like a tour guide, the only one who can see the big picture, who knows the itinerary and what has to happen to ensure everyone reaches the next destination. Every so often, you have to get your passengers back on track, but most important is that you help them find their bearings and feel secure about what needs to happen and when. You radiate confidence as their tour guide, because your inner voice is telling you, "I'm familiar with this situation. I know what has to happen. I know how to grocery shop."

You might be even more than a tour guide, at least for the first couple of years. Until about preschool age, your child sees you as someone who knows and can do *everything*. You get their shoes on every time. You warm them up when they're cold. You know how to magically turn things that come in a box into yummy food. Just act like you know what you're doing and that you have your child's life under control. In moments of leading, do not ask them what should happen next—at most, they can help decide trivial details.

Only then can your child follow you with ease, without ever having to take over. Do not allow a vacuum to arise while leading, otherwise they will have to fill it, which puts tremendous strain on those involved. When the person leading lacks a sense of the big picture, it's a challenge for everyone.

Whenever you're in a situation with a goal, exude the confidence of a tour guide. State what's about to happen, break the situation down into many small steps, and facilitate the transition from one step to the next.

For the first couple of years, this entails a lot of concrete action and modeling, as language is of lesser importance to very young children. You'll be able to lead better with language later on, but even then, your child won't do what you want without your modeling it first. You can't expect them to do something you won't do. The example you set is more powerful than anything else.

To recap: You take the lead in goal-oriented situations. You are the only one who can see the big picture, so you take charge. *How* you lead will depend on your child's age, as you gauge how much they should participate in decision-making, for instance. Clever leader that you are, you know how to include other people and what can be expected of them.

We'll examine that in greater detail in the chapters on development.

I've called these *moments* of following and *moments* of leading because they alternate, and can pass in an instant. Most situations will contain both leading and following, but with a distinct emphasis on one or the other.

Your Child Follows You

Imagine that you're dressing your child. If we take a Marte Meo approach and break this situation down into its "social atoms," here's how it looks:

1. First, you establish a warm connection with your child, because it's impossible to lead without connection. You do this with other people all the time—after spotting them, you look them in the face, assess the situation, and (ideally) smile.

2. Then, you clearly indicate the start of the interaction. Most people say "Okay" here. (You might try tallying how often you use the word every day!) These intuitive "okays" break the complexities of life into manageable portions for your child. It's a wise move. "Okay" signals to them that something is about to begin.

3. Then, you describe exactly what your hands are doing. That will give your child the exact information they need from you right now. Maybe you say, "Okay, I'm holding your shoe. Stick out your foot, please!" Your child extends their leg, which might take a minute, as they still process verbal cues very slowly. You put their shoe on and continue narrating whatever you do next. Since toddlers' attention spans are extremely short, yours might notice a shiny zipper and want to take a closer look. You sense intuitively that this is a moment of following and say, "Oh yeah, look at how shiny," and for a few seconds you study the zipper together. After this (very brief) moment of following, you redirect their attention to the task at hand and say, "Okay, now it's time for the other shoe. Look, I'm holding it out for you. Put your foot in—nice job!"

> 4. Each small task is completed with a quick acknowledgment, like "good," "nice job," "all done," "all right," or any other phrase you use to wrap things up—you might even use "Okay" again. Done. This is how you divide any moment of leading into finer details that your child can understand and put into action.

Observe yourself over the course of a day: You're likely leading and following automatically, because these are natural skills. But try doing them on purpose too, because even intuitive skills can go out the window when things get stressful. You have to create structure, otherwise your child will get lost in this exciting world full of impressions. You are in charge of this little world, helping your child to get their bearings and to feel safe.

On days when you do a lot of leading, your child will need some space after their capacity for cooperation is spent. If that moment coincides with a trip to the store or some other demand, it can be pretty rough going. It might even turn into a tantrum or meltdown. What your child urgently needs at that moment is the freedom to play on their own terms. Maybe they want to go outside or go home, to cuddle, recharge, and tend to their own needs for a spell.

Interestingly, toddlers can get really cranky on days when they do most of the leading, with few opportunities for following. It's hard for many adults to comprehend why their child is unhappy when they lovingly cater (if not bend over backward) to the child's wishes. Parents often feel disappointed and deem it ingratitude, when what was missing were moments of parental leading.

Children need to find their bearings and to feel safe. You are the missing partner in this social dance if you don't assume your role in moments of leading.

Work–Life Balance for Toddlers

Your child is searching for balance between moments of leading and moments of play, just like the rest of us. It's comparable to the work–life balance that we find in the adult world. These moments are just shorter for kids. You can work for three hours straight, then take a one-hour break. Then again, maybe not: If you studied yourself at the micro level, you would discover that after a period of intense focus, you'll often look out the window, let your mind wander, or "play" a little longer, say, with a trip to the coffee shop.

The younger your child is, the less closely they can follow your lead. Work–life balance for toddlers might mean that after cooperating for a few minutes (or even seconds), they switch to a moment of following, in which you watch them play, letting them recover and enjoy a nice interaction with you.

That's all there is to it. See how long your child is currently able to focus, and at what point they need to take a breather.

Whatever the interaction, these are the only tools you need: understanding your child's current developmental stage, and deciding whether you've got a moment of leading or following on your hands. If there's an objective, then you need to lead. Whenever that's the case, you narrate exactly what is happening, as it happens, in small chunks. And when it's your turn to follow, you get to enjoy your child's playful impulses. The social dance between you and your child is fun—you each get a chance to lead and to follow.

This foundation is important to your child's healthy development. Everything else is up to you and your family. There are no rules here, and no right or wrong ways.

Summary

At the heart of it, life with children comprises two moments: those of leading and those of following. Every situation determines its own course of action: In moments of leading, you lead. In moments of following, you follow.

Moments of leading occur in *all situations with a defined order of operations and a goal*. Activities like getting dressed, personal hygiene, shopping, arts and crafts (if making something specific), cooking, picking up, and household chores all have a goal and a series of steps to accomplish that goal.

Ask yourself: Do I have a goal in mind? If so, then your child needs you as their tour guide, clock, and coach. The question is never *whether* you're leading, but rather *how* to lead in an age-appropriate way. You're the only one who can see the big picture, so it's up to you to take charge.

In moments of leading, you exude the confidence of a tour guide and break the situation down into details your child can follow. In concrete terms, you do the following:

1. Establish a warm connection with your child—look at them.
2. Clearly mark the start of the task, maybe using the word "Okay."
3. Say exactly what your hands are doing or what your child should do.
4. Complete the interaction with a clear, friendly word to wrap things up.

Moments of following occur in *open-ended situations without any goal*, when your child is playing, discovering something new, or experiencing emotions. Follow them and keep your own impulses in check. You're just along for the ride, your loving presence communicating an appreciation for what they're doing, which allows them to develop on their own. With toddlers, you occasionally provide language for what they're doing, like, "Oh, you're using the green block."

Depending on your toddler's age, they might want you to play a role in the game. If they do, of course you might do so: What's important here is that your child continues to lead the game and follow their own mysterious developmental path. You are helping them build soft skills.

Leading and ***following*** are not mutually exclusive elements—some moments call for both at once. You and your child are partners on equal footing in the social dance known as interaction. Sometimes you lead, other times your child does.

Quick Reference—Moments of Happiness

What Does Happiness Look Like with Kids?

Before we launch into the chapters on development, here's the first "Quick Reference" to reflect on happiness with children. Most families just want to be happy, after all, but happiness often gets lost in the hustle and bustle of daily life. Maybe you'd like to draw your awareness back to feeling happy every now and then. Your child cannot make you happy—you have to find happiness together.

"Happiness" is a big word, and it's not possible to feel happy all the time. We contain all sorts of feelings, and happiness comes and goes like the rest of them. Let's refer to "moments of happiness" instead. Maybe the goal could be to recognize (or even deliberately create) moments of happiness in everyday life. When we seek out moments with this intention, we can recharge our own happiness.

Your child can help you in looking for tangible, everyday moments of happiness. This kind of happiness requires us to shift the level on which we're operating, because it's found in the details, in our senses, and in perception. If you stop trying to push your child to conform to the timelines, rules, and endless to-do lists of the adult world, they can teach you how to be happy.

Observe the way your child perceives the world. Look at the love and fascination on display as they study a beautiful beetle on a leaf. Or how they enjoy letting sand run through their fingers. Or the way they simply watch and perceive, plunging into the world of senses and giving in to the moment. Watch, feel, and listen closely.

Give in to the moment of happiness when holding your child, sensing their warmth and connection, maybe sniffing their head or neck, the best smell ever. Happiness is sensory.

The mind often gets in the way of happiness, as it's focused on goals or to-do lists. It wants the whole world cleaned up before it can allow itself to be happy.

In this respect, your child really can "make" you happy, if you let them help you rediscover the world. Make a point of seeking out such moments, pausing, and perceiving them fully. Shift the level on which you're operating and study the details like your child does. If you're stuck in your thoughts, do what you can to return to your body. This is how happiness happens. What do you see, smell, hear, or feel?

Look at your child. They're like a seismograph for quakes within the family. They'll show you exactly what's happening. If your child is often stressed, cranky, whiny, sad, or angry, it's because—aside from basic needs—they aren't experiencing enough moments of happiness. The message they're sending is, "Mom, Dad, and everyone else—we are perceiving far too little of life."

If you follow your child in this process, happiness can become enduring, with only occasional lapses. It's possible for many individual moments to weave together into a blanket of happiness, plush and secure, to wrap around you and your family.

One of the main tips for infancy:
"Say what your hands are doing."

PART 1

Your Baby

Please do not compare your child too closely with our "average" child, Alex. Development does not follow the law of averages. Your child is probably slower in one area and quicker in another. They might not display certain traits or behaviors, whereas others are highly pronounced—all of that is normal. Your child is unique.

1

Development from 0–6 Months

Thinking and Play

It's extremely hard work to enter this world, so Alex needs some time. His parents, John and Julia, have a leg up—they had the entire pregnancy to prepare, whereas he was busy with basal matters like developing organs and growing. His parents' preparation led them to form certain expectations: After all the baby pictures they looked at, they expected a beautiful, smooth, smiling newborn. When Alex finally arrives, he looks haggard, wrinkled, and withdrawn. It will take weeks, even months, before he is able to respond to other humans. The first real smile can take up to two months to appear, a painful wait for his lovestruck parents. They're looking for positive feedback—and they want Alex to show them what he wants and how they can make him happy. Unfortunately, their baby can't immediately provide that information.

Alex just came from a world in which everything was bathed in a mellow reddish light, sounds were muted, movements weightless. Neither hunger nor clothing existed. Gravity was not a concern, as he floated comfortably in fluid. Toward the end of the pregnancy, the space got a little tight, but Alex didn't mind. In fact, it created his preference for constraints and closeness. The transition to glaring light, unfiltered noise, and the constant battle with gravity are new to him. He discovers the sensations of wetness, cold, warmth, and different textures of fabric on his skin.

And what the heck is that biting, pinching feeling in his stomach every couple of hours? It makes Alex scream! His parents call it "hunger," and sometimes he has to endure it for a little while before he's fed. The path the food takes through his body—with all the attendant bodily sensations—is yet another new thing for him to experience and manage.

Sorting Out the Senses

One of Alex's first developmental tasks is to sort out his senses. In the first months of life, he can hear, smell, taste, touch, and feel things, but seeing is a different story. Mom and Dad are blurry figures at first, because at the start of his life, he can't see farther than about twelve inches ahead. He can only make out his mom's face when he's nursing or when she leans over him. His eyesight improves quickly, but it's a challenging project. Alex's vision won't be as clear as a grown-up's until around the time he enters school.

Alex has a general preference for faces and loves it when people talk to or smile at him. It isn't so easy to react, though, because Alex is still working hard to get both his eyes to look in the same direction. John and Julia sometimes notice one eye lagging, then jerking into place to look at them. Colors won't appear for the next few months. For the first few weeks, all Alex can see is the difference between light and dark—which is why he loves contrasting colors and shades, reflections of light, shiny objects, and shadows on the wall.

His sense of smell is highly developed. In fact, he responds more strongly to smell than grown-ups do. He loves smelling Mom and Dad best and doesn't mind one bit if they don't have time to shower. Perfume, soap, or other artificial scents really bother him.

Differences in temperature are still hard for Alex. Being undressed is similar to how his parents might feel if they were transported suddenly from their cozy living room into a snowy tundra.

Things get interesting around the third month, when Alex's brain starts to connect all the different points of perception: Not only does a rattle make a sound, you can also see its shape and feel it in your hand—all these qualities are what makes the rattle a rattle. It would seem that various levels of experience come together to create this object—very interesting. At three months, Alex turns his head toward the rattle as soon as he hears it.

Perceiving the World Through Play

Alex's brain develops primarily through play. During the first eight weeks, he discovers his hands—the start of a new life for him.

Everything happens by coincidence at first: He's lying on his back, arms and legs flailing, when suddenly a hand comes into view! He's amazed, because it's completely unexpected. He keeps fidgeting, the hand disappears from sight, and since he doesn't yet know that what he can't see is still there, he doesn't go looking for the hand. He gazes peacefully into space—and there's the hand again! He soon realizes that this strange thing has a habit of appearing.

At some point in his flailing, Alex touches something and it moves. After about eight weeks, he realizes that he can make things move and purposely tries to make it happen. He's learning the basics of cause and effect: When I bump an object, something happens.

At three months, Alex can consciously bring his hands together in the middle—until that point, what the right hand had to do with the left was a mystery to him. He realizes that these two hands are always there and can hold things.

By four months at the latest, Alex directs objects straight into his mouth, which now does the work of his eyes. He feels every side of the object with his lips and tongue, thus generating an image of this thing in his mind. He wants to know what it tastes like too. Most important, however, is its appearance, and he uses the sensitive organ of the mouth to figure it out.

Take a look around the room you're in. You know how it would feel to lick each and every object you see. You can imagine the shape, surface, temperature, and taste exactly. You probably didn't put all these things in your mouth as a baby, but you learned to create and transfer patterns. For instance, doorways are always smooth and cool on the tongue. Same goes for a metal bookshelf, which appears to be made of a similar material, so you don't need to lick both. Alex is making discoveries like that right now. He's acquiring a whole world by means of his mouth, hands, and eyes.

Alex will expand his experiments in the coming months. Soon he no longer uses just his mouth to feel objects, but studies them more thoroughly. He feels, shakes, and throws things. This teaches him the properties of various objects. He is now using all his senses. For instance, he shakes his rattle, then pauses, listening. Then he does it again—will it rattle again? And again? Alex must repeat this many, many times before his brain registers a concrete connection. These are advanced physics experiments; Alex deserves to win the Nobel Prize in science for his unbiased, comprehensive research projects.

Traces of memory gradually form on Alex's brain from all these experiments, and he begins to recognize objects. Repetition is very important for him, and will be for years to come. His brain is like a massive rail network to every corner of the globe, but in the coming years, only the regularly traveled routes will remain.

The Experience of Time

Alex's sense of time in the first months of life are especially interesting, because he lives exclusively in the present moment. John and Julia have started noticing strange things happening to their own sense of time since they arrived in the universe of baby-time. On the one hand, time sometimes drags so slowly, they'll glance at the clock, incredulous that only ten minutes have passed. On the other hand, the days fly by, and in the evening they're stunned to discover that yet another day is done. They wonder how it's possible to accomplish so little, and why there's still so much to do. The new tasks facing them are just so new. Like Alex, they will need a few months to begin developing routines. They might even be able to relate to Alex and what he's going through, while they struggle with unusual waking hours, lots of laundry, unaccustomed physical contact and carrying, complicated new procedures, unexpected bodily fluids, Alex's needs, and their own regular obligations. Meanwhile, Alex is busy getting to know his surroundings and five senses. Both parties—parents and baby—are negotiating complex tasks and need some patience.

Feelings and Relationships

Alex feels . . . well, he doesn't really know. Feelings are not fully formed yet, but will develop over time. At first, Alex feels either okay or not okay, and he cycles between the two. His state can change abruptly. Something's pinching or tight: not okay. Everything warm and cozy again: okay. Over the first weeks, he slowly learns to differentiate between hunger, fatigue, and other states.

All John and Julia want to do is make him happy, but they're uncertain how to do so. They try to guess at his desires, feelings, and needs. Their main question for Alex is: What do you want from us?

What *does* Alex want? He doesn't really know. He's busy learning to differentiate between his various states. At the moment, Alex feels displeasure, which he expresses clearly. It's perfectly reasonable for his parents to feel helpless and lost, because he feels that way too. The often impossible request is, "Help me, only I don't know with what or how." We venture guesses and try things out. The small family has to get to know each other—and that takes time. It's like any new relationship.

John and Julia have a hard time understanding their baby's needs in the first months, since he can't use words, body language, or facial expressions to guide them. As adults, they're used to exchanging information through conversation or at least a telling look. Alex's facial expressions need to develop first, and he's still a long way away from speaking. In the first months, Alex's parents need to "read" him physically. In other words, they are connecting "body-to-body."

Alex's slowly developing feelings require teamwork. Initially, all he can do is express the feeling, then he needs an adult to help him regulate it. This arrangement will remain in place for the next couple of years. John and Julia intuitively do a great job of helping him with his feelings—they pick him up, rock him gently, and make comforting sounds when he expresses displeasure. In most cases, that's exactly what Alex needs, but his parents often think that they need to do more.

Alex gradually discovers his emotions. At three months, he can express happiness, curiosity, interest, attention, shock, fear, sadness, and surprise. He is becoming aware of these feelings, which you can see in his facial expressions. He starts to express his feelings verbally, like babbling and chortling when he's happy.

At five months, he expresses happiness by laughing and squealing. He has also learned to get worked up, which is an important step. He understands his needs better and can express the feeling of rage when, as far as he's concerned, those needs are not met. For instance, he protests when someone unfairly (in his opinion) takes things away from him. Only by experiencing such feelings can he begin to learn how to manage them. For years to come, Alex will be grappling with the question of "How do I calm myself down in a reasonable manner?"

Crying

Like their baby, John and Julia are busy finding their footing in their new life with all its new territory. They don't register many of Alex's challenging developmental tasks, as he's not great at communicating them yet.

His parents want the very best for him. They did their homework and read a lot about early childhood development, so they know that his brain needs to be stimulated. Whenever he cries, they usually assume it's due to either hunger or boredom. From the outside, it *does* look boring: Alex can't do anything yet and depends on others for help. He's either lying down or being carried.

But to Alex, life is like a thriller, full of sudden noises, light, smells, bodily sensations, changes in location, and much more. He is consumed with trying to get all this under control. Nothing is boring for the first few months. Were Alex to describe these developmental tasks to a stress coach, he would be encouraged to improve his work-life balance.

Alex's primary issue during this period is overstimulation, not boredom. Because he can't filter, contextualize, or block out sensations yet, even a trip to the supermarket can be a lot for him to handle.

One of the first misunderstandings arises between Alex and his parents: they respond to his crying with more activity. Distraction can work well with babies six months and older, but in those first few months, it's totally overwhelming. When distracted, Alex tries to absorb the new stimulus and quiets down, but only briefly, as this method is not suited to reducing tension. Frequent repositioning—first on Mom's shoulder, then in her arms, then on his back or belly—also worsens his stress. Quick changes in position are hard for Alex. If his head tips back even slightly while being turned on his back, he experiences a sudden lurching sensation of falling and startles (see Moro reflex, page 36).

John and Julia determine that rocking Alex calms him somewhat. Understandably, they use that as a method to calm him when he's crying. Too much rocking, however, sends Alex into something of a trance. He experiences so many sensations in that trance that he might briefly quiet down, but in the long run, it overstimulates him even further.

A vicious cycle emerges for parents and baby alike: rocking and distracting Alex calm him down immediately, so his parents keep it up. These things briefly quiet him but lead to more crying later. It's tough to see the direct connection here, because there's often a delay. As things become habitual, Alex's parents need to come up with new, longer, more complex modes of distraction and rocking.

Alex isn't a "big crier." He cries a normal amount, but of course his parents would love for him to stop. They want the best for Alex and read that you shouldn't let a baby cry alone. Their stress must have blinded them to the word "alone," because they think that Alex shouldn't cry, period. Did they do something wrong? Is that why Alex is crying? Does this mean they're bad parents? They take his crying personally. They want to prevent him from crying—an impossible goal that causes huge amounts of stress.

Alex cries to express hunger or other forms of discomfort. But there's an additional reason: Alex cries to blow off steam, to relieve himself of accumulated stress. Maybe he's still working through the stress of his birth, difficult developmental tasks, or a busy afternoon of errands and appointments.

Like his parents, when he's stressed, all he wants is to find a quiet corner and curl up under a blanket. When stress-crying, Alex wants the stimulation to stop. He wants physical closeness from someone who will "listen" to him and let him cry until it passes. He just wants someone to be present, so he doesn't have to cry alone.

This is a tall order for Alex's parents, because a baby's crying is powerful, loud, unbridled, and often very dramatic. It's a biological alarm that screams, "Do something already!" Alex's parents feel forced to take action and desperately try to figure out what it could be.

They make an appointment with their pediatrician right away to see if there are health reasons for Alex's crying. That's important. He's healthy, but they learn about colic. The doctor explains that a stomachache is more often the result of crying than the cause, and that the crying will let up over time. This provides them some comfort but doesn't help them "prevent" the crying.

Alex's parents are inundated with messaging that tells them they need to prevent their baby's crying. They've heard it all, from unsolicited tips and tricks to subtle reproaches like "chill parents have chill babies." They eventually take Alex to a physical therapist, who discovers some areas of tension. Physical therapy seems to help, and he's crying a little less, but it never stops completely. What is going on?

Everyone around them treats crying like some minor catastrophe. No one would dream of just letting it happen. They don't see it as an expression of emotions that are simply making themselves known. No one tells them that Alex usually just needs a quiet corner of the couch, some time on Mom's or Dad's chest, a comforting sound, gentle hands, or a few words of understanding. Most importantly, he needs time and physical contact, someone to weather the storm with him, until he can relax again because he's relieved the stress. Since feelings transfer rapidly between people, it would be wonderful if his parents breathed calmly—or as calmly as possible when there's a baby howling in the room. The more peaceful his surroundings, the more quickly Alex can calm down, just like adults. The main thing he needs is time to relieve tension.

No one tells John and Julia about this response to crying, but they do read that in the first months, anything reminiscent of the womb is comforting to babies: physical contact, the pressure and compression of a tight space or embrace, and quiet. They discover that the baby sling works well for Alex. It's important that they carry Alex during the day, *before* he starts crying, otherwise it doesn't work as well.

Like most babies, Alex doesn't cry much in the first week or two of his life, then his crying begins to increase, especially in the evening. Crying is most intense around six weeks, then slowly begins to decrease. It drops off significantly around three months. As more time passes, Alex is crying less and for shorter intervals, which makes John and Julia very happy.

Establishing Human Contact

Alex loves faces and eye contact! Close physical contact with another person is his favorite, especially when that person is also moving.

After learning to control his eyes and hands, as long as he's not tired, Alex eagerly wiggles his whole body when someone talks to him. His way of communicating leads John and Julia to do what makes sense: They become more deliberate in the signals they send. They smile at him. They speak more gently, slowly, and in a high-pitched voice, arching their eyebrows, repeating themselves, and simplifying their sentences for their little one. They also pause between sentences to give him more time. They intuitively adapt to his limited language skills, allowing him to build them up gradually.

As thrilled by human contact as Alex is, it's a lot of work for him initially. He gets tired and averts his eyes or, later, turns his head away. Since John and Julia don't tire as quickly, they often try to catch his attention and offer something new and exciting to reestablish the connection. It usually works, but it's actually too much for Alex. First he has to make sense of the many simultaneous stimuli—looks, light, smells, sounds, emotions, and bodily sensations. Averting his gaze is his way of signaling, "Cool, thanks, that was great, but I need to take a break now. I'll let you know when I'm ready."

But Alex can't say that yet, so John and Julia feel rejected at times. He won't even look at them—versed as they are in adult body language, they assume that his averted gaze means he's uninterested, bored, or even annoyed by them. Could it be that Alex doesn't love them? He can't say much on the matter at present, but if he had a lawyer, they would object and explain that their client is merely acting out of self-preservation in temporarily terminating contact.

Around this time, physical contact is best for Alex, plus occasional eye contact. Between six and eight weeks, he can finally start returning people's smiles. He studies faces with great interest and learns to read facial expressions. Looking at older people's faces not only makes Alex happy, it's also very important for him, because he has to learn what different facial muscles do when expressing emotions.

Within a few months, his own facial expressions become much easier for grown-ups to read. By five months, he can even "greet" people by kicking his legs and bouncing. When someone he knows wants to pick him up, he lifts his arms. He can maintain contact longer now and sometimes cries when the adult is the one to break the connection first.

He is just starting to understand cause and effect, but it will be a long time before he understands or tries to influence human behaviors. It is impossible for him to manipulate others at this point, because that requires deep understanding of connections. He can't "impose his will" on anyone, because he is not yet in possession of it—only his needs. Developing personal volition is extremely complicated and will prove plenty challenging for Alex in about two years.

Movement

Alex begins to work on his body. His development moves from top to bottom—first his head, then arms and hands, while legs and feet come last.

To ensure the most important things are always taken care of, Alex has a few handy reflexes: When something touches his cheek, it triggers the rooting reflex and he turns his head—food could be there. And when the area around his mouth is touched, it triggers the sucking reflex.

Alex doesn't have conscious control over his feet yet. When someone touches the soles of his feet, he spreads his toes. When something touches his palms, his hands close. At first, he can't open them again and hangs on tight until the reflex subsides.

The Moro reflex can be a tough one for Alex. If his head tips back, even slightly, or there's a burst of sound or bright light, he startles: Alex's arms fly up and out. This reflex makes sense for baby mammals carried by their mother: When running from a saber-toothed tiger, it's best to hang on tight to Mom. As part of everyday human life, though, it can be pretty unpleasant. It takes Alex a little while to settle down after startling, so he likes it when his parents support his head when picking him up or laying him down. Whatever they can do to keep his head from tipping back is great, including turning or adjusting his body so he's on his side or belly when they pick him up.

Human Babies Are Meant to Be Carried

At first, Alex's legs are mostly bent and fall open to the sides, a position that looks super uncomfortable to his parents. When someone picks him up, he spreads his legs as if squatting, because he's about to straddle another person's body or, later, actively sit on their hip. For now, it's very pleasant for him to hang on that person, flat as a little bug. Alex's instincts are ancient, so he doesn't realize that the stroller has been invented and grown-ups often find it more comfortable to move around without babies on their bodies. He's attuned to physical contact and loves hanging on an active person, maybe one who's doing housework or other regular tasks and takes him along for the ride. It doesn't have to be all the time, of course, just every now and then. His parents' warmth, breath, smell, movement, and closeness make him feel so secure. Like riding as a passenger on a motorcycle, being carried teaches him to move along with the adult's body—in other words, to passively learn the movements, shifting to find balance and dealing with changes in position.

John and Julia read that it's good for babies to be carried once in a while, but since they weren't carried as children, sometimes they secretly feel their bodies are under siege. Whenever they want their bodies back to themselves, they use the stroller. This really bothers Alex, who loudly expresses as much. Something inside him knows that the best place to be right now is attached to a grown person. And contrary to what John and Julia think, the grown person doesn't always have to be one of the parents. Alex is usually fine with other people carrying him. All is well, as long as that person is active, because he starts to learn how life works through the mundane actions they perform.

It's a few months in, and John and Julia are eager to show Alex as much of the world as possible by carrying him facing outward. Alex is totally into it. He gets very quiet, because the incoming information creates a lot of tension. He just looks and looks and looks. He lacks the opportunity to regulate these many impressions for himself. Normally, when there's too much going on, he likes to bury his face in the grown-up's chest and take a short break. He'll fall asleep or nuzzle his parents' clothing and breathe in their smell. He doesn't have that option anymore. It's hard for his parents to connect his wailing later that evening to the overstimulation caused by all the input earlier in the day.

Being carried while facing outward puts pressure on Alex's sensitive pubic bone and creates a hollow in his lower back, sending a jolt through his spine with each step. Depending on the design of the carrier, it can also increase the risk of his legs dangling straight down, rather than assuming the natural "spread-squat" or "M" position, in which his knees are above his bottom. It's best for Alex's hip health to be carried face-in, like a sweet little bug pressed against Julia's or John's chest.

Alex's parents have no way of detecting this. Their little one is looking around with great interest and is much quieter. Besides, lots of parents do this. Alex is fine with just about everything offered to him, so it's all good from his end too. He's happy hanging on his parents and taking in the view.

It's only after bumping into their physical therapist while taking a walk one day, and her explaining a little about the structure of Alex's hips, that they start carrying Alex facing inward again. He fusses for a few days, because he's gotten used to all the input. He has to readjust and can't accept that less is better for him. It will be years before Alex can gauge when something is too much for him. He always wants as much as possible.

Alex was a real acrobat in the womb, so he's already practiced a lot of movement. Now he has to assert himself with gravity. It all starts with the head. In the first month, he learns to lift and turn his head briefly.

He's lying on his back, and his body feels very far away from him. At three months, Alex manages to touch his hands together and put them in his mouth. Then he goes back to kicking and notices, hey, there's something else down there. Once his abdominal muscles develop somewhat, he draws his legs in and discovers he has knees! Fancy that. Alex is astounded to find more of himself—there are *feet* past his knees! He keeps working his abdominals until he can put his feet in his mouth too. He jams them straight in his mouth to investigate. While doing so, his body rolls to the side, and Alex discovers that he can turn. He practices turning, because something that he wants comes into view. How to get there? At first, he makes it onto his tummy but can't get back. He complains; he could use some help returning to his back. It's best to hold his thighs to turn him over. Still, he needs tummy time to practice propping himself up—because that's what he wants. After turning, it's all about preparing to crawl, whether commando-style or on hands and knees.

Alex works on these developments at his own pace. All he needs is the opportunity to try things out. If an adult tries to sit him upright, for instance, he would love to be able to say, "Nice of you to try, thanks, but I'm not there yet. Please give me space to lay the groundwork, okay? I still need to strengthen my abs to hold me up, so it doesn't strain my back. I've been working on my six-pack to help . . . and I'm just going to put my feet in my mouth again . . . and again . . . and again."

Speech

Hearing develops in utero, and from birth, Alex can differentiate between his mother tongue and other languages.

He loves human voices. When his parents lean in to talk to him, he squeals and coos excitedly. He begins to have "conversations" with his parents. John says something to him, then pauses, and Alex responds with cooing, squealing, kicking, or facial expressions. Then John says something else or mimics the sounds that Alex made. Alex responds, and they happily go back and forth like this. Alex also listens very carefully when his parents explain what's happening. He looks at John and Julia, observes their facial expressions, and hears the intonation and flow of sounds.

At three months, he starts trying more with language. John and Julia marvel at all the sounds Alex produces. He practices gurgling, humming, babbling, squealing, shouting, cooing, and sometimes he makes bubbles with his tongue and lips. His "language" is universal at this moment—he could converse for hours with babies around the world. At five months, Alex introduces smacking and hissing to the repertoire—and eventually starts producing syllables and strings of syllables that sound increasingly like his mother tongue. He tries the syllables "ba," "da," "ma," "pa," and "boo," in preparation for real words.

John and Julia sing lots of songs and nursery rhymes, which Alex eagerly absorbs. The unique emphasis in these ditties teaches him a lot about speech rhythm and intonation.

Nursing

Julia decided to breastfeed. She's read a lot about it, and experts seem to agree that across the board, breastfeeding is best for babies. After Alex was born, Julia's midwife showed her how to nurse, but Julia was pretty out of it and couldn't keep track of all the details. How does it work again? Shouldn't it just happen naturally?

Julia and Alex figure it out together, but after a while, breastfeeding starts to hurt. Julia tries to grin and bear it—surely it will pass. But when it gets worse, she starts looking for a solution, because she doesn't want to stop nursing so soon. A girlfriend encourages her to post about it in an online parent group or talk to a lactation consultant. She learns that breastfeeding shouldn't hurt and isn't something to be "endured," and that small mistakes in positioning could be causing the problem. In Julia's case, she has to adjust the angle, whereas a friend of hers has to put more of her breast into the baby's mouth—after that, both women continue to nurse without any trouble or pain.

Lactation counseling helps Julia, and over the following months, she comes to appreciate the benefits of nursing, which has gotten easier. She is enthralled by the mysterious process of breastfeeding. She's fascinated by the notion that her body is producing antibodies for Alex that he can't make for himself yet. It's also helpful that she never has to worry about his nutrition: Her body and baby communicate independently, so when Alex wants more, she automatically produces the milk he needs. She doesn't need to worry about hydration, either, because nursing provides both food and drink.

Julia likes that her milk is always the perfect temperature and free of pathogens. She and Alex are gradually becoming a great team, even at night.

Despite these benefits, Julia lives in a society that privileges adult needs and creates many obstacles to breastfeeding. There are few quiet places to nurse outside the apartment, and not everyone accepts how bound she is to her baby in those early months—even she thinks it's a bit much sometimes and wishes for greater freedom.

Quick Reference—Nursing

Far More Than Food

Written in collaboration with Regine Gresens, a midwife and lactation consultant

Breastfeeding is considered an essential part of parenting because babies have not finished developing by the time they're born. But what exactly makes breastfeeding so important?

It's generally accepted that when a baby regularly experiences a feeling of fullness and comfort at their mother's breast, a bond is created. A tight bond, initially with one person, is important for your child and basically happens naturally through nursing. Breastfeeding releases high levels of oxytocin—the hormone of love, comfort, and bonding—in both mother and baby.

Breastfeeding has another, lesser-known superpower: It helps babies build their immune system, which they couldn't do in utero; coming into contact with the outside world is their first exposure to pathogens. When a baby is fighting a pathogen, the mother's body receives this information through their close physical contact. Mom's immune system most likely recognizes the culprit and within hours produces the appropriate antibody, which is passed to her baby through the milk.

Reducing illness is one of the primary reasons the World Health Organization (WHO) recommends breastfeeding exclusively for the first six months of life.

WHO also recommends continuing to breastfeed, with complementary solid foods, up to the child's second birthday or beyond if mother and child so choose, though very few people do this. FYI: If you want or need to send your kiddo to day care from a young age, continuing to nurse can help prevent them from getting sick during the notorious first winter in day care, because their body is still telling your body what it needs. Statistically, breastfed children get sick less frequently, experience milder symptoms, and bounce back more quickly.

Naturally, this doesn't mean that breastfed children are always healthy and bottle-fed kids always sick. Breastfeeding simply offers a special shield against sickness for both you and your child.

Breast milk adapts to the needs of the child; its composition even changes over the course of a single feeding. The time of day matters too: At night, it contains calming substances, whereas during the day, it's more energizing.

The amazing elixir of breast milk also contains maternal stem cells that can develop into other types of cells. Does your baby need muscle, bone, or brain cells? No problem: Breast milk can deliver. The contents of breast milk are specifically suited to the optimal development of the human brain and body.

Not only does breastfeeding benefit babies' health, it also improves their motor and cognitive development: another reason nursing is recommended. Mouth muscles are stimulated by the sucking action, which is great preparation for speech.

Breastfeeding helps mothers recover from the physical tolls of pregnancy, and in the long run, it helps protect against conditions like diabetes, breast cancer, and cardiovascular disease.

Remember: Breastfeeding is not an all-or-nothing situation. Even combination feeding (feeding your baby both breast milk and formula) or a short nursing period benefits mother and child. Every drop of breast milk is worth it.

If you want to nurse but struggle with it, seek out a lactation consultant as soon as possible. In many cases, the issue is minor and you just need a personalized solution. If you experience pain, be proactive in determining the cause, because nature intends for breastfeeding to be a pleasant experience for both parties.

Sleep

Sleep! There's nothing John and Julia want more than for Alex to be a good sleeper. But the universe has other plans. Alex's sleep schedule is complete chaos at first.

In utero, Alex would sleep now and then, resting in small units of time that had nothing to do with day or night: Steady darkness surrounded him—how could he know that any difference existed? For now, Alex simply sticks to his prenatal habits, sleeping here and there over the course of twenty-four hours. He tires quickly and often falls asleep in exciting situations, when things get to be too much for him. Sometimes he's only awake for ten minutes. Sometimes his reflexes make him jerk or thrash in his sleep.

At three months, he gradually—very gradually!—starts sleeping longer at night. Alex has noticed that there seem to be differences, because when he wakes up sometimes it's dark and his parents are just lying around, not doing anything. There are far fewer sounds and less human contact—everything is hushed. But he's still hungry, and sometimes needs a fresh diaper, but the whole vibe is different than during the day. Nevertheless, he continues to divide his sleep between day and night, and at four months he's still getting tired every ninety minutes to two hours. This window is smaller in the morning, whereas in the evening, he manages to stay awake a little longer. He's taking three or four naps a day at this point.

Alex's two issues with sleep, which he'll be working on for some time to come, are:

1. How do I fall asleep?
2. How do I connect periods of sleep?

All humans experience multiple periods of sleep or wakefulness. Adults wake up repeatedly during the night too, only they've learned to seamlessly stitch these periods of sleep together, so they aren't even aware of having woken. Alex can't do that yet. When he wakes up at night, he has to check: Is everything okay here? Am I hungry? Am I too warm or too cold? Am I safe—or am I lying here all by myself, just waiting for the saber-toothed tiger to come along and gobble me up? Alex does not associate being alone with rest and relaxation, but with peril. He likes having an adult close enough to hear their breathing, occasional movement, and smell.

It will be a while before he can self-soothe and fall back asleep on his own. John and Julia can help him with this, but not as much as they like to imagine. Alex's individual sleeping patterns are connected to brain development. Though his parents can provide support in certain areas, in many cases they have to accept how little influence they have on things. They will have to be flexible and very, very patient.

Sleep develops differently among babies. In Alex's baby group, there are "better" sleepers who fall asleep easily and sleep most of the night. John and Julia feel a lot of pressure, because in their world, a "good sleeper" is a parental badge of honor. They would love to announce that their infant is sleeping through the night. It feels like a test of their performance as parents. But sleep is not a parenting goal. As elsewhere, Alex takes these developmental steps at his own pace. Sleep is just more front-of-mind: John and Julia aren't as acutely concerned about when he'll start crawling as they are about when they'll finally get a full night's rest again.

John and Julia can provide external support by showing Alex the difference between daytime and nighttime. At night, they can keep the lights low, move slowly and quietly, and generally do less around the house. Routines and regularity help a lot, as he learns to connect falling asleep to certain signals. Which signals could unmistakably herald bedtime for Alex? And what might help him relax? How might he self-soothe?

It's also helpful when his parents notice early signs of tiredness and put him down then. Alex yawns or rubs his eyes and ears when he's sleepy. He might get fussy too, or start crying. His body starts going slack and his eyes glaze as he stares into the distance.

John and Julia are confused, because Alex doesn't slow down when he's tired—he's the kind of baby who becomes active when tired. If Alex were older, he might be described as "hyper." At first, they thought he wasn't getting enough input, so they showed him lots of exciting new things, talked and laughed more with him, acted silly or took him someplace new with interesting stuff to see. It was all so thrilling!

Curiosity usually gets the better of Alex's fatigue. It would be such a shame to fall asleep before he's had a chance to check out this cool new thing. He's not unlike a tired adult who's scrolling social media and just wants to watch this next video . . . then maybe the next one . . . but then really, just one more . . .

John and Julia discovered that, to avoid Alex getting worked up, they have to put him down much earlier. It's best if they can avoid overstimulation, because it's best to ease into sleep—a tall order for Alex if he's worked up. But it's also tricky if he's too awake—a difficult balancing act for his parents.

There is no single correct path. John and Julia have to work with Alex to figure out what he needs to learn in order to fall asleep by himself.

John and Julia also consider how they might get enough sleep. Whenever possible, Julia starts napping at the same time as Alex. For a little break, they ask their own parents to take Alex on a walk from time to time. Their pediatrician told them that formula—which many parents hope will help their baby sleep—doesn't make any real difference, so Julia has focused on optimizing breastfeeding. She and John opted to co-sleep using a bedside sleeper, which allows Julia to nurse at night without having to get up. They've made nighttime diaper changes less of a production and sometimes skip it altogether. They've even changed Alex's diaper right there in bed to make for quieter nights. This helps them get through these early months in decent shape, while Alex continues to develop his sleeping patterns.

At a Glance: 0–6 Months

Thinking and Play
In the first months of life, Alex is primarily concerned with sorting out his senses, especially eyesight. He begins exploring his world by putting objects in his mouth or experimenting with shaking and throwing. This is how he learns about cause and effect.

Feelings and Relationships
Alex doesn't really know what he's feeling—and definitely not what he wants. During this period, he learns how to express feelings by means of facial expressions and sound, but he can't regulate them yet. Crying expresses needs like hunger, fatigue, or overstimulation—or it might connect to something in the past, and Alex is howling to release stress.

> Alex and the ball: Alex puts a ball in his mouth and moves it around. *What might this be?*

Alex loves human contact! In the first three months, this primarily means physical contact and being carried. Alex loves faces, voices, and having "conversations." When he needs a break, he turns his head to the side.

Movement
Movement develops from top to bottom—first Alex learns to hold up his head, then comes control of his arms and hands. At some point he turns over for the first time.

Speech
Alex starts with universal sounds, babbling, squealing, yelling, humming, cooing, and blowing bubbles. He then starts forming basic syllables.

Sleep

At first there are no discernible patterns to Alex's sleep. It takes a few months for him to discover that daytime and nighttime even exist. He takes several short naps a day and gets tired every one to three hours.

2

Development from 6–12 Months

Thinking and Play

Alex is a brilliant scientist. She is open to surprise, eager to learn everything there is to know about her world, tireless and unbiased in her pursuit of knowledge. She was born with some knowledge of physics, like an awareness of gravity, but over the next six months, she really digs in and expands her knowledge of the world through experimentation.

What's the deal with falling objects? Some make a sound when they hit the floor, but others don't—interesting! She throws something and listens . . . it's louder in the kitchen than in bed. What's the difference?

Alex is riveted as she beats the tabletop with a spoon, then wants to try it with a cup or anything else within reach. She does it all the time and discovers that solid objects cannot pass through other solid objects, no matter how hard she hits them together. Aha. Meanwhile, liquids move past other things, like water on her hands, which moves very quickly and sometimes all over the place. Well! Why is that, and what can be done to change it? When she balls up her hand under the spout in the bathtub, suddenly the water goes in a totally different direction. And sometimes it makes the grown-up talk in a loud voice and grab towels. The floor is wet. Did she have anything to do with that?

It's necessary for Alex's brain development to make these discoveries, as they create the foundation for her entire life. Without these experiments, she wouldn't be able to draw more complex conclusions or move through the world with much success later on. She is forming neural pathways constantly, but that relies on her *doing*. She literally has to "grasp" things to ensure functioning pathways.

At seven months, Alex starts using her eyes more. After studying an object from all sides, she'll touch it, rub or whack it against the table or floor—then chuck it! She is baffled when Mom or Dad says, "Stop throwing." Her learning requires it, and she would love to remind them not to interfere with her intermodal perceptual process, thank you very much.

She still uses her mouth to investigate, because her tongue and lips provide a good spatial sense of objects. It's amazing that after checking something out with her mouth, she can recognize it with her eyes.

Sometimes this is hard on her parents, because they worry about hygiene and wonder why Alex insists on putting absolutely everything in her mouth. Alex would love to tell them, "Listen, it's all still new to me. I'll be investigating with my mouth until I'm eighteen months old, plus I've added my hands now too. Everyone uses their hands to check out new objects. They even have to put up signs in museums that say 'Do Not Touch' because the impulse to touch new things is so powerful."

As the months roll by, Alex's experiments lead her to make connections, and her brain begins to create categories: There are humans, there are animals, there are inanimate objects. Okay. You can tell that something is alive if it makes noises and moves. Cool. Got it.

To Alex, anything with wheels is a car. Anything with four legs is a dog. But Mom calls Grandma's dog "Olive," and Olive purrs and meows. When they see another Olive on the street, Mom says "kitty." There are lots of "kitties," but only one Olive. Huh. Very complicated. How does that work? Is "kitty" its own category, separate from dog? She needs to do more research and keep honing her categories.

Everything Must Go!

Once Alex starts to move—whether by rolling, or crawling commando-style or on hands and knees—she explores a larger radius. She opens and closes doors, over and over and over again. Opens and closes drawers, over and over . . . these are different than doors and require some force in pushing and pulling. Or she'll press buttons and flip light switches repeatedly. Does the same thing always happen? Alex wants to understand the underlying principle. There's a pedal you can push to open the trash can in the kitchen—does her diaper bin do the same? She takes books off the shelf, pulls clothes out of the closet, and empties drawers of their contents. She's practicing motor skills and learning about positional relationships—things can be *in* other things. How fascinating! Can you take those things out? How do you do that? And is it the same every day? Alex tries to draw conclusions from her experiments and tirelessly continues her research. Experiments must be performed many times before you can be sure of the results.

John and Julia read that their baby is not consciously trying to "make a mess" when she empties cupboards and drawers of their contents. They show Alex that you can put things back after taking them out. She manages to put one or two things back, but sometimes she'll just take them out again. It doesn't make any sense to her. Why should it matter if this object is here, instead of there? And why should it just sit there, isn't the whole point to do something with it? But actually, it's okay when something *is* just sitting there, because then you can practice getting close to it and seeing what's *behind* it. So what's the problem?

Alex's parents rearrange their apartment during this phase, keeping safe objects down low and moving anything breakable up and out of reach. Alex has her pick of bowls, pots, plastic lids, spoons, old magazines, socks, laundry, and other exciting things to investigate.

Alex is never looking to "finish up" what she's doing. She wants to be doing something at all times. Alex needs to develop: Her schedule is jam-packed and doesn't include any breaks. Development is going full steam ahead!

Oh My Gosh, It's Still There!

At some point during this period, Alex has a major breakthrough with what's known as "object permanence." She now knows that objects and people are still there, even if she can no longer see them. This is an important skill. She's created an image of the thing in her mind and knows what to look for if it suddenly disappears. Her short-term memory has also developed enough to assure her: I *just* saw that thing, so it's got to be around here somewhere. Julia tests this skill for fun by covering Alex's toy with a blanket to see if Alex pulls it off or loses interest and turns her attention elsewhere.

When Alex plays, she is not yet inventing storylines for her toys, but rather exploring her world to lay the foundation for flights of fancy. There are times when she becomes utterly engrossed in something new. She is fixated as she fiddles around with it. It's great if she can do this without interruption, as she's starting to learn concentration and how to play by herself.

Alex also likes it when a grown-up pays attention to her playing. Adult attention helps her concentrate a little longer. Plus, if the grown-up names the thing she's currently holding, she effortlessly builds her vocabulary—fabulous!

She starts to become interested in containers. Take this Tupperware container: How much does it hold? At what point does it overflow? What can be squashed into it, and what's too rigid to fit? What happens when you shake the container? Alex wants answers to all these questions.

She loves making a racket, whacking things together or squeezing a squeaky ball, because she's now able to link sounds to their sources. For instance, she looks at the door when someone knocks.

Alex is fascinated by mirrors now too, and will sometimes greet the child she sees there. She does not, however, understand that the image in the mirror is her own. She does not yet have any concept of "I" or "me."

The Right Toy

John and Julia researched which toys are appropriate for Alex at this stage, and they are constantly reading about how important various playthings are for her development. Their families and friends want to give Alex gifts too, and they start piling up. The new parents are amazed to discover that the toys do not captivate or hold her attention for nearly as long as manufacturers promise. She is far more fascinated by everyday objects.

Aunt Toni recently gave Alex a nice new toy, but all Alex wanted was the box it came in. Her parents were mortified and tried to get Alex to play with the toy. No dice. The box is a large container that Alex discovers fits over her head—*and* it's dark inside. Huh! The best gift Alex receives is from a creative friend of her parents: a big yellow salad bowl, along with salad servers. Alex can play and experiment with this toy, and her parents can use it in the kitchen later.

Alex is most interested in whatever Mom and Dad are using: cell phones, keys, remote controls. These seem to be important to getting ahead in life. Her parents use them to do amazing feats, like opening the door. It's like magic, and Alex wants to learn how to do it too. She loves when her parents are doing regular stuff around the house and they give her one of the objects they're using. When John is stirring in a bowl, Alex would love to check out the spoon. When Julia unlocks the front door, Alex becomes curious about the key.

If an object is off-limits, Alex would like an appropriate alternative. It can be tricky for her parents to find something she won't immediately reject as a worthless substitute. A cell phone swapped for a boring wooden ring? Dream on! She figured out the wooden ring ages ago. She is not easily duped, certainly not when it comes to the challenging job of understanding the world around her. She supposes the least her parents can do is to provide reasonable support in this endeavor.

To help make this very confusing world a little easier to understand, John and Julia establish routines for Alex. These really help her find her bearings, as she has some sense of time now and can make connections. The sound of dishes tells her: Time to eat! John and Julia discover that Alex is more relaxed when various processes are completed in the same order. She quickly realizes what comes next. By ten months, she can participate—for instance, she might lift an arm or leg to help her parents change her diaper. She likes helping.

Feelings and Relationships

Feelings are the engine of learning. Without them, development stalls. If Alex didn't experience such curiosity and delight in discovery, she would have no reason to develop something like motor skills. And why should she? What's wrong with just lying around? But because she is eager to investigate that toy *just* out of reach, she learns how to move her body.

Alex can now express feelings like happiness, rejection, anger, grief, amazement, disgust, and fear. She uses facial expressions, sounds, and different behaviors. Though she can express feelings, she can't regulate them yet and needs an adult to help. The last thing Alex wants is for the grown-up to get rid of the feelings or get them "under control." Feelings just want to be felt. Unlike many adults, Alex still understands that. All she wants is someone to use simple sentences, like "I know, that makes you sad," to tell her what she's feeling, then maybe make some comforting sounds to help carry the weight of the feeling for a little while. That's it. In time, this will teach her how to manage her emotions.

Managing Distance and Nearness

Alex begins to develop fears, including the famous "stranger danger," which can apply to situations and objects as well as to people. Alex's rule when it comes to new things: Approach with caution. Many friends her age are different; depending on their personality, they might be more adventurous or even more fearful in unfamiliar situations. Alex is often scared of strangers and might start crying. Having a familiar person there helps to comfort her. Sometimes she makes friends with strangers quickly, while other times it takes her longer to warm up. She has no concept of politeness, and she has offended Aunt Toni a few times, when Toni swooped in too quickly and Alex refused to engage. Rejection like this is usually in response to details like unfamiliar body tension, a different voice, or an unfamiliar smell.

Alex adapts her physical distance to adults based on how well she knows them. For us adults, what we deem a comfortable distance from other people is fairly constant. If someone disregards that buffer and gets too close, it quickly feels uncomfortable to us.

A "safe distance" for Alex, on the other hand, can change from minute to minute. She might cuddle a trusted adult or cling to their legs, which adults generally don't do. When she meets someone new, however, she usually keeps her distance at first.

Alex is generally very curious about new things, but she is also scared. When someone approaches her, she'll regard them with curiosity first, but if it goes too fast, she'll turn her head away. That's her sign for "You're coming in too close—we don't know each other that well yet." If the adult takes just one step back, Alex immediately turns her head to look at them. The adult can try this a few times: When she turns her head away, take a step back, then watch her turn her head again. This is her "safe distance" for the moment. It's really nice for Alex when people respect that distance, especially if she's being held and can't regulate the distance herself. She wants human contact, after all, but it can also spook her when it's too quick and too close. It usually takes just a few minutes before curiosity gets the better of her and she turns her attention to the new adult and gets a total kick out of connecting with them.

Alex has separation anxiety. It is terribly unsettling when her caregiver leaves the room. Then she's all alone. What will she do if the saber-toothed tiger comes in? She only feels safe when she's near a person who could scoop her up and make a run for it. She is not yet aware that there haven't been any saber-toothed tiger sightings in her neighborhood for quite some time.

This separation anxiety makes a lot of sense for Alex's survival. Because she is currently getting to know her surroundings, it's important that she not stumble into any life-threatening situations because she's too far away from her adult. She uses eye contact to assess danger levels—whenever something weird happens that she doesn't understand, she looks at Mom or Dad. If they look relaxed or supportive, then she'll keep doing what she was doing, whereas a look of concern makes her stop or be more careful.

In addition to body language, Alex is learning to read people's faces. This is a very important skill for assessing what's going on around her. It will help her navigate situations for the rest of her life. To practice, Alex needs people who will look at her, display and mirror emotions, and maintain eye contact. Alex is confused when her parents look down at their cell phones. All she sees is neutral, distant facial expressions, and since she does not understand the connection between her parents' faces and the phones in their hands, she thinks it has something to do with her. Did she do something wrong? Why isn't she getting any response from her parents? Why is she suddenly all alone? Alex does whatever she can—making sounds, smiling, even crying—to put an end to this very unpleasant state of noncommunication (we've all been there and know how it feels) and to reestablish contact with her parents. She can't assess the situation. All she can do is read the face.

What Is "No"?

As she practices reading emotions during this period, Alex becomes an expert in recognizing her caregivers' feelings and starts to recognize their preferences and goals. She gains experience in what they seem to think is okay—and what isn't. Stroking their hair, for instance, seems fine, whereas pulling it is not. It's helpful for her to receive clear signals here. Since language doesn't really register for her yet, she won't respond to a long, gentle explanation, like, "Sweetie, I don't like what you're doing right now, though I understand you're not doing it to be mean." But Alex *does* want to figure out if what she's doing is acceptable or not. And if not, is that always the case? Is it a hard and fast rule, like gravity? Why is it sometimes okay and sometimes not? What determines that? The more undefined the answer, the more often she has to test it out. It was so much easier with drawers, Alex might sigh—with drawers, open is always open, closed always closed.

And what's the deal with this word "no"? What does "no" mean? Does it refer to the wall, the electrical outlet, the potted plant beside it? "No" comes up in so many different situations, including when she reaches for the big bread knife in the kitchen. It's hard to figure out which part is "no." Actions are better for Alex's learning, anyway: Being moved away or having something pointed out helps her to understand much better than individual words. She picks up on tone of voice, bearing, and facial expressions.

Even when she learns what "no" means, at nine or ten months, she doesn't really respond to it. She usually goes ahead anyway, because it's so hard *not* to. Halting an impulsive action is almost impossible for Alex at this age. Sometimes she resists the impulse briefly, only to end up doing it later. The developmental drive is stronger than anything else.

Alex currently mirrors many of the emotions she encounters in others. For instance, if another child in her playgroup starts to cry, there's a good chance she will too. If someone acts aggressively toward her, she might respond aggressively. None of this is planned, because she can't plan yet. She simply mirrors in response to whatever comes her way. A loud, aggressive "No!" can prompt her to pull that person's hair again, simply because the atmosphere is so charged—after all, the person is glaring at her and basically expects her to do it again. Alex responds to adult expectations. If they assume she's going to behave in a certain way, in all likelihood, she will.

Sometimes Alex tries to change whatever the adult is feeling. For instance, if she hears an angry "No!" because she's near the electrical outlet again, she might smile. It works like a charm. When she smiles, the adult always smiles back—she's been doing this since she was eight weeks old. It smooths things over, and everyone goes back to being in a good mood. Unfortunately it doesn't seem to work as well this time, because the grown-up mutters, "When she smiles like that, I can tell she's doing it on purpose, just to push my buttons." But Alex is incapable of provocation. All she can do is respond to impulse. She is concerned solely with how her body turns impulse into action.

Playing with Friends

And what's the story with Alex's friends in her playgroup—do they play together? Alex thinks other kids are very interesting and observes them with curiosity. Sometimes she makes contact, crawling around with them or banging spoons on the table in stereo. But she is completely oblivious to the feelings, objectives, and needs of other children. She plays by herself. Alex can't concentrate long enough to develop a sustained, shared game. It is far too difficult to coordinate with another person, so she happily plays by herself or with an adult. She likes the game where she hands her parent an object and then takes it back, or interactive nursery rhymes like "Pat-a-Cake." She also loves throwing games, where she throws an object and John or Julia pick it up and give it back to her—over and over until everyone has had enough.

Movement

Alex quickly mastered rolling from her back to her tummy and back again, and after scooting around in a circle for a while, at around seven months she starts rolling or crawling commando-style. She is determined to become mobile and move in a specific direction.

John and Julia make sure Alex gets plenty of tummy time. It can make her grouchy, because it's strenuous, but her hard work pays off: Around eight months, she successfully pushes up onto all fours. She wobbles back and forth on her hands and knees, trying to distribute her weight equally. Sometimes she moves backward instead of forward—very frustrating—but at ten months, she succeeds. Attention: Alex is crawling! Meanwhile, she's been practicing sitting and there she is, ten months old and sitting without support. Ta-da!

Not once did Alex let failure get her down as she worked on these skills. She could be the keynote speaker at any management conference, because Alex can do what many adults cannot: She can fail her way to success. She keeps trying, mistakes be damned. Maybe she needs to try a different approach, or to strengthen certain muscles, but giving up is not an option.

Some of Alex's buddies choose different ways to get around. Instead of crawling, they discover it's just as effective to slide, roll, or even slither to get from point A to point B. No problem. They do it for months.

After that, Alex tries to pull herself up on all manner of things, though she doesn't have much sense of what can (or can't) support her weight. Eventually she's ready: From her knees, she plants a foot and pulls up to standing. Her stance is short and wobbly, but she's standing! The way down is still tricky, so she usually just plops back onto her bottom, which she doesn't mind one bit. This worries her parents a little, and they try to help or stand behind her, ready to catch her. At this point, she could turn around and dispense some wisdom: "That's very nice of you, thanks, but please let me make mistakes. Falling is fine. I won't learn anything if you do it for me. Gravity is my best teacher. It never changes, so I can let it guide me. Falling shows me that the way I was doing it was wrong, and I need to try something else."

At the same time, Alex has been doing more with her hands. She's currently practicing the pincer grasp, picking up tiny things—crumbs, lint balls—between her thumb and index finger. How hard does she have to squeeze to pick the thing up without squishing it? How best to aim for that crumb? Her eyes and hands have to work well together. She sticks her fingers into holes one at a time and digs into her bread, learning how to use individual fingers.

John and Julia had to make some real adjustments. Alex is increasingly mobile, and they had to baby-proof their apartment to keep her from hurting herself. They know they can't teach Alex these skills yet, because that would require insight into her own behavior, which remains in her distant future.

They still carry Alex around during everyday activities, though they now prefer a baby carrier to the sling. They find it a good way to get the chores done and to encourage her development.

Quick Reference—Carrying

Discovering the World from a Parent's Arms

Written in collaboration with Frauke Ludwig, a babywearing consultant and parenting educator

Carrying makes sense—literally—as it engages all the senses. Let's take a little walk to see it in action.

Baby is being carried in a carrier or sling (tactile system: Baby senses the outer limits of the body). Mom is in a hurry because she made plans to meet a friend. Thanks to the snug wrap, Baby goes through the same movement patterns as Mom, though the little one occasionally needs to push back to find balance (kinesthetic system: As Baby's musculature moves, the pressure and pull create a steady stream of new stimuli).

Mom and her friend stroll past a food truck (olfactory stimulus), and she can't resist the smell. She accidentally drops her wallet on the ground when she goes to pay. She stoops to pick it up, while Baby adjusts (vestibular system: sense of balance).

Mom snacks as they continue their walk, and Baby sucks on the sling (gustatory stimulus). Then a police car speeds by, sirens howling (auditory stimulus). Mom keeps cool. Her calm physical bearing assures Baby that it's not dangerous. Baby looks at Mom (visual stimulus) while Mom covers Baby's ears and says that everything is okay. Then Baby goes back to snuggling (tactile system). Baby's visceral system has been running at top speed this whole time: The sensory organ receptors send signals to the brain for evaluation.

As we've discussed, humans are biologically programmed to be carried. A baby's instincts and reflexes are perfectly calibrated to being carried, so there's no need to worry about spoiling our little ones by carrying them too much, or about hurting our backs or theirs. The opposite is true: When the sling or carrier is positioned comfortably—so you aren't in a contorted position to compensate, and your baby isn't slumped—carrying turns into a great workout for both of you.

Trying out different carriers or slings is time well spent, because they're like a pair of jeans: We need to find the pair we like, the pair that fits like a glove. If you're feeling lost, a babywearing consultant can help find the best solution for you and your child.

Speech

Alex loves how much the grown-ups are talking to her in simple sentences and the way they explain what they're doing, step by little step. She listens closely and adores the human voice. "Chatting" with adults is just splendid. Drawing on syllables like "ba," "ga," and "boo," she delivers impassioned monologues that make John and Julia smile. When she needs a break from human contact to process all this information, she actively disengages.

Alex soon knows her own name. She also recognizes the names of things around her, as indicated by her looking at the object when someone mentions it. She mysteriously manages to organize this stream of endless sounds into individual words and sentences and occasionally understands their meaning. Repetition and pauses in speech are helpful.

By ten months, Alex can understand short, simple instructions like "Give me the ball." She still needs some help, though, which is provided by the context and her parents' body language. Alex needs to understand situations with all her senses—she has to see and feel them before she can add words to the mix. Long sentences remain meaningless to her.

The months Alex spent with basic syllables pays off: To form the words "Mama" and "Dada," all she has to do is repeat the sounds: "Mamamamamamama!" When Alex first utters the words "Mama" and "Dada," the person in question responds enthusiastically. Julia beams and says, "Yeah, Mama!" and repeats it many times. This is how Alex learns the word.

Toward the end of year one, Alex is busy building her vocabulary. She wants to learn the names of all the things and people around her and holds forth in gibberish. She starts picking up words on her own. "Banana" becomes "nana," while "ball" becomes "baba."

Around this time, Alex also starts using gestures, like waving goodbye. This can lead to funny situations: One afternoon, Julia is carrying Alex around the apartment when a neighbor stops by. Alex is following conversations closely these days, trying to figure out when they're ending and it's time to start waving. She interprets her mother's body language, and because Julia is in no mood to talk to this neighbor and keeps trying to wrap up the conversation, Alex takes it as a sign and suddenly starts waving. She's perplexed when both adults start laughing.

Sleep

Alex has developed a daytime/nighttime rhythm and even slept through the night a few times. John and Julia now realize that Alex's "sleeping through the night" means five or six hours. During the second half of the night, her sleep is lighter and she wakes up more often.

For whatever reason, John and Julia assumed Alex would easily sleep twelve hours a night, say from eight to eight. This is not the case. As ever, Alex breaks up her sleep over the entire day, but settles into a longer sleep phase at night and two or three naps during the day. She can now stay awake for two to three hours before getting tired again.

Routines help a lot, but any disruption—teething, for instance, or other changes—can throw everything out of whack. When Alex goes to sleep past her bedtime, it's as if she had jetlag—rather than sleep late the next morning, she just sleeps worse. It's all a mess. It isn't easy to develop regular sleeping patterns! Alex must learn to give in to sleep and feel safe and relaxed doing so.

Around eight months, Alex starts doing something that really worries her parents. Before going to sleep, she's been banging her head rhythmically against the hard side of her crib. John and Julia think this behavior signals much more serious issues—but at Alex's age, this isn't the case. She is still just looking for ways to self-soothe, however illogical her methods might appear to adults. This habit passes as soon as Alex realizes it doesn't work. John and Julia can help her with self-regulation, but not as much as they might have thought.

At a Glance: 6–12 Months

Thinking and Play
Alex learns how things behave and whether there are connections between objects by trying them out. She studies objects, puts them in her mouth, turns them over, bangs them against other things, or throws them to discover their properties. She practices concepts like "open" and "closed," "on" and "off," "in" and "out." She is interested in the objects that she sees her parents using, especially kitchen utensils. She starts creating basic categories, like Cars or Animals.

Feelings and Relationships
Alex can express nearly any emotion but can't regulate them yet. Sometimes she is scared of new people or situations and experiences separation anxiety. She loves human contact and is learning to read people's faces and emotions. She's also learning that certain behaviors are not allowed, but her understanding relies heavily on clear communication. She rarely chooses on her own to avoid behaviors that are off-limits.

Alex and the ball: Alex now understands that a ball is smooth and round.

Movement
During this period, Alex practices crawling, first commando-style, then on all fours. She also works on sitting and grabbing—she can pick up tiny things like crumbs. She is on the move, and by the end of the year, she's pulling up to standing.

Speech
Alex is a real chatterbox and loves having "conversations." She strings syllables together, like "Mamamamamama." She is building her vocabulary, and by the end of the year, Alex is using a few simple words that she

adapts to match her abilities (e.g., "nana" for "banana," "baba" for "ball").

Sleep

As the rhythm of daytime and nighttime emerges, Alex sometimes sleeps for five or six hours straight at night. She and her parents continue to search for what she needs in order to fall asleep (and stay asleep) by herself.

What to Know in Year One

If you don't remember what defines moments of leading and moments of following, please reread pages 7–20. When it comes to raising children, there's really just one question you need to ask: "Does my child need me to lead or follow?"

Moments of Leading in Babies

As you've seen with Alex, the first year of life is very confusing and challenging for babies. They could use a lot of leading.

But how do you lead such a young child? During these early months of life, your baby looks to you for security. "Creating security" is a big, abstract directive, and it's hard to know what it looks like concretely. Fortunately, it's pretty basic: When you pick up your baby, maybe to change their diaper, tell them exactly what you intend to do. Your baby is busy with very different internal processes and appreciates your saying, "I'm going to pick you up now." During the first weeks of your baby's life, you can create an important sense of security by supporting their head or picking them up from their side, to help avoid the unpleasant shock of the Moro reflex. Little moments like these are what constitute life.

When changing your baby's diaper, you can give short, basic descriptions of what you're doing, as outlined in the chapter summary on page 18: "I'm unsnapping your onesie . . . it's going to get a little chilly . . . now I'm wiping you."

One of the most important tips for parents to remember is: Say what your hands are doing.

Your baby is trying to create connections and to establish some kind of meaning and structure in this strange world. They want to understand the flow of different processes and to learn to orient themselves. It's a tremendous help when you assign words to your actions. Whether you're bathing, dressing, or changing your baby—or whatever else you're doing!—simply let them know.

It makes a difference to your baby whether a hand appears out of nowhere to grab their nose and wipe it with a tissue, or whether that big person up there respectfully says, "Okay, I just need to touch your nose for a second . . . hang on, don't move . . . and we're done. Good job!" You're creating the conditions for your baby to learn to trust you. Down the road, this will translate into better teamwork and cooperation.

Although your baby doesn't understand many words yet, they do recognize when something new is happening and gradually learn to predict what comes next. You become predictable to your child, creating a sense of ease, trust, and security.

During the first few months of your baby's life, they deal with stressful fluctuations in temperature, sudden changes, unfamiliar bodily functions, sounds, smells, loud noises, and blinding light. These experiences are easier for your baby if you help to prepare them.

If you'd like, for added benefit, you can adjust the speed of your actions. Your baby's brain is still developing, meaning it takes much longer for stimuli to make their way through the tangle of neural pathways. When it comes to big changes like picking up your baby, you could tell them what you're about to do, then count "One, one thousand, two, one thousand, three, one thousand," before acting. It takes several seconds for your voice and words to truly register.

Identical processes are important for establishing security and for understanding the world. Right now, your baby is learning to create connections, and if they notice that you always feed them first, then change their diaper, then put them to bed and turn off the light, they will soon learn to predict this step-by-step process and relax into it. They will internalize these routines, though it will probably take longer than you'd like. Your baby needs instructions to be repeated many, many times.

Another thing your baby wants from you is less. Consider this rule of thumb: If something is mind-numbingly boring to you, it's probably just right for your baby, as they absorb stimuli without any filter.

The next time you're at the supermarket, pay attention to the number of external stimuli you filter out. You hear the music and smell different aromas. There's the beeping of the cash registers, the cold air of the dairy aisle, the rustle of greenery in the produce section, the general vibe, the feeling of your jacket on your skin—you might notice these things, but you also block them out. To a certain degree, you decide how much or how little you take in. Your baby, meanwhile, perceives everything all at once and at full volume. They need you to be a good manager of that input.

If possible, try to limit the number of daily errands or activities, at least during those first few months. Your baby is still consumed with self-organization and other internal processes.

As the months go by, you'll start getting to know your baby. Observe them carefully. What's their personality like? Do they dive into new situations, eager to discover and learn? Do they often cry because they're easily overstimulated and overwhelmed? Or do you have a "chill" baby who knows their boundaries and simply falls asleep or disengages when things get too intense?

It will take several months—as in any relationship—to figure this out. Enjoy the fascinating process of getting to know your child as a person. As you lead, take your child's personality into account, anticipating if they need to be shielded or if they easily manage lots of input.

How Do I Comfort My Child?

During the first three months especially, your baby will respond to anything that reminds them of being in the womb: tight spaces, being carried, human closeness, warmth. Regarding the tight spaces, your baby loves being rolled up, with a rounded back, just like they were in utero. It's calming. Babies who are carried more tend to cry less than others. This is not the case, however, if your baby is already crying when you start carrying them—it's better to incorporate carrying or wearing your baby earlier in the day. What if you used the stroller to hold the groceries while you carried your baby? Maybe you'll even enjoy doing household chores with your baby in the sling. When they fall asleep, you can take a break too.

Let's take a look at what babies need, so you can spend less time wondering what on Earth yours wants right now.

These are the *basic needs*:

- Is your baby hungry or thirsty?
- Are they too warm or too cold or wet?
- Are they tired, in need of a nap or a break?
- Does your baby need human contact and closeness?
- Have they been carried yet today?
- Are they in acute pain?

Then babies have *developmental needs*. In the first three months, these needs are primarily quiet time, connection with you, and physical contact. Between three and six months, developmental needs expand to include experimentation, eye contact, and "conversation" with you. The range of needs broadens further around six months: Experimentation now features locomotion, as your baby moves their body to reach things. Most babies also need structure and routine. That's it. For now, that's all you need to keep in mind.

It's easy to lose track of your baby's need for sleep during the day, since your sleeping patterns are so different—within an hour or two or three, your baby will get tired again. In the first weeks of life, it might even be within ten minutes.

And what are your needs? Other than sleep and some quiet "me time"? Because these needs are often overlooked, I implore you: Ask for help. Build up your network. If it works for you and your extended family is interested in baby time, get them involved. If that isn't an option, hire professionals and babysitters. There are many options for professional or community support, yet too few parents know about or use them. Postpartum doulas can help for several months after birth; birthing centers offer classes and support groups; "Mommy and Me" programs, many of which are open to fathers and other caregivers as well, create opportunities for bonding and development outside the home; public libraries may offer baby-friendly story hours, a great time to meet other families; many YMCA branches provide childcare while parents exercise; parenting chat groups and forums can connect you with other parents, near and far; parenting classes can be found online or through local charities or community colleges; your favorite coffee shop may host kid-friendly meet-and-greets. If none of that appeals to you, then start building your own network of parents. Compare notes. Seek out people who can help provide support and relief.

Your baby is definitely attuned to receiving care from other people. Throughout history, humans lived in tribes or large extended families, so babies were always raised by multiple adults. You've probably heard the proverb, "It takes a village to raise a child." For a long time now, Western society has veered in the opposite direction, putting undue stress on the nuclear family unit and mothers in particular. My students frequently ask if a few hours apart from their baby will damage the bond. I am here to tell you: No. If anything, the time apart will benefit everyone. Start building a happy village for your family now.

Time apart is all the more important if you're feeling stressed—which is to be expected during this phase. Be targeted and tenacious in your search for relief, even if it's hard. Where can you create little oases for yourself? What can you hand off, postpone, or drop altogether from your day-to-day? This is just a phase, and one that will seem very short in hindsight. Life won't always be like this—even if it feels that way sometimes.

We tracked Alex's development during this period and saw that babies in their first year are concerned with fundamental needs.

Your baby cannot manipulate you. Not even a baby genius is capable of thought as advanced as manipulation. Your baby simply mirrors and responds to all the emotions swirling around, which is why they're more likely to cry in situations that are already stressful for you. Lots of parents will think, "The baby just *had* to start shrieking, didn't they? They do it to get under my skin." These are normal thoughts, but they are the product of an adult mind. Your neighbor might do something to bug you on purpose, but not your baby. Babies react. Make an honest assessment of the mood in the room. Your baby can detect mood like a seismograph and reliably signal what's really going on. Don't worry—this doesn't mean you always have to be cheerful. That's a fool's errand. All emotions are acceptable.

How Do I Change Things?

You will want to change certain things—your baby's sleep patterns, for instance—and my hope is that you will check here first to see if what you want to do is even possible, developmentally speaking.

I led parenting groups for a few years, and whenever a mother proposed a potential change in her baby's life, I usually followed up by asking, "Who wants to make or see that change? And why?" Lots of moms had heard, read, or seen online that a certain behavior "should" be happening now.

But your baby doesn't care what they "should" do. Thoughts, ideas, opinions, or concepts are inaccessible to them. The only chance you have at success is if you, your partner, or your baby has a real need for change. Then patience is required, because your baby must relearn, and that takes time.

How Do I Create a Strong Bond?

We've touched on this, and I'm sure you're aware: It is very important to build a solid bond with your baby. Yes. True. But you don't need to worry about it too much. I don't understand why so many parents these days fret over bonding. I fear that, over time, we parenting experts got into people's heads and somehow created a problem where one doesn't exist.

A bond between you and your child forms naturally through everyday routines and interactions. The little things count—don't let the big, nebulous notion of "bonding" scare you. Say what your hands are doing, so your baby comes to trust you and feel safe. Carry them when you can. Give them lots of friendly looks. When you feed your baby, keep them warm, and talk to them, they will come to trust you and realize that you provide security and protection. You'll discover it's almost impossible *not* to behave this way toward your baby. It happens automatically.

Moments of Following in Babies

A bond forms in moments of following too—in other words, bonding occurs when you take both moments of leading and following together. You're not just talking to your baby—your baby is talking to you too. Wait for it. Stillness, more than action, gives rise to bonding. While you wait, so much is happening in your baby's brain. You're just there. Your presence is enough.

As the months pass, the two of you come to "converse" more. You say something, and your baby responds with sounds while you listen. You imitate the sounds your baby makes, then your baby responds with more sounds, and you continue back and forth, just like in a real conversation. It's wise to repeat the sounds your baby makes, because it's the beginning of language. It makes your baby think, "Amazing, I can already speak! I'm going to do more of this. I seem to be headed in the right direction!" It encourages words to gradually develop.

These exchanges are so happy, they automatically give rise to another important dynamic between you two: fun. The value of happiness, laughter, and fun cannot be overemphasized. If I had a single tip for parents, it would be: Just have fun! Your child doesn't want much more from you than that, given how much love and connection are found in having fun—it's more than enough for a happy childhood.

How Do I Handle Unpleasant Feelings?

Lots of parents think they need to "get rid of" every unpleasant feeling that comes along, and they'll go to extreme lengths sometimes to accomplish it. This is both normal and understandable, as it is very, very hard to hear your baby cry.

Try to remember that everyone cycles through moments of anger, grief, or stress over the course of a day, and your baby is no exception. All they want is to be allowed to feel these feelings—they want to experience the full spectrum. Your baby de-stresses by crying and screaming. It makes sense.

If you're able to stay with your baby while they cry, that's great, but don't become overwhelmed. It's like the oxygen masks in airplanes: Why do they instruct you to put yours on *before* you assist your child? You're the helper, which means you need oxygen first. If you can't breathe, soon there won't be anyone there to help. If you feel overwhelmed, do whatever you need to get some "air." If that means putting your baby in a safe place and stepping outside for a minute, please do it. You have probably read that shaking your baby or even picking them up too roughly in a moment of elevated stress can be life-threatening. If your stress spikes, simply leave and practice some form of self-care. Calming down can also help your baby—feelings are contagious.

One practical tip: Lots of parents tell me that noise-canceling headphones help them ride out crying fits.

Any way you cut it, though, it's not easy. Especially because very few of us received good care during these spells when *we* were babies. It's very likely that when you cried as a baby, your behavior was not treated with love and acceptance. People just didn't know better. There's a good chance that your baby's howling triggers very old feelings and you suddenly find yourself with two babies on your hands and a lost sense of your adult self. That is entirely normal.

How Do I Create Shared Moments?

Most moments of following occur during play. At this stage, play is more of an exploration—after all, toys have to be examined thoroughly before playing with them is of any interest. You don't need half the toys that you have—everyone you love is just so eager to give your baby presents. You don't actually need much more than what's already in your home. Your baby will discover different colors and textures on a wool blanket, bare floor, or bedsheet. They want to examine everything, so regular household items are fascinating. The kitchen—with its spoons and pots, jars and boxes—is a treasure trove for babies. Let your baby try everything out at their own speed, giving them time and space to examine. Your baby knows what to do, and you don't need to be part of it.

It's great to pay some attention to your baby while they play. Just watch and enter the remarkable world your baby inhabits, where they make the most of every opportunity, turning up new discoveries by the minute. It's wonderful to adopt your child's perspective, as it gives you a chance to rediscover the world for yourself. Feel free to share a few words. Narrate what your child is doing. It will make them feel that they're doing something important and doing it right, plus they'll start learning the terms for individual objects. "Yes, you're shaking your rattle." That's all you need to do here, because your baby will always seek out the next challenge they need on their developmental path.

Please allow yourself time to grow into and shape your new role in whatever way works for you. All you need is time. Truly, far less is required of you than you might think. Your baby will handle most of their development on their own—you're there as the audience, companion, and to manage their surroundings.

BONUS

Sleep in Babies and Toddlers

Babies start by taking lots of short naps over a twenty-four-hour period. As their nighttime sleep grows longer, babies will go from three daytime naps to two, then down to one. Many kids transition to just one nap around eighteen months, and by the time they are two or three years old, they will stop napping and sleep only at night.

Bedtime activates your child's need for bonding, because falling asleep is a form of separation. Being alone remains perilous as ever—what if the saber-toothed tiger shows up? By this point, your child has developed awareness of the fact that Mom and Dad really *can* go away.

For many families, co-sleeping solves the problem of going back to sleep at night. Every time your child wakes up, they check to make sure everything is okay—and the nearness, warmth, breath, and comforting smell of their parents is a huge help here. From a child's perspective, there isn't a single benefit to sleeping alone.

If you can't get a wink of sleep with your child beside you, then co-sleeping doesn't make any sense. As an option, your child could fall asleep on a floor bed in another room with you there, then come to your room in the middle of the night if need be. Being able to take matters into their own hands in case of "emergency" goes a long way toward your child's reassurance.

Nighttime disturbances caused by sickness, changes to daily routine, bad dreams, night terrors, and "monsters under the bed" will come and go in phases. Sleep tends to be a roller-coaster ride during the first few years. Starting day care, or other life changes like a move, or simply a new fear cropping up can have a huge impact on your child's sleep. Sleep differs from night to night, just like it does for adults.

If you want to change the sleep situation in your family, it can be useful to work with a sleep coach or consultant, with whom you can create and implement a personalized approach to your concerns.

Falling asleep cannot be forced. It's tied to trust, letting go, and letting yourself *fall*. It requires subtlety and sensitivity. Nonverbal messaging and feelings play a big role.

I remember once sitting on the edge of my son's bed when he couldn't fall asleep. I was desperate to leave. I didn't want to help him fall asleep that night. All I wanted, at long last, was a little "me time." I wanted to be free of my child for just one night.

At some point I thought, "How is he supposed to relax and fall asleep when Mom is clearly anxious to leave? That's scary for a little kid. I'm teaching him to fight sleep because he has to make sure I don't run off. I am explicitly teaching him how *not* to sleep."

I couldn't change how I felt that evening, but acknowledging what was happening helped a lot. I could be honest. All my clever sleep tricks were just that—ways of tricking my kid into falling asleep so I could get to that "me time" quicker. Once I admitted this, but without guilt-tripping myself—stress got the better of me, and I was overwhelmed—I made a silent apology to my son. That night, I made my peace with simply sitting there. Before long, my son fell asleep.

Let's be honest: We often wish our kids didn't just sleep whenever they were tired but would instead adapt to our hours. Ideally, they would go to bed early and sleep late. Sleeping in the car is a no-no, and they shouldn't nap so much that it keeps them up at night—we work hard to control their sleep. There are so many theories and rules to bedtime, falling asleep becomes a complicated ordeal.

Of course, finding a rhythm for sleep is a big help, and it's important for your child to grow accustomed to that rhythm. It's also perfectly reasonable for us to want to call it a day at some point, especially when that day was long and stressful. But does that always coincide with sleep? We have to give in to sleep; we can't force it to happen at a specific time. The need for sleep is like the need for food—a little different each day. On certain days, you'll be tired earlier (or later) than on others. Surely that's happened to you before. It takes patience, flexibility, and love to support your child until they learn to fall asleep on their own.

Rosy

Sleep can sometimes turn into a yearslong battle with your child. Perhaps this shift in perspective could help.

In search of non-Western approaches to parenting, Michaeleen Doucleff, an American journalist, spent several years visiting Maya, Inuit, and Hadzabe communities with her toddler, Rosy, in tow. See Further Reading for more information on her book, *Hunt, Gather, Parent.*

When it came to sleep, Doucleff had a similar experience with her daughter as I had with my son. She realized that she had been teaching Rosy (who was a little older at that point) how *not* to sleep. Bedtime was a nightly battle.

During her travels, Doucleff discovered that these three Indigenous groups approached parenting very differently. How do you teach your child with ease? A new skill emerged from the principle of modeling how it's done, encouraging the child to practice it, and acknowledging their results. Doucleff questioned why she'd never thought to apply this to sleep.

So how do you teach your child to sleep? There are just two things to learn:

1. What does tiredness feel like in my body?
2. What do I do about it?

Doucleff became a model for Rosy. How do you know when you're tired? She described and then demonstrated that when she felt tired, her whole body felt worn out and limp, and she would yawn and rub her eyes. Then she got ready for bed and lay down. If Rosy joined her or changed into her jammies at the same time, Doucleff acknowledged her behavior. She smiled and cuddled her daughter. Then they practiced being quiet and slowing down together. There was no pressure, just an invitation to sleep. The lesson was about sleeping when you are tired, regardless of the time.

After many nights of practicing calming down and feeling fatigue, Rosy began to do it on her own. Going to bed slowly transformed from a battle into a welcome opportunity to cuddle, rest, and recharge for the new day ahead. Rosy learned to interpret and respond to the signals that her body was sending, and she began going to bed when she was tired—around the same time as before, but much more easefully now.

Don't forget to have fun with
all the parenting you're doing. Love
and connection are all your child
is after. Just have fun together.

PART 2

Your Toddler

Please do not compare your child too closely with our "average" child, Alex. Development does not follow the law of averages. Your child is probably slower in one area and quicker in another. They might not display certain traits or behaviors, whereas others are highly pronounced—all of that is normal. Your child is unique.

3

Development from 12–18 Months

Thinking and Play

Alex more or less has a handle on his body now, allowing him to explore new areas at home. What will he do with these new options? He's kind of pressed for time too, as most of his development will occur over the next four years—time is of the essence.

He needs to spend all his time exploring and trying things out. His brain needs him to *grasp* things—literally.

Alex learns about objects by putting them in his mouth, banging them against something else, studying, turning, rubbing, or throwing them. He was born understanding certain laws of physics. For instance, he knows that objects always fall down. Calculating the exact flight path of various objects, meanwhile, will take some practice. Why does his blankie fall right away, whereas a ball soars through the air? What does it take to make any object fly? What muscles does Alex need to use, and what angles? He needs to have these experiences many times over to ensure functioning neural pathways and connections in his brain. He knows instinctively that trying things out makes him smarter.

Doing Something "Wrong" Is Right

Alex learns by trial and error. John and Julia would love it if he just sat quietly on the rug and played with the expensive shape-sorting cube, spending hours trying to slide the triangle into the square hole. As far as they're concerned, that's how you learn things. As far as Alex is concerned, meanwhile, the apartment is filled with exciting shapes, colors, textures, and objects whose qualities require thorough examination. He doesn't understand how his parents could call what he's doing "making a mess," or why they insist he's using things the "wrong" way—he's working on discovering the world here. How can they expect him to learn to use an object the right way if he hasn't run through all its other possible uses first?

Alex poses countless scientific research questions every day as he experiments: How much OJ fits in this egg cup? How do you pour liquid, anyway? Where's the tipping point, then how do you stop the momentum? Do liquids behave differently than courser things like sand or flour when you pour them? When does it overflow, and how do you avoid that?

Can you stick a finger into things other than bread? Can you use it to flip the light switch on and off? Do fingers fit in the crack when the refrigerator door is open? Does the remote control only slide under the TV sideways, or does it fit lengthwise too? How much strength does it take to lift a water glass and put it back down? How does an empty glass differ from a full one?

Alex is starting to learn about boundaries. He knows that certain experiments are okay, while others are not allowed. It's important that boundaries are clearly set—after all, he wants to find out what's allowed in this world and what isn't. Constraints are part of that. Alex is learning on all levels. It's apparent to him that physical constraints exist, and sometimes it's humans setting the boundaries. Hmm, okay. Are human boundaries as reliable as physical ones? Are they the same every day, like gravity?

Although Alex is starting to understand that certain behaviors aren't allowed, it doesn't mean that he can follow the rules yet. He hasn't developed impulse control. In other words, *doing* is still much easier than *stopping*. What's some silly rule compared to the opportunity to discover and learn something new?

It's extremely frustrating to Alex when things are off-limits, because he *has* to try them out in order to understand them. What he needs in these situations is a similar alternative. It's galling when an adult tries to pass off a boring wooden block for what he's *actually* interested in—say, the riveting ventilation holes on the computer.

Someone tells John and Julia to pay close attention to what Alex is learning right now. They observe him at play and conclude that, for instance, he's in his containers phase. Their child wants to check out everything he can about containers: what they're like empty, full, half-full, whether it's liquids he's pouring or solids he's jamming in.

Alex's parents try to identify the learning need behind his action, then figure out a permissible alternative. Playing with water in the sink or tub is always an option, because water is so changeable. It will take several years, until about preschool age, for Alex to understand the behavior of water.

Planning and Doing Things On His Own

John and Julia feel like they have to do everything for Alex, but their service doesn't mean much to him. He's interested in learning. He wants to help! It can be so frustrating when his parents give him a piece of toast, already cut in two, because *he* wanted to do that. Someone stole the process from him! He isn't aware of the underlying reason for his anger. All he knows is that he's frustrated. John and Julia try to guess what's wrong, and eventually he just says "Yeah." Reasons don't register yet, nor does language. For now, his parents think he wants his bread cut in a specific shape, a preference they don't understand. They're upset because Alex makes such huge demands on them, while Alex feels wronged because he wasn't allowed to try things out at his pace and according to his abilities. He wants to know what it takes to smear peanut butter and jelly on his toast. What are the steps to learning that? Curiosity gnaws at him.

His parents have a hard time letting Alex do things himself, aggravated as they are by his learning process. It's just so much quicker and more efficient when they do it themselves. At the same time, they definitely want Alex to become self-sufficient and capable—it's a constant juggling act.

By about eighteen months, Alex masters a tough skill—he can use tools. Standing at the kitchen counter, curious about what's going on up there, he now realizes: I'm too short. The counter is way up high. So I need to make myself taller. How tall am I? What do I need to get up there? Here too, he has to try out different ideas: Does it work to extend his arm holding a spoon? No, he still can't see. He'll have to get his head higher, and since his head is attached to his body, he'll have to climb onto something. Hmm. What would work? He looks around for options . . . then spots the chair. It's over by the table. Alex knows that he can make the chair move, but not the table, so he happily pulls the chair to the counter and climbs up. Ta-da! Finally, he can see what he wants to see. This is a huge cognitive leap. He's starting to imagine things before trying them out. Picturing and playing out scenarios in his head is a crucial life skill. It doesn't happen that often, though. For the most part, Alex still has to try out what works and what doesn't.

He can now remember successful experiments and repeat them as needed. His mind has the capacity for memory. He recognizes people, objects, and places, like the sandbox at the playground.

When Aunt Toni comes by, Alex pulls out the puzzle they did

together the last time she visited. This aunt and this puzzle evidently go together. Aunt Toni brought another great present, though, and to her delight, Alex is actually excited about the gift this time, not the box. Whatever this gift is, it lights up so brightly and makes such a loud noise that his parents immediately agree not to replace the batteries once they run out. And who knows, things do have a habit of disappearing.

Learning How to Get Dressed

John and Julia largely underestimate how quickly Alex learns practical skills. Thinking will take some time, but he is more practically skilled than they realize.

Alex wants to help his parents dress and undress him, which he indicates by tugging on his clothes. He can't do it himself yet, but he can try: He just needs his parents to break it down, helping him put on his jacket step-by-baby-step. He understands and can follow basic directions like "Stick out your arm" or "Give me your foot." He learns something new from it every day.

Changing Alex's diaper can be tricky these days, because he has no interest in what he's already figured out—this is precious time he could be using for research. He wants to do more when getting dressed, but since it takes so long and there's so much he hasn't figured out yet, his parents usually do it for him. But just lying there is boring. As soon as a new trick is introduced, though, like pulling a sock on over his toes, he is 100 percent on board. What parts of getting dressed or undressed can he practice on his own? How can he join the team? Learning to get dressed takes months, but once Alex learns how, his parents never have to do it for him again.

Learning by Doing

Alex is practicing walking these days, and once he's got that under his belt, he'll start carrying (big or small, light or heavy) objects from point A to point B. He's passing two milestones at once—walking and carrying—and over time, his mind starts working out the notion of lines, or trajectories. A line happens when you transport an object from here to there. He is practicing with his whole body the form he will later be able to draw on paper. And this is what a curve looks like physically, a form that registers mentally. From the outside, it looks as if he were picking up and moving items at random, but Alex always has his reasons. There are usually multiple developments happening at once—in this case, he's practicing new thought processes, sequences of movements, and many other skills. Alex usually has some cryptic reason for what he's doing.

Quick Reference—Play Schemas

Actively Discovering the World

Did you know that your child never makes a mess? Making a mess is intentional: Your child would be strewing things around the room simply because they felt like it. But they have earnest and important reasons for what they're doing.

Most kids engage in what's called "schematic play" or "play schemas." Your child uses objects in certain ways to figure out the nature of the world around them. Think of it this way: In order for your child to understand division in math class later on, they need to tear bread into pieces as a toddler. They need to learn that a whole can be broken into smaller parts. To understand that conceptually, a child needs to experience it concretely.

Children take on the exact projects they need for whatever developmental step comes next. There isn't a specific age for your child to play according to this or that particular scheme; in their own personal fashion, they will play their way through countless schemes. They'll combine schemes, expand upon them, skip some altogether, and immerse themselves deeply within others.

Let's say your child disassembles a new toy, rather than using it the way it's supposed to be used (according to you and the manufacturer)—they are practicing the "transforming" scheme, an important step for brain development. Or maybe they're working on the "positioning" scheme, arranging the pieces in a row. Or they wrap the new toy in a towel, thus practicing the "enveloping" scheme. Maybe they carry the toy around the room, learning more about "transporting." You can be certain that however they're using the toy, it makes the most sense for your child's current development.

Here are the most common play schemas.

- **Positioning:** Your child will line up cars or stuffies, roll a toy truck along the edge of a rug, drop objects or toss them in the air. This teaches a sense of length, height, distance, quantity, and (later on) timelines.
- **Transforming:** Children love making things change or watching them change. Cooking eggs, for instance, transforms egg whites from translucent goo into an opaque solid within seconds. Your child is gaining experience in chemical processes and physical qualities.
- **Connecting:** Your child practices tying or sticking things together, connecting train cars, and of course building with Legos or blocks. This shows them what fits together, and they starts gaining experience in stability, stasis, and construction.
- **Enveloping:** Children wrap up objects in pieces of fabric or paper. They might even wrap themselves up. This scheme teaches them all about size and materials and develops their sense of touch.
- **Transporting:** Your child hauls toys, sand, or pieces of furniture from point A to point B. They're testing the limits of their physical strength and learning about quantity. The fact that an object or quantity stays the same, regardless of where it is, is very tricky—it can take until preschool age for a child to understand object permanence.
- **Dividing and Scattering:** Children like making piles of things:

Legos, stuffies, sand, cookies, leaves, flour—then dividing them into smaller pieces or scattering them. A piece of bread can be divided into smaller pieces, whereas cookies can be crumbled completely. The pieces of a puzzle are always the same, but when you cut up an apple, the pieces can be different sizes. There's lots to learn here about geometry and math, quantity, shapes, and volume.

- **Sorting:** To learn about structures and categories, your child enjoys sorting objects according to various characteristics. These are some of the first experiences they'll have in organizing principles and the criteria we use for them. While immersed in this scheme, your child may not want different foods to touch on the plate.

- **Filling and Transferring:** Children dump sand or pour water from one bucket into another or stuff solid items into a box. They're discovering volume, quantity, what (and how much) different containers can hold, the speed at which various liquids flow, tipping points, and other physics concepts.

- **Orientation:** Your child hangs upside down, bends over to look back through their legs, lies under the table, or crawls onto the flat bottom rack of a grocery cart. Exploring different perspectives now may prepare them to consider various points of view in the future.

These are the primary play schemas, although others do exist.

What Can Parents Do?

As you might imagine, play schemas become wildly complex in practice. They overlap and complement each other. Your child might not do some of them and might do others concurrently. In some cases, schemas will emerge in different situations or at different ages and your child will investigate them in new ways. Even as an adult, when you tidy up your desk, for example, you're expanding on the sorting scheme.

If you enjoy this kind of teaching, you can observe your child at play and figure out which scheme they're currently exploring. At times, they might be more interested in specific aspects of an object, while other times engaged in the underlying scheme. As part of the "rotation" scheme, for instance, you might see your child studying clock faces with fascination, twirling around in circles for fun, watching the spin cycle in the washing machine, and trying to crank on whatever steering wheel they can get their hands on. If you like, you can provide objects or situations that lend themselves to this scheme.

Or you can just lean back, give your child the time and space to explore, and trust in the mysterious inner workings of their development. Your child knows best when it comes to what they need to learn right now, and they'll seek out experiences to get there. Give them the freedom to try things out and as much free time to play as possible.

By now, John and Julia have bought a lot of building blocks for Alex. Like other kids his age, he learns how to build in the same order: First he stacks the blocks, then he lines them up, and months later he'll combine the two.

Currently he can stack two or three blocks. It isn't easy: He has to aim carefully when placing one block on top of the other, which takes lots of concentration. As always when learning a new scheme—in this case, connecting—he won't limit himself to objects designed specifically for that purpose, but will instead stack everything within reach. As long as he can practice the scheme with all sorts of objects, he's good. Equally important is knocking the tower over, almost immediately after its completion. After all, Alex isn't interested in the final product. It's all about practice.

Alex also loves taking things out and putting them away—though rarely where they came from! Some objects can be *inside* other objects, a fact that simply must be explored. Socks that he plucked from the sock drawer may very well end up in the stock pot. He pulls clothes out of closets, books off shelves, and every day he empties the bottom kitchen cabinets. Alex repeatedly clears out the same spots in the apartment—a specific drawer or bookcase—until he fully understands what's going on there and can move on to the next area.

Alex needs to repeat behaviors many times in order to learn. Whether it's the puzzle he does the exact same way every day or emptying drawers, shelves, and cupboards of their contents—repetition is the name of the game. It's already taught him a lot, like which objects go together. His doll goes with the dollhouse, for instance, or his spoon with his plate. Every day he discovers another little piece of the world.

The best toys for Alex now are sponges, pots, bowls, mixing spoons, and all sorts of kitchen utensils. And we're talking the real deal here—forget about "baby-proof" imitations that clearly aren't meant for actual use. How can Alex be expected to play for hours with a plastic stick of butter when an actual stick of butter is sitting on the kitchen counter? Real butter is sometimes soft, sometimes solid, and has a smell. You can poke a finger in it, unwrap it, and make yummy foods with it. Alex can see that Mom and Dad don't use the pretend butter, a sign that it won't help him with growing up.

Alex adores helping around the house. He wants to feel useful. He wants to be a valuable member of the family and do whatever he can to contribute in meaningful ways. He wants the experience of making things happen. To his parents they're little things, but to him they're huge. He can hold out his arms—all by himself!—when getting bundled to go outside. Great! He's a big kid now. He can fetch his shoes, peel a banana (as long as someone gets it started), put the butter in the fridge, help sort socks, take groceries out of shopping bags, sweep things away or pick them up. It's nothing short of a party for Alex when he gets to stir the pot of food his family is about to eat. Alex loves all of it. He doesn't view any of it as "work." He does not distinguish between "work" and "play" the way grown-ups do and doesn't see one as better than the other.

Books and Drawing Take Time and Effort

John and Julia look forward to bedtime reading and try to spark Alex's interest in picture books, but unfortunately all he does is flip through the pages. They worry that he might not be interested in reading, which would be a shame—they would love it if Alex grew into a big reader, just like them. But books, like any other object, have to be "worked out" before Alex can turn his attention to the story. That means he has to turn page after page after page until he's understood the nature of the book. He does, however, recognize everyday objects in the illustrations. Some kids his age have moved on from the flipping phase and love reading and pointing at things they see in the pictures.

If presented with a piece of paper and crayon, Alex will scribble wildly. It's fun. He's not looking to draw anything specific yet; he's just trying this out. He holds the crayon in his fist and pounds the paper with it, punching holes. John and Julia don't love that. They'd pictured drawing differently, but Alex's artistic career starts with scribbling: first featuring lots of hitting, later moving on to zany back-and-forth strokes.

Feelings and Relationships

Alex is unbridled, clear, and direct in expressing his feelings. When he's upset, everyone around him knows it. When he likes someone, he'll hug them or offer them his prized possessions. When his mom holds another child on her lap, Alex will emphatically push them. Although Alex can now express his feelings, it will take another couple of years before he can regulate them.

He is still learning to read faces, and he pays close attention to how people show their feelings. He tries to make eye contact and loves human interaction.

When Alex sees other kids crying, he tries various ways to help them. He goes to them, comforts them, and maybe gives them one of his toys to make them feel better. This behavior is unmediated: Alex sees someone crying, so he acts. And that action reflects his knowledge.

It will be a while before Alex develops "real" empathy: the ability to imagine what other people are feeling and respond accordingly. His parents see that Alex can't tell whether his friend wants the form of comfort he's offering. He forces his toy upon the other child because he's learned that toys help, whether his friend wants it or not. Resistance is not accepted. Alex will sometimes press the toy into the other child's body.

Alex learns a lot by trial and error, but also by imitation. He observes his surroundings closely and starts imitating what he sees. He makes phone calls. He cooks, stirs, touches the screen of the tablet. Alex wants to do whatever the grown-ups are doing. He likes playing give-and-take games with adults. It's great to hand something over . . . but not if it isn't given back. He feels uneasy until he gets it back. The game is all about going back and forth.

Riding Out Frustration

It's wonderful that Alex understands so many rules at this point. At the same time, he freaks out when the rules suddenly change.

It can be little details he's picked up from his surroundings. For instance, John usually wears black shoes, but one morning he puts on brown shoes, and Alex starts crying. He *just* grasped the black shoes, now suddenly they're different? Why? John and Julia are thoroughly confused and can't figure out what's wrong for the longest time. Alex can't articulate it and just keeps pointing at the shoes, tugging at the laces, and crying. It takes a lot of imagination these days for his parents to get into his brain, where things still look pretty different. And their attempt doesn't always work. His brain simply functions differently than an adult brain.

And it doesn't always *have* to work. Alex currently feels a lot of frustration. Because things don't behave the way he wants them to. Because people don't understand him. Because a boundary is put in place or he wants to do more than he is capable of—there are lots of reasons.

His parents think it's their job to keep Alex's frustration at bay and cheer him up quickly, to which he would respond, "Listen, it's important for me to learn how to cope with frustration. How am I supposed to do that if I'm never frustrated? I want to know what it feels like, and how to deal with it." Alex also wants to learn that there isn't anything you *can* do much of the time; you just have to endure and wait for the feeling to go away. Things don't always work out in life. It's good, then, that life is so frustrating currently, even if Alex hates it in the moment.

When Alex feels mad or sad, he's still just looking for understanding and a grown-up to ride it out with him. Sometimes he wants a solution, but being allowed to feel is more important. Raging is a fantastic way for Alex to relieve anger. The frustration passes, and it's like nothing ever happened. Alex doesn't bear grudges.

Besides learning to deal with anger and sadness, Alex is also battling separation anxiety. He thinks it's great to keep his parents within earshot. He regularly faces the dilemma of wanting to explore the world and venture out on his own, though it can be scary. If something happens that he can't quite make sense of, he rushes back to Mom or Dad. But if they can't hear him, it's even scarier. He keeps a close eye on them in unfamiliar territory, crawling or running directly behind them if they try to leave.

Understanding Rules

Alex is starting to understand rules. He might stand by the electrical outlet, shake his head, and say, "No-no." It's like the drawers: He had to empty them out many times before he understood. He'll look at Dad and move toward the socket—how does Dad respond? Is his reaction consistent or does it change daily? Humans are so much harder for Alex to understand than drawers. Some rules seem set in stone—like the one about the socket—whereas others do not. Sometimes he hears the word "exception"—what the heck does that mean? It will take more time for Alex to understand variable rules.

Then there's the pesky fact that, although Alex might know this or that rule, he can't actually follow it yet. He can only experience one thought and one feeling at the same time—old thoughts or feelings are completely replaced by new ones. Even if he intended to follow the rule, the feeling and thought promptly vanished. Besides, his developmental drive and impulse to investigate are much stronger, so he might end up doing what he's not supposed to. It just sort of happens to him. Something similar happens to his parents when they're eyeing the candy dish or an empty wine glass. They know they shouldn't . . . but the impulse is so strong . . . they resist for a while . . . then end up finishing the chocolate or polishing off the bottle.

Alex often smiles after breaking the rules, because as an infant he learned that smiling fixes everything. Usually when he smiles, the grown-ups smile back, and everyone's happy. This is not the case after breaking the rules, though. Instead, his parents think Alex is provoking them. Aunt Toni calls it his "naughty smile," and tells his parents they have to "nip it in the bud, otherwise he'll walk all over you." The adults discuss it at great length. John and Julia try to explain where Alex is at developmentally, but Aunt Toni isn't convinced. She prefers to trust concrete fact—in this case, that smile. She did things differently in her day and doesn't buy all these newfangled explanations, which to her sound less like Alex's inner life than a load of excuses. Toni loves Alex and wants the best for him, but the path she would take is very different.

Playing with Friends

What's up these days with Alex's playgroup? Alex loves interacting with other kids, but he is not yet capable of forming friendships. He likes crawling or toddling with other children. He'll greet them and hand over his toy (then get mad when they don't hand it back—they don't follow the same rules as his parents). He watches other children intently and can learn a lot from them, as their behaviors resemble his more closely. He's still awkward in this kind of interaction and doesn't have any sense of etiquette. True collaborative play is still too complicated. He's not there yet. If older kids with a more developed sense of play are around, joint play can arise, but Alex can't concentrate on any one activity for very long, so the game will be brief. Still, contact with other children is wonderful for Alex; it just doesn't look exactly the way that his parents expected.

Movement

Alex can walk! At some point, he takes his first steps. This looked different for everyone in his playgroup—most started with crawling, but others scooted on their bottoms, rolled from point A to point B, or even snaked around the room. Whatever path they took to get there, Alex and his friends trained their muscles and mobility for many months until they finally managed to start walking.

When Alex first starts to walk, it looks like he's falling from one leg onto the other. He raises his arms for balance. Sometimes he likes to hold a grown-up's hand while walking, just in case. Other playgroup parents advise John and Julia not to hold both hands and guide Alex from above, because that teaches kids to lumber side-to-side like a bear. Alex would prefer to walk like a human, arms and legs crossing, meaning he'll need at least one free hand to practice his balance.

Stopping is another matter altogether, one that requires practice, so at first he just plops down or grabs hold of something to be on the safe side. As for Julia, she needs to practice not overprotecting him. One day, she sees Alex reaching for his marble run, and she rushes to steady the toy so it doesn't tip over. As a result, Alex thinks it's a secure spot and heads toward it at full throttle—only to fall down, marble run and all. He needs to learn these things for himself.

As he learns to walk, Alex loves pushing objects around. That includes heavy objects, because he's trying to build muscle. His parents are tempted to take away heavy objects, but Alex protests loudly. Even when crawling, for instance, he opts for the most challenging path over, under, or even through obstacles. His parents laugh and wonder why he doesn't take the easier path, to which Alex would respond that he's busy learning again. He seeks out challenges to teach him every variation that a certain movement might have. He wants the exertion. People only look for more efficient options when they're big and know what they're doing.

Alex now has a good grasp—literally—of the use of his hands. He can use individual fingers deliberately, which is a new accomplishment. Naturally this too needs practice, so for now he burrows his digits into all kinds of spaces, scratches the carpet, or runs them across smooth surfaces.

Alex has the "pincer grasp" down pat: He can pick up small items (like crumbs) between his thumb and index finger.

It's becoming evident that Alex favors using his right hand. There's a little girl in his playgroup who seems to be left-handed. Her mom tells Julia that handedness is inborn and should be accepted, however it turns out.

Feeding Oneself: A Real Feat

Alex loves doing as much as possible on his own. Eating is especially awesome. He clenches the spoon askew in this fist—the only way he can—and makes a big mess. It will be a long time before he manages to hold the spoon level and travel the great distance from plate to mouth without spilling. He is determined to do it himself and has little regard for losses in transit. How do you get your spoon—which is tippy by nature—to your mouth when you can't really bend your wrist yet? Alex has to learn by lots of trial and error. Besides, he needs to play with his food, because if you're going to put something in your mouth, you have to check it out with your hands first. Alex's parents notice that he becomes extra absorbed in squishing and smearing his food after he's full, so they give him other squishy things to play with during the day to satisfy that need. That way he won't need to play with his food as much in the long run.

John and Julia let Alex try drinking from a cup now too, which leads to lots of spilling until he finds the tipping point.

Speech

Alex is beyond determined to decode the weird noises the grown-ups around him make all the time. He is learning lots of words, as John and Julia always tell him in detail what's going on and what they're doing when they're with him. By sixteen months, Alex's passive vocabulary is around two hundred words, but he still understands demeanor, voice, body language, facial expressions, and gestures much better.

Alex is now using what could be called the "key word strategy." While he listens, he watches the facial expression and gestures that go along with whatever the person is saying. He can get away with recognizing a few words and filling in the rest with body language. "Give me the cup" is a great example, even if he doesn't know the words "me" or "cup"—he sees Dad holding out his hand expectantly and looking at Alex's cup. He can even understand longer prompts using this approach, although he often misunderstands. When his mom says, "Careful, the knife is sharp!" he responds, "Wah!"

Alex tries to speak and makes increasingly purposeful sounds and words—soon he can say about ten. Alex adapts the words according to his skills, making changes that allow him to use them. For instance, he says "nana" for banana or "bzzz" for bees. His parents learn to simplify and shorten their own speech for Alex.

Alex can't form complete sentences yet, but he has a clever workaround—he alters his tone of voice and body language to express full thoughts using a single word. A quizzical "Car?" might mean "Are we leaving soon?" whereas an enthusiastic "Car!" suggests a new car-related discovery. His parents interpret his tone and respond with, "Yes, we're about to go for a ride in the car," or "You're right, there goes the new Audi. Or did you mean the Nissan?"

At a Glance: 6–12 Months

Thinking and Play

Alex is exploring his surroundings more closely these days. He learns by trial and error as well as imitation, meaning he needs to check objects out thoroughly before using them the "right" way. Repetition (lots of repetition) is key. Alex is learning about rules and boundaries but can't follow them yet, as his developmental drive is too powerful. He's happiest playing with everyday objects.

Feelings and Relationships

Alex is unbridled and direct in expressing his feelings. He's learning to cope with frustration, so the frustrations of everyday life are actually very important. He loves helping around the house and wants to tackle small tasks on his own. Although Alex is curious about other kids, he's still awkward in interactions.

Movement

Alex has learned to walk. He can climb onto chairs and carry things. He can use individual fingers and pick up small objects between this thumb and index finger. And he is hell-bent on feeding himself—though a fair amount winds up on the floor. Practice is hugely important for the brain and muscles to learn how these things are done.

Speech

Alex is steadily building his vocabulary and can soon say a few words. He adapts the words according to his skills, like saying "nana" for "banana" or "bzzz" for bees. He can follow short instructions but gains the most from gestures, facial expressions, tone of voice, and bearing, then infers the rest from the situation.

4

Development from 18–24 Months

Thinking and Play

At some point during this period, Alex makes a significant cognitive step: She begins to identify as "I" or "me." She recognizes herself in the mirror, as proven by the "rouge test." If a grown-up sneaks a bit of blush on her cheek, then holds up a mirror, Alex will rub the makeup off her face. Until quite recently, at the sight of herself in the mirror, she would have either greeted the child or looked behind the mirror to find them. Now she knows: Hey, that's me!

This is an extremely exciting realization that will influence all areas of her life. Alex now sees herself as her own person. It turns out she's not part of her parents—she's her very own "me." She can act of her own accord! Alex is bowled over by this newfound awareness, and she will test its scope extensively in the coming months and years.

However fabulous the notion of independent action, Alex soon discovers just how many obstacles can get in the way.

First there are her motor skills: Alex's mood sours when she fails at something. She rarely musters the patience she exhibited in her first year of life, when she would gladly try things over and over until they worked. And a lot doesn't work out, because her physical skills simply can't keep up with the amazing plans in her head. Here, all she's trying to do is help cook dinner, and she knows the steps—but it falls apart because the pan is too heavy. How frustrating!

But that's not the half of it. Then there are the boundaries set by people. For instance, Alex's parents refuse to let her use the big bread knife or work the stove on her own. Alex cannot make heads or tails of it, because she is convinced that she has all the skills she needs.

Free Will

Alex is developing her own free will, though it doesn't come easy—first she needs to become aware of what she wants. This is a new feeling in her body. She wants something . . . but what? . . . Maybe this thing . . . or maybe not? It will take Alex many months to sense what she wants with certainty and then stick to it. She's initially overwhelmed by personal choice and goes back and forth on what she says she wants.

John and Julia read that it's important to let her make decisions as she begins to develop autonomy. They view their toddler's autonomy much like they do their own: as an opportunity for Alex to direct the course of her life. They are happy to give her as much freedom as they can to make her own decisions and chart her path.

Alex defines autonomy differently: She wants to be independent at a very practical level, as often as possible. Her parents underestimate her ability to learn practical skills quickly and well. Meanwhile, they overestimate her mental maturity and ability to make decisions.

This leads to strange situations for our little trio. It starts first thing in the morning, when Mom or Dad gives Alex the choice between cheese or jam on her toast. Alex gets in the way of her own brain, which hasn't developed enough for this: She doesn't understand the concept of "either/or" yet. "Do you want this or that?" is an unanswerable question for her. Since she still relies mostly on gestures, facial expressions, and tone of voice to communicate, Alex looks at the foods that her mom put on the counter. There's the jam, and beside it some cheese. And Mom just said both words. Based on Mom's tone of voice and gestures, Alex can tell that her mom wants some kind of response. Okay—what might that be? Since this is a regular occurrence, Alex soon learns that she's supposed to point to one of these two items, so that's what she does. She points to the jam, then Mom takes away the cheese. Red alert! What's the big idea? Why is that other thing suddenly gone? Alex complains and Mom asks if she would rather have cheese. Alex says yes. Then the jam disappears, sending Alex back into despair.

If only Alex could tell her parents, "You know what I would really love is to prepare my toast myself. That's all I care about. I want to learn how it's done and go through as much of the process as I can. I'm very hands-on—thinking and decision-making aren't really my thing."

Alex and her parents are routinely stymied by their differing takes on autonomy. Eating is fine, because it's a concrete action with direct consequences, so Alex learns it quickly. But her parents ask her to make so many decisions. John and Julia discovered that doing so can prevent (or at least delay) a meltdown through distraction. Alex can only concentrate on one thing at a time. Being asked to mull over a choice distracts her from her feelings. Other distractions—"Look, a bird!"—would also accomplish this.

Certain decisions, like how long to stay at the playground, can send the entire family into a tailspin. John and Julia want to respect their one-year-old's freedom of choice: If Alex really wants to stay at the playground, her parents try to grant her that, even if it means a more stressful evening for them because they have so much to get done. They do it for Alex, to make her happy. Unfortunately, Alex can't appreciate that yet.

Were we to hand the mic to Alex, she might say, "Mom and Dad, it's nice of you to offer me so many opportunities to make decisions, but I'm not there yet. It's too soon. I won't be able to make good decisions until I'm able to anticipate the consequences. I can't decide if it's best to stay at the playground. Do I know what will happen if we head home too late? That there will be all sorts of important things we don't get to, and everyone will feel overextended? No, I don't know that. You two need to manage that big-picture stuff for me. You need to make the decision, and yes, there's a good chance I'll make a fuss. But that isn't reason enough to hand off the decision-making to me. It's too much responsibility, and it's overwhelming."

Although Alex often tries to take the lead, she isn't actually looking for it to work. She's more interested in the attempt. She's trying her hand at resistance and exercising free will. But leading her whole family? No thanks. As a consequence of Alex's wish to stay at the playground, she and her parents are sweaty, dirty, and tired when they get home, and it's *late*. But that's what Alex "wanted." Her parents are openly (or secretly) annoyed with Alex and her "demands." Now pressed for time, they try to rush through their evening routines. Alex has no idea why things feel so weird. She seems responsible, but how? She is beyond tired, far too exhausted to be in a good mood. Alex's desire to stay at the playground totally did her in, because she couldn't anticipate what it would mean for her.

Navigating the Day-to-Day, Plus Drawing and Painting

Alex is still imitating lots of everyday actions, which are gradually becoming more complex. She especially loves making "pies" in her sandbox and "selling" her seemingly endless supply to the grown-ups. The game goes like this: The customer says, "Mm, yummy pie!" then buys another crumbly pie. Alex has a loose interpretation of "selling" and might give some customers their pie *and* some money, because she doesn't quite understand that it's an exchange—money for pie. What matters most to her is that the game repeats many times and always goes the same way. It takes a long time (way *too* long for the adults involved) for Alex to introduce tiny new variations of her own accord. Her brain simply wants the process repeated as many times as possible. Alex is learning. The adult brain is unfortunately bored stiff by this game, meaning her parents' interest in buying sand pies soon wanes. They prefer variety and would love to switch it up, which is still beyond Alex.

Alex is making countless new sensory discoveries. She gleefully smears and smooshes all sorts of matter, like sand, clay, bubble bath, lotion, paint . . . she's got to try it all out. She laid the foundation for drawing and painting as a baby, when she would scatter, spread, and smear anything soft.

Alex now starts drawing—or rather, scribbling on paper and other surfaces. She does it for the pure pleasure of rhythmic movement. She sweeps her arm back and forth, without lifting her hand, typically holding the writing implement however she pleases. Crayons (the sturdier, the better) are her favorite. Clenching the crayon squarely or askew in her fist, she'll press or bang it into the paper, making dots or in some cases punching holes. The movement is fun, whether Alex is scribbling in wild circles or back and forth. She has no time for the adult question, "What are you drawing?" She isn't drawing anything in particular; all that matters is that it's fun and she gets to practice the movement.

Alex continues to work on understanding the world around her, grouping things by rough categories. All women are called "Mom," anything that drives is a "car," and round objects are broadly referred to as "ball." The grown-ups laugh when she makes mistakes in categorizing, like when she calls a sheep a dog. It's too bad Alex can't assume a dignified stance and say, "Excuse me, but I am still working on the global-to-basic level shift in my categorical thinking, meaning I will occasionally apply the superordinate level of 'animal' to a subordinate object. I have to rely on the limited information available to me in day-to-day life, so please, show some respect."

Alex has explored shapes enough to know that a square object will not fit in a triangular hole. She can easily match shapes and sort things—for instance, she can put forks with forks and spoons with spoons in the silverware drawer. It's something she does with abandon, as it checks two major boxes: She gets to help *and* learn more about sorting and categorizing.

Help Me Do It Myself

Alex loves helping! She wants to know exactly what's happening on the kitchen counter. Her parents are getting a little tired of constantly having to pick her up, because she would otherwise whine and tug at their pant legs.

John and Julia see a "toddler tower" at a friend's house and love the idea. It's a wooden step stool with a safety rail that Alex can climb on and off by herself. From that height she can watch and learn what's happening on the counter. It's important that she can climb up and down by herself, because her attention span is so short. She just wants to take a quick peek, learn, maybe try something out herself . . . and then she loses interest. But she'll be back a little later to check in. Alex takes in what her mind can handle, and thanks to the tower, John and Julia don't have to plan some big presentation, only to feel disappointed when their toddler leaves two minutes later.

Alex loves having a job. She can't always approach a task methodically or finish it, but she certainly can practice cracking or whisking eggs, filling things up, or fetching items. She loves doing dishes—hooray for water play! She also likes shoveling snow, raking grass, vacuuming, matching socks, taking laundry off the line, mopping, sweeping, and watering flowers. Alex is also practicing personal hygiene like brushing her teeth, combing her hair, and washing her hands.

Alex occasionally hears the grown-ups talking about how messy and chaotic she is, which is baffling to her. If only she could explain that she needs someone to teach her tidiness. She simply doesn't know how it's done. As she grows out of her "take everything out" phase, she's ready to start learning about structure. This definitely does not happen overnight but is instead—like so many things—a months-long process.

What Alex needs here is a bird's-eye view. She needs someone to break down tidying up into very small chunks. She needs to hear: The red block goes in here. Now the blue block. That goes in here too. Aha. Will it be the same tomorrow? What about next week? She needs a reliable structure to learn.

Alex can only be tidy with a small number of items—full shelves, for instance, are completely overwhelming. Alex would do best with just a few toys, though these can be switched up. When she spots a toy that she hasn't seen in a while, it can spark new interest. Alex can't handle excessive input, however well-meaning, though she *will* of course try—and the effort to check everything out leads to chaos.

Extending Thought Through Play

Alex is still puzzling out the way things work and has accomplished another major step in cognitive development: She can now pretend, which is also known as "symbolic play." She doesn't need the actual object but can, for instance, hold a wooden block to her ear and in her mind it becomes a telephone. This was a difficult step for her brain, using imagination to transform a concrete object into something else. Alex uses this symbolic object as she would the real one, in this case babbling into the block held to her ear as she toddles around the room. She also continues to imitate everyday actions. She plays with her toy cars, puts a stuffie in one of them and drives it around, cooks, or goes grocery shopping. Alex demonstrates that several everyday routines have cohered for her in the way that she plays. For example, she'll feed her stuffie, then tuck it in, just like her parents do with her.

Containers remain a source of fascination. Alex fills buckets with sand, water, acorns—whatever she can get her hands on!—then dumps them out. She also loves loading rocks into her toy dump truck and dumping them out. At times, she becomes utterly engrossed in play, talking to herself in her own language.

Alex likes building towers, piling things high. She can stack about three or four blocks at this point. She's following the mysterious internal pattern that all kids do, first piling things vertically, then arranging horizontal rows before combining the two and building more complex structures.

Generally, Alex follows certain patterns of play. Currently she's spending a lot of time with transporting and piling. She carries objects from point A to point B and puts them in piles. This teaches her that you can pile or amass objects, then divvy them up—a fundamental of mathematics. Alex is also learning all sorts of lessons about transporting, like how much she can carry in her hands or a bucket, how far she can get, and how long it takes. These are the tricky research questions she's working on right now (see Quick Reference—Play Schemas, page 86).

Another important point: Alex's response time is still slow. When giving instructions, it's best to wait. Maybe count to ten, then look for her response, because it might take that long. Alex needs time to sort through the images, smells, sensations, and voice cues that just rained down on her: Someone wants something . . . what was it again . . . how do I . . . oh yeah, that's right.

Feelings and Relationships

With newfound awareness of being "me," Alex's emotional range has expanded. She now experiences the "secondary emotions" a person can only have when they see themselves as their own person. These emotions are tied to a sense of self—like shame, pride, envy, and guilt. Life is about to get more complicated, as Alex has never felt ashamed or guilty before. That's slowly changing. On the other hand, she also feels proud of her accomplishments, which she likes.

These days Alex's biggest struggle is that she wants to do things herself, but it doesn't always work out. Then, whether she likes it or not, she has to accept help—and she is *not* okay with that. She's big! She can do it herself! She's her own person, and she can take care of her own stuff! Alex gets super frustrated when she has a hard time putting on her jacket and can't get the zipper to work, or when she's not allowed to try because her parents are in a hurry. She shrieks, refuses to cooperate, and momentarily views the world as a cruel and cold place.

Perceiving Desire and Setting Boundaries

It isn't easy for Alex to feel so uncertain at times—and to get people to believe her when she *does* know what she wants. Sometimes she cranks up the volume and vehemence to compensate—if she screams loudly enough, surely then they'll know that she's serious. It further complicates matters for everyone involved that within minutes, something else comes along that Alex feels just as strongly about. Perceiving exactly what you want is just too difficult!

Sometimes Alex will take a stand against something for no good reason. As it is, reason or rationality is hardly involved during this phase, which is all about Alex learning to perceive and assert free will. She practices on little things. The reason doesn't matter. Just as she tirelessly emptied out drawers for practice, she's now practicing taking a stand in conflict with other people. It's not too convincing yet, but she'll get better at it (see Autonomy and Boundaries, page 126).

This is the first phase of Alex's distinguishing herself from her parents. She can come across as surly, but it's only for lack of practice. In quiet moments, Alex would say, "Mom, Dad, my big feelings are not directed at you. Please don't take it personally. I'm in search of myself. In search of what I like and don't like, what I can and can't do, and I'm unable to express that appropriately yet. Things are constantly going sideways, and I'm overwhelmed by the corners that I keep painting myself into. You have to take over for me in those moments so my emotions don't escalate. I need boundaries. Sure, I'll get mad about that too, but it gives me something to hang on to. I need to know that I'm not completely lost, and that someone else still has a handle on things when I definitely do not."

John and Julia have a very hard time with this, because their one-year-old's feelings are so extreme. Situations escalate quickly and unexpectedly these days—everything was fine, now suddenly the child acts like it's the end of the world. Plus these emotional outbursts never occur when the scene is relaxed but always seem to coincide with stressful, difficult situations (see Feelings and Tantrums, page 182).

Playing Together

There are many magical moments when Alex and her parents play movement games, like "The Itsy Bitsy Spider." Or Alex might just cling to one of their legs and shriek with glee as they swing her back and forth. These games are tons of fun for her, and romping encourages sensory learning!

Alex likes turning the pages of the picture books Mom and Dad read to her—so much that she often turns the page before they finish reading it. She's also in it for the cuddles.

Playing together is great, though Alex and the grown-ups still have different notions of what that looks like. To her, an amazing game is when she repeats something many, many times while a grown-up watches, or if they smile and say a few words about what she's doing. That's plenty. That, to Alex, is a perfect example of "playing together."

Around other kids, Alex is growing out of "solitary" and into "parallel" play. In other words, she will play *next to* other children doing the same activity. She and her buddy might swap a toy now and then. Alex might bring something to another child in the room, or maybe they scoot or run behind each other.

Alex might desperately want what her buddy is playing with. Since neither is talking yet, they can't exactly have a measured discussion about who gets to play with that toy right now. Instead they solve it physically. Whoever is faster or stronger gets the toy. Alex doesn't get why this makes the grown-ups yell. She hears them say the word "share." What the heck? Why does she have to give up her toy? She is desperate to play with it, and her impulses are powerful. What possible reason could there be for passing it up? Alex hasn't developed empathy yet, so the notion that her buddy might want the toy as badly as she does is the furthest thing from her mind. She'll need to have it explained and, more importantly, demonstrated concretely many times over. If sharing is something she experiences in everyday life with her family ("Let's share the last piece of pizza"), she'll learn. Just not quite yet.

Fighting!

Alex's social skills are middling at present. Here too, she employs trial and error to work them out: Kid won't give toy? Push kid, take toy. Awesome. Uh-oh, the grown-ups are responding—maybe not so awesome. Is there another method? How does it go? Alex needs role models here. She needs to see (repeatedly) how grown-ups would solve the situation. Saying "stop" or "please" or waiting or apologizing . . . this is complex and will take Alex a long time to learn.

Her parents wonder why Alex shoves and hits other kids. Is she maladjusted? They're very worried. This isn't the example they've set for her, so where does it come from? Alex would assure them, "It's all good. I'm still learning. You don't worry about me being dumb, just because I can't do math yet. I'm not maladjusted—I'm adjusting. Not antisocial, but pre-social. Playing with others is difficult, and I'm just getting started. I can't speak much yet, nor can I really empathize with others or gauge their reactions. Hang tight, it's in the works. It'll just take another year or so!"

A friend informs John and Julia that most toddlers go through a phase of pushing, hitting, or biting themselves or others. It's just important to keep track of the behavior. They have to intervene right away (and repeatedly) to show Alex clearly (and calmly) that what she's doing is wrong, then immediately demonstrate what an appropriate response would be. Mom and Dad act as her role models and coaches. Discipline doesn't accomplish much when you don't know why you're being disciplined or how to act instead. Their friend assures them that they're on the right track; it's just a lot slower than they'd thought. (Let's remind ourselves: Learning social rules takes months—years, really.)

Movement

Alex now walks with confidence. She works up the courage to try the stairs, provided she has something to hold on to. At this point, she's still using the step-to pattern, one foot leading and the other following, both landing on the step before she moves on to the next one.

Another trick she's working on is kicking a ball without falling down. Not as easy as it looks! You have to balance on one leg, then correct for the movement of the other one. Wild. Alex can throw a ball now too, though it can be hard to predict the direction.

Alex is great at climbing on furniture, play sets, ladders, and the like. Fascinated by her own climbing skills, she unfortunately has no concept of danger and could easily wind up someplace high above the ground. Her parents sometimes need to act quickly.

Alex is gaining dexterity in her hands. There's so much to learn from zippers: You need enough strength to pull it evenly all the way to the top. If allowed to practice, Alex can soon unzip and remove certain pieces of clothing on her own. Getting dressed and undressed is a great game. It teaches Alex lots of new skills.

Alex can eat on her own now too! It's very slow and very messy, but it works. She has great physical awareness of satiation. Her body sends a clear signal when she's full. Sometimes that moment comes right before the last bite of food, and she will stop eating. Alex's parents try not to make her eat that final morsel. They want to encourage her to listen to her body and not to ignore the feeling of fullness for the sake of a clean plate.

Alex's food needs change almost daily, depending on how active she is or if she's growing or sick or worked up. It worries her parents when she doesn't eat much, perhaps because she's growing less quickly during that period. Alex could reassure them that she has a good sense of what she needs. It's a decision she's well equipped to make because it isn't mental. She simply feels it in her body and acts accordingly. She doesn't think "I should eat now" or "I shouldn't eat now" or "I should eat something different." Hunger means eat. Full means stop. End of story.

Speech

Alex's comprehension is gradually improving, but she still relies on gestures, facial expressions, tone of voice, and context for help in decoding. Speaking is harder. Alex can say around twenty words now, and by the end of the year, around fifty. There's a wide range in her playgroup: Some kids actively use lots of words, whereas others use far fewer. Both are normal. And "words" still mean Alex's personal version of the "actual" word. It's of no use when John and Julia fix her mistakes, because she learns by modeling. One option for her parents is to eagerly repeat the correct word, so Alex can hear it again the right way. It isn't necessary to do this every time, though. As long as her parents keep talking to her, answering her questions and generally engaging with her, Alex will figure it out.

Alex is pleased to discover that she can get across to grown-ups (and get what she wants) by saying phrases like "want car" or "more milk." It's very frustrating when they don't understand, or when she can't find a way to communicate her needs and feelings and brilliant ideas.

It's hard to differentiate between sentences like "Please close the door" and "Please do not go near the door." If "door" is the only word she understands in the latter, Alex might just fill in the rest and beeline to the door, though it's the very thing she is *not* supposed to do. As it is, Alex doesn't really understand the word "not." Spoken language creates a picture in her mind, so "door" conjures up a clear image, whereas "not"—well, there's not much to land on there. It's best for John and Julia to tell Alex exactly what they *do* want, and not what they *don't* want.

At a Glance: 18–24 Months

Thinking and Play

Alex now sees herself as her own person—"I" or "me"—and wants to be a free agent. In practical terms, she wants to do as much as she can on her own. Making decisions, however, remains a challenge, because she can't see the big picture. She loves helping out around the house, which is like playtime to her. She can now use symbols and tools.

Feelings and Relationships

Alex experiences a lot of frustration these days, as she often wants to do more than she's capable of. This can unleash big emotions and sudden mood swings. Her sense of free will or desire is new to her, and she is slowly figuring out what she wants. She is highly ambivalent: One min-

> Alex and the ball: Now she knows that a ball will always fall down and roll away if she lets it go.

ute she wants this, and the next minute she wants that.

Alex is interested in other kids, but she has to develop her social skills. She hits and pushes sometimes, because she doesn't know how else to behave toward others. She mostly plays alongside her peers, rather than with them. Longer-form joint play is still too complex.

Movement

Alex is confident in walking now. She climbs on furniture and other structures and has little sense of danger. She's getting better at using her hands. With some practice, she can do things like close a zipper. She can feed herself and is great at knowing how much food she needs.

Speech

Alex understands about two hundred words and can say between twenty and fifty words, though she simplifies them. She can form one- or two-word sentences. She still relies on facial expression, gestures, tone of voice, body language, and situational context for understanding.

What to Know About 1-Year-Olds

If you don't remember what defines moments of leading and moments of following, please reread the summary on page 18. There's really just one question you need to ask when it comes to raising children: "Does my child need me to lead or to follow in this situation?"

Moments of Leading in 1-Year-Olds

At one year of age, your child is up against three major frustrations.

1. They experience strong, often sudden emotions that they don't really know how to handle. On top of that, they're not great at impulse control.
2. They're getting to know their own desires and free will. It doesn't work well at first, though, and they waffle between wanting this and wanting that.
3. Their speech hasn't developed enough to solve problems, explain themselves, or negotiate. They learn and communicate primarily by means of action.

For the most part, these three frustrations just require more time and development. Remember: There's no easy remedy. Development is underway and far from over. Things aren't easy for your child right now, because their feelings are getting so mixed up.

It's still important for you to give your child a sense of security and orientation. Just remember: Say what your hands are doing.

Look closely at the specific details of what you're doing. "Okay, we take the toothbrush. . . . Now where's the toothpaste? . . . There it is. . . . We squeeze some on our toothbrush. . . . Now we're done."

Whenever your child is learning a process—whether it's changing diapers, getting dressed, or eating—tell them about it. When you're about to do something unexpected, like wiping their nose or picking them up, tell them before you do it. It's a way of observing boundaries and treating them with respect—while teaching them these very lessons.

Say what you're doing, even if it feels boring and you've said it a thousand times and your child already gets it—as you know, repetition is important. Your child may remember specific details, but they're still working on all the different steps to all the different routines. How do you wash your hands again? First soap, then water, or the other way around? What's the first part of brushing your teeth? What's my job while my diaper's being changed? When it's time to eat, do I grab my spoon and plate first, then sit down, or the other way around? By saying what's going on, your child gains a sense of security and finds their bearings. At the same time, you lovingly take the lead. You know what comes next. You're extremely competent and trustworthy.

Your child is picking up the words for objects and routines and can start working with you, because they know what to expect. Teamwork truly starts on the changing table. Your child supports what you're doing as best they can.

Your child still processes information very slowly. You might need to count to eight or ten before they react to directions like "Hold out your arm." Give them time. As often as you can, give your teammate a chance to contribute. They're eager to do so.

How Do I Create Structure?

All your child wants to do these days is to learn. In order to grasp things, they have to literally *grasp* them. Take the lead here and help your child fulfill this powerful need. Too many "nos" will slow your child's developmental drive and are very frustrating to them. We don't want to shield them from all frustration, but being allowed to try things out is simply too important. Your child can't handle excessive constraints. They'll either find a way to do it anyway, dissolve into regular tantrums, or act so quickly that you won't have the chance to say "no."

Create a "yes space," a term from early childhood education. Rearrange your living space in such a way that you rarely have to say "no." Place vases out of reach. Keep pots and plastic bowls in lower cupboards. Consider all the ways in which you can "child-proof" your home, beyond the electrical outlets and stove (though they're important too). Your child can register and respect a few designated "no spaces," though it will take some time. They won't be able to follow the rules if you make too many of these spaces, though; they'll either forget, or impulse will get the better of them.

If you value tidiness, don't despair. Some people might think that little kids are messy, but they actually love structure and order. Like the rest of us, they prefer to know what's going on. To instill a sense of structure and order, you need to have a set place for everything and to repeat yourself many, many times.

Your child quickly loses track of what's going on when there are too many objects around. Toddlers respond to simple structure, as outlined in the Montessori method; see Further Reading. To be clear, a one-year-old cannot maintain order consistently, but they can work toward it slowly if someone repeatedly shows them what to do—for example, the blue block goes into a certain bin after playtime or at the end of the day.

If you're less concerned with overall tidiness, your child can still learn that it's nice to pick up together now and then. That too needs to be broken into small chunks. While you do the lion's share, see to it that your child puts away maybe two items. Tell them exactly where the items go, and accompany them in the process. Over time, they'll learn to put more and more things away. Repetition is very important in this context as well.

It can take months for the things you say (or better yet, do) to take effect. Don't think your efforts are in vain. They *are* making a difference, just not immediately. Leading often requires patience. It's completely normal for your child to point at an electrical outlet, say "no-no," and still reach for it. Their impulse control simply isn't developed enough. Don't take it personally. You're like the sock drawer that your child won't understand until they've emptied it a few hundred times. Now, it's your response that needs testing. This understanding is much harder won. Even harder is resisting the impulse to investigate and discover just because of some silly rule against it.

Boundaries are key at this age. Try to memorize this line: *All feelings are allowed, but not all behaviors.* For more on boundaries, see Autonomy and Boundaries, page 126.

After you've gained a bird's-eye view of your child's developmental stage, you'll save yourself a lot of stress by learning to anticipate many difficulties. When you have a tough day, take some time to reflect on what went wrong. Be honest with yourself: Was it a good idea to swing by Home Depot after a stressful afternoon? Was it obvious that my child was in no shape to come grocery shopping with me? Did I overtax my child's willingness to cooperate? Were there too many plans? Can we do it differently next time? Can I really let them play with others and expect it to work without my coaching? How can someone with no impulse control be expected not to make a mess if I don't tuck things away? As a good leader, you have so many opportunities to manage everyday situations preemptively to ensure they run smoothly.

How Do I Support Independence?

It's a widespread assumption that parents have to serve their child, to take care of every last thing for them in their first years of life, until they can do it themselves. It seems that everywhere you turn, parents are bending over backward to give their child the best life.

Lots of times, though, your child isn't able to appreciate the effort and parents come away feeling frustrated. Go that extra mile if and only if it's fun for you.

Your child isn't interested in the end result; they care about the process. This year, they're learning to use tools, and they can learn and do a lot more than you might think. Have faith in what your child can do at the practical level.

Your child requires a learning phase in which they watch you, then gradually start doing part of the process themselves. These steps add up quickly.

I generally don't think you need to buy many toys for your child, but toddler towers are a pretty brilliant invention. This step stool with a safety rail encourages self-regulation (ultimately allowing your child to decide how long they want to watch an activity and whether they want to join in). You can also use a chair with high armrests. As we saw with Alex, children know how much they can absorb and when they've had enough.

I'll keep stressing this: Kitchen tasks and household chores are child's play, literally! Your child doesn't differentiate between work and play the way you do. Everything is a game to them. They play while doing the laundry, making dinner, and building a tower of blocks; they make zero distinctions between these activities. At this age, all that matters is being allowed to choose freely, because your child is the only one who knows what developmental step to take next.

Your child loves nothing more than to help out, and they like having a job. They want to feel useful and to be an important part of the family. They don't like being far from the adults and kept busy just so they're out of the way. Although plenty of children happily "cook" in their play kitchen, most prefer the real deal, especially if it means hanging out with you.

If playing with your child bores you (true for many adults, though they seldom admit it), then do tasks around the house together. Tackle that to-do list as a team. Yes, this slows the process at first, but it's worth the slowdown in the long run. While these tasks promote your child's development, you get to enjoy the feeling of productivity. Add a little fun to the mix, and it's the best kind of nurturing.

A few small purchases may be wise here—for example, an affordable kid-size broom, mop, and other cleaning tools.

Eating is another important action that your child will want to do on their own. Once your child is using a spoon, you can start to expand on food items. But keep the relative size of these items in mind—it's hard to pour a glass of milk from a gallon jug when you're a toddler. Imagine trying to pour yourself a drink straight from a five-gallon water-cooler jug—as big as you are, you would struggle to find the tipping point and to control the flow. A creamer container is the perfect size for a toddler to practice pouring.

If the creamer is breakable, all the better! How can your child be expected to encounter danger if no one teaches them about it? If all they ever use is plastic, they'll think it's okay to throw things around because nothing will break. In the coming years, teach them how to handle glass and other fragile or dangerous items. Toddlers need to learn to be careful. Your child is more competent with practical skills than you might think. Trust them.

Sleep

If sleep is a concern, which would be perfectly normal, see Sleep in Babies and Toddlers, on page 74.

> ### Quick Reference—Thinking It Through
>
> **Working Together to Find Solutions**
>
> Now and then you can play around with something called "sustained shared thinking." The term is typically reserved for moments of true joint reflection, but you can start practicing this skill with your one-year-old. In the coming years, you will nurture your child's intelligence by allowing them to share in everyday problems, encouraging them to "think along." This may sound complicated, but it's really quite simple: Think out loud when you encounter an everyday problem. "Hmm, there's a lot of dirt on the entryway floor by the shoes. What can I do? Can I sweep it up? No, the dirt is wet, so I need to use a rag or wait until it dries. Where is that rag? Here it is. Let's wipe this up, then rinse out the rag. Wow, look at all the dirt that comes out. I'll hang it here to dry. Okay, that's done."
>
> By introducing everyday processes to your child in such a regular way, they can start thinking in tandem with you. At some point, they'll start presenting their own solutions to you, and this is the goal. Show enthusiasm for their suggestions, even if the solutions aren't perfect. If your child presents an imperfect solution, take some time to explain why it wouldn't

work. They need to learn the way things work now, if you want them to bring you coffee in bed in a few years' time.

"Metacognitive dialogues" gradually develop between toddler and preschool ages, as questions become more complex and you figure out the answers together. When your child asks a question, you could say something like, "Good question. I've wondered that too." You could venture a guess, saying, "I think it might work like this or like that," then pose the question back: "What do you think?" This exchange teaches your child how to approach and solve problems on their own.

Remember that your child is looking for love and connection. Just have fun together. Most children love to laugh, though their understanding of humor is different than yours. Verbal humor is lost on them, because language is still too new. Your child is amused by seeing something familiar suddenly turned on its head: wearing a colander as a hat, pulling a sock onto your hand, making a broom speak with a funny voice. These are great ways to amuse your child, reconnect, and make unpleasant moments a lot easier.

Moments of Following in 1-Year-Olds

The social dance between leading and following is challenging for us grown-ups this year, because a one-year-old's feelings are often volatile. Your child needs you to lead in situations that have a goal and a sequence of steps. When your child is playing, discovering new things, or experiencing strong emotions, they need your loving support. These are moments of following.

How Do I Support Emotions?

This is a tough year for your child when it comes to their newly awakened sense of volition. Imagine experiencing a powerful emotion but having no idea what to call it, how to express it, or how to regulate it. All you can do is stand there and scream or cry.

Your one-year-old often finds themselves in this position. Something doesn't work or looks different than usual. You make a change in routine. They're not allowed or unable to do what they want. Here come the big feelings. Life feels catastrophic. What would *you* need in moments like that? You'd need someone who simply sees what's going on, who understands you, and who might offer words for the situation or explain what your options are.

When you simply say what your child is feeling, they acquire words for this strange condition. They see your face and gaze, and they hear, "Yeah, that was hard. That makes you sad." This teaches your child that we have a word for their agitated state. They will gradually learn how to make sense of what's going on inside.

At this point, you can't ask your child what's wrong yet. First, they need the words for the emotional state. It is completely overwhelming for your child to be asked what they're feeling, and on top of that, what they want. That's the whole issue: They don't know. There's something they *don't* want—that much is clear—but the rest is one big question mark.

You know your child. Just look at them, read their face, and say what you see. "You're sad." "You're angry." "You're scared." Respond to their condition; identify and name it. They're learning basic emotions, so stick with sad, scared, mad, happy. That's plenty.

Having someone there who knows the ropes is so important to your child. It reassures them that this state of being has a precedent, which provides a tremendous deal of security. Your child feels seen and understood, which helps them to calm down.

Frustration is an important emotion these days. Your child needs to feel angry sometimes. Don't shield them from all the frustrating moments that life offers us. Emotions like joy and fun are much easier to handle than anger, annoyance, and sadness. This is called "frustration tolerance."

Simply saying what your child is feeling may seem inadequate. We often want them to feel better instantly and will take further steps to stop their frustration. It's enough to make a few calming sounds or gestures, provide physical contact (or space), and ride it out together, allowing time for the strong emotions to pass. You can also try deep, slow breathing, which helps to calm your child. They need someone to help carry the weight of their feelings, which are too big for them to manage alone. Sadness and anger will arrive, stay a while, then leave, and we can move on with our day. Your child wants to experience this process. It's part of maturation.

The intensity of your child's emotion has far more to do with their personality than with your "good" parenting.

Providing support for strong emotions can be challenging. For more information, see Feelings and Tantrums, on page 182.

How Do I Support Play?

Your child is discovering a lot this year, exploring every last detail of their surroundings. Follow your child, and say what they're doing or holding in their hands. Simple phrases like "That's a red block," or "Yes, the triangle fits there," provides them with the right words for the objects. Your child can tell by your tone of voice that you value what they're doing. You're not only building their vocabulary, you're bolstering their self-awareness and self-confidence. Your child is getting to know their own personality and preferences. When you lend your attention, their attention span increases incrementally. In the long run, this will boost their ability to concentrate.

You can incorporate this simple trick into daily life, because it doesn't take any extra time. Just say what you see in passing. Sit with your child while they're playing and say what you see. The trick is not to interfere or take over, because your child is the leader during play. You follow, signaling to your child that they can move at their own speed and do their own thing.

One major challenge for you might be boredom. Let's be real: Adult brains can be under-stimulated by a one-year-old's play. You are well beyond this point of cognitive development. Your child repeats actions over and over, whereas adults mix things up to make the game more complex. You can always do something productive on the side, like fold laundry or tackle another task you've been meaning to do.

You don't need many toys, because your child is most interested in regular household objects. Since your child is focused on exploration and discovery, you can rotate their toys. Having a few toys in the room and swapping them out once a week is better for your one-year-old than having all their toys on display.

Give your child space to make discoveries. They want to explore the world, and you set the boundaries for where that happens. They want to test and expand on their skills. What they can't do this week, they might master next week. Development is swift.

Your child is steadily developing a personality, with unique preferences, interests, and emotional states.

Your child's brain has not developed enough for them to play complex games with others, but this year they're slowly transitioning from solitary to parallel play. In other words, your child will occasionally come into contact with other kids. Usually, the focus is a toy. Please don't expect your child to make friends yet. They need to develop more social skills first.

Your child is unpredictable around others, so you probably find yourself facilitating with some frequency. When your child hits, shoves, pinches, or bites, it usually comes down to the fact that they can't speak yet and need to practice interpersonal skills. Don't worry; 80 percent of toddlers exhibit signs of social "maladjustment." Rather than call their behavior "antisocial," I prefer the term "pre-social." You can't be antisocial if you haven't learned yet how to be social.

Repeatedly show your child how to treat others, because it's a tricky skill to learn. Your modeling is key, because showing is better than telling at this age. It's pointless to give them some long-winded explanation about how to behave. Your child learns by observing your actions.

What Do I Do If There's a Fight?

If your child starts fighting, it's important to respond with kind but clear action. Intervene in the dispute. Don't say too much. Say "stop," and maybe remove your child from the situation if they don't stop on their own. If they're fighting over a toy, you might say, "That belongs to someone else," and give it back to the other child. If necessary, apologize to the other child. During this phase, it is truly best for *you* to apologize to the other child.

Apologies are still too much for your child, and even if they do apologize, they don't understand the meaning behind it. They're missing the criteria for a real apology: regret, insight, empathy, and a desire to make amends.

If your child is the one whose toy was taken, first assess how they're dealing with the situation. Do they care? Or is it you who has a problem with it? What is your child doing? Let them explore the options here. If they're upset, comfort them and try to clear things up. Never attempt to teach the other child a lesson—that's for their parents to do.

Model for your child the behaviors you wish to see. In a few months, they'll be able to put these behaviors into action, after seeing them enough times and developing the necessary skills. But first, they need this long phase of observation and learning.

Mediating conflict is a great example for the interplay between moments of leading and following. Play is generally a context in which you can follow your child's impulses, unless it unravels into a fight, in which case you immediately take the lead.

"It takes a village to raise a child." Always remember that. You can't do everything yourself. Sadly, many parents still try.

Are you creating a village for your family? At least a small one? You need to work actively at it, because today's society doesn't provide much in that regard. We were never meant to spend all day inside with a million things to do *plus* the raising of a child.

Most of us aren't used to living in large groups; instead, we've either lived alone or as a couple. We aren't accustomed to Grandma stopping by as frequently as she has been lately. Perhaps you'll devise a model that suits you, because you need all these people, and your child does too. Your child needs to meet different people, to help develop different aspects of their life. You have your personality to offer, but your child needs the input of various personalities to develop their sense of comparison among different people. For many, day care is a great place to make friends and grow your village, swap stories with other parents, arrange playdates, and seek help and advice from early childhood educators. If you're currently debating whether to send your child to day care, see Quick Reference—Day Care, page 155.

BONUS

Autonomy and Boundaries

Autonomy begins to emerge in toddlers. This developmental phase is one of the most important—and for parents, most difficult—features of these early years. Terms like the "terrible twos" or "toddler defiance" are misleading, though still used in some parenting forums. In this phase, your child is not defying you and your wishes, though it might feel that way. Your child is just taking the next step toward developing their personality. It's incredibly hard to become your own person with unique preferences and skills. At some point during the second year of life, your child realizes that they can act independently of others. This is a massive step, one that alters their entire worldview. After that sinks in, they have to figure out how to be their own person.

The Autonomy Phase in Three Obstacles

Obstacle 1: Natural Limitations and Set Boundaries

Natural Limitations: Your child relied on you for everything when they were a baby. As the months passed, they acquired practical skills and got their body under control. They would love to use these skills, only their attempts don't often work out. Your child has countless great ideas that can't yet be put into practice. For instance, they want to dress themselves but can't work the buttons. Or, to help you cook dinner, they try to take out the saucepan but it's too heavy. Lots of limitations come up every day.

What You Can Do: Trust your child's self-reliance. They've accomplished so much this past year, including learning to sit and walk without your help. Now they could use your support in acquiring practical skills like cooking and getting dressed. When it comes to these skills, your child is much more teachable than you might think.

As always, when it comes to leading, you simply need to break down the process into small steps.

Observe what's difficult for your child. Socks, for example—socks are very floppy. Then you have to pull the elastic *apart* at the same time as you pull the sock *up* and *over* your foot. This involves too many steps at once. As the leader, you could start by practicing with pulling the socks up. Get the sock onto your child's foot, then let them pull it up as far as they can. Do a little more each day.

Consider why your child struggles with certain everyday tasks. Is the object too big? Do you have a smaller one you could offer? Are there any prior skills to learn? To put on socks, for instance, you need enough strength in your hands to both open the top of the sock and hold it open. Is that the challenge your child is facing? Maybe give them an elastic hair tie to practice with.

Or do they not grasp the concept yet? Do they simply drape the sock across their foot and call it good? If so, model the action again. The Montessori approach can help here; see Further Reading. If that feels overly complicated, it's fine to keep demonstrating how to put on socks, describing exactly what you're doing. Your child will likely find their own way.

To start, let your child complete the final step of whatever you're doing. It gives them a sense of accomplishment. Closing Velcro straps, zipping or unzipping—if you allow them to practice, they will get better every time.

Set Boundaries: During this period, your child also butts up against your boundaries, which they rarely anticipate. In the mind of a toddler, there aren't multiple ways to go about a given task—there is just the one way, plan A. Plan B doesn't exist. Alternatives must be provided externally.

Remember how powerful the developmental drive is. Any disruption to that drive is hugely frustrating to your child, so you need to provide plenty of opportunities for practice. Give your child space, otherwise a state of permanent frustration can set in.

At the same time, it's important to become acquainted with frustration and to practice riding it out. Limits and boundaries are a fact of life, so your child has to learn how to deal with them. It's not your responsibility to clear every path for your child. This is impossible—and unnecessary to boot. Instead, focus on developmentally appropriate boundaries.

What You Can Do: You need a "yes space" at home for your curious little explorer. Create a space in which you can permit lots of activity to happen. You'll drive yourself (and your child) crazy by saying no all the time. Rearrange the rooms, putting the vases up high, pots and pans down low.

Certain "no spaces" will remain, like the stove and the stairs, but try to limit these areas, as your child has a hard time keeping track.

When your child approaches these areas, say "no" or "stop" over and over again. Don't expect immediate success. Your child learns very slowly by lots of repetition. Be as reliable and consistent as gravity. That's how your child learned to walk—they knew they could depend on toppling forward if they bent over too far.

Your child doesn't respond well to words yet, so action is usually required. Say "no" or "stop," and if they don't stop, physically remove them from the area. You will probably have to do this repeatedly. They're learning, but instructions need to be repeated literally hundreds of times. It can take weeks or months for your child to understand a boundary *and* respect it. We'll explore this in greater detail shortly.

A big plus during this time is that your child doesn't question rules and limits yet. Communicate your rules with confidence. It can help to use visual aids for these rules. Print pictures that represent your evening routine and hang them where your child can see. It's great if you can turn the pictures over or cross them out after completing that task. This communicates something along the lines of: "At our house, we eat first, then brush our teeth, then go to bed and read bedtime stories." This sequence is a fact, as irrefutable as the fact that objects always fall down and not up.

Keep the number of rules and boundaries to a minimum, but communicate and implement them consistently and calmly.

Obstacle 2: Desire and Free Will

Your child's newly discovered volition hasn't fully developed yet. They're just starting to explore it. If someone offers or asks something, your child will say yes or no without any sense of consequence. Is this really what your child wants right now? They'll only find out once the outcome is clear—and often, not even then.

Initially, your child taps into opposition: Being against something is the first and easiest feature of free will. Your child sees what you want them to do and says no. Don't take it personally. Right now, they're just practicing saying no. Usually, they don't have a good reason for it. In many cases, it doesn't even make sense. It takes months—years!—for children to figure out their own free will, perceiving what they want, finding a way to make it happen, little-kid-style. This is a hard-won accomplishment that they'll work toward throughout their toddler years and beyond.

One major misunderstanding of the autonomy phase occurs when parents think that their child is making these decisions deliberately. Viewing autonomy as freedom of choice is an adult interpretation. This may be what autonomy means for you, but you've gone through puberty, questioned the world around you, and forged your own path. Furthermore, you can anticipate consequences and make good decisions. As we saw with Alex, your child is unable to imagine the big picture when it comes to making decisions. They are overwhelmed by most decisions. Although your child is more competent at a practical level than you might think, their brain is still developing.

Perhaps you've read or heard about the importance of letting your child make their own decisions. Now you're trying to follow through. Unfortunately, this excellent (and well-intentioned) advice rarely specifies the appropriate age for the child to begin. I firmly believe children should be allowed to decide for themselves, but first they need big-picture understanding of the consequences.

Can your child assess these scenarios: Whether they need a warm hat to go outside? How long to stay at the playground? Whether to brush their teeth? Whether to get dressed now? The likely answer to these questions is no.

However, your child *can* make certain decisions, but only about what's happening right now and not ones with big future consequences: what today's T-shirt color should be, how much they want to eat, whether to use the yellow or blue toothbrush.

In most cases, leading your child makes the most sense. They need to find their bearings in the world. Show them how things work. Your child is very insecure during this phase, though it may not show. Their unpredictable volition sends them this way and that, and they often wind up at a crossroads of their own making.

Security and a sense of their bearings are hugely important for your child. Freedom is not useful to someone who doesn't feel safe.

In unfamiliar situations, establish your own sense of security first. Think of a time when you arrived at the airport or train station in a new city. Do you remember how it felt? You tried to find your bearings: How do I get to the hotel? Can I get a taxi? Where's the bus stop?

This is how your child feels every day. They frequently encounter this "new city feeling." Most of their life is like an unfamiliar metropolis, day after day. They need you to provide signposts for trying out desires and free will. After all, your child wants to learn to make good decisions, but first they need someone to provide feedback on whether a decision makes sense in a given situation.

If your child truly doesn't want (to do) something, they'll stop you or say no. Regularly allowing your child to make decisions as a preventive measure won't, in fact, prevent them from saying no or having a tantrum. If a tantrum is on deck and your child just needs to cry, they'll take whatever occasion presents itself—just as we all do.

What You Can Do: When your child wants something or says no, the first thing to do is assess whether this is a moment of leading or following. It's important during the autonomy phase to maintain balance between moments of leading and following. A participant in my parenting course drastically reduced the number of her child's tantrums when it dawned on her that she had been doing all the leading. Her child was forced to follow, and the sense of teamwork was unbalanced.

If you're in a moment of leading—a situation with a goal and sequence of steps—consider the current possibilities. Will everyone be okay if you let your child lead instead? If there's no chance of harm, then go for it, because sometimes your boundaries need to bend in favor of your child's developmental drive. Still, hang on to your role as leader here. You could say, "You know what? That's a great idea. I changed my mind. Let's do it your way." This elevates your child to a capable teammate with great ideas. But you're still in charge.

If deferring to your child would be disruptive or detrimental to others, your job is to keep leading—and your only question now is how best to guide your child. What do they need? Is the underlying cause fatigue, hunger, thirst, or the need for attention or snuggles? Is the sense of teamwork unbalanced?

Often, all it takes to defuse these heightened emotional situations is decisive action: Take clear control. Believe in yourself, and radiate confidence. Take tiny steps to guide your child through the situation. If emotions are riding too high, see the tips in Feelings and Tantrums, on page 182.

Obstacle 3: Big Feelings and Impulses

Your child is on a developmental mission and doesn't have much time: They have to get through the lion's share of overall development within the first four years of life. They are driven to try, test, and explore. The intensity of this drive varies based on a child's personality. Your child has far more energy than you do, which you're probably reminded of nightly. Development is always driving forward.

On top of everything else, your child is currently experiencing the full emotional spectrum. The prefrontal cortex, with its moral authority that says "You can't do that," hasn't formed yet.

Besides, your child has no idea how to regulate powerful emotions that swell up and take hold. What do you do when that happens?

Be understanding of the fact that impulses will shoot through your child, and they have no way to regulate or control these impulses. When you say "no," it's incredibly difficult for your child. In order *not* to do something, they would need the ability to stop. Stopping is in direct opposition to the forward thrust of their powerful developmental drive. The drive is so powerful that the best you can do is to divert it.

What You Can Do: Respond to what your child wants right now by finding an alternative. When you say "no," you want your child to stop, but then they're left with nothing to do. This is asking far too much. Take note of what your child is exploring right now. What's the underlying goal? Is it the practice of pouring things? Figuring out what fits where? Determining what something feels like? You don't have to know exactly what's going on—many root causes can coexist, and it often remains your child's little secret why they absolutely must do what they're doing at that moment. Try to find a similar activity, and if your child rejects it, try something else. If necessary, set a boundary and accept the powerful emotions that the boundary might prompt.

Smiling After Breaking the Rules: Many kids will smile after doing something that's not allowed. This smile might mean "Sorry," or it could be an attempt to restore the mood. When your child sees your unhappy face, they engage the strategy that's worked since infancy: smiling. In their experience, this makes the grown-ups smile back. Their smile could also communicate uncertainty or fear in response to the tension that just took hold of the room.

When children smile after breaking the rules, adults often interpret it as a "naughty smile." Instead, view it as an earnest apology or flash of uncertainty and the desire for everything to be okay.

This phase will pass much more smoothly if you help your child to find their bearings and if you don't avoid the attendant emotions. Your child will start to recognize your boundaries and know that they can depend on you. You've got the lay of the land. You can be trusted to lead and to do what's best for them.

The autonomy phase is an amazing developmental step for your child—an important step toward becoming human. It's actually cause for celebration!

Whenever you get frustrated by moments of defiance, remember that your child has also learned to agree! They can respond to requests now. Pay attention to how often your child cooperates and does what you ask, which happens far more often than you might realize.

Your child is small. There's only room for one thing at a time. One thought. One feeling. When the next thing comes along, the old one's got to go. There isn't room for both.

PART 3

From Toddler to Preschooler

Please do not compare your child too closely with our "average" child, Alex. Development does not follow the law of averages. Your child is probably slower in one area and quicker in another. They might not display certain traits or behaviors, whereas others are highly pronounced—all of that is normal. Your child is unique.

5

Development at Age 2

Thinking and Play

Alex is two years old, and she has made so many developmental steps. She can walk, almost run, climb, form two-word sentences, eat on her own, and use tools. There's a lot about life that she understands now.

Exploring the World, Down to the Last Detail

Alex engaged all her senses to discover the physical qualities of objects, whether by throwing, touching, or banging on them. Now it's time to study the details.

For example, Alex has been investigating the openings of different objects. What fits in there? What doesn't? Her toys aren't enough—she has to test a wide variety of items to understand what's going on. She picks up a small, hard, angular object and tries to find a good opening for it. Where does this weird thing go? Eventually Alex finds a sort of triangular opening and puts the object in there. It fits! Perfect! She can't get it back out, unfortunately, but that's one more discovery for the books. Her brain learned something. Hooray!

Alex isn't aware that she just dropped the mailbox key into the milk carton. She doesn't understand that the key is "important," or that not having it to check the mail could be a problem. Nor does she realize her parents don't stand a chance of finding it. Alex doesn't see the big picture yet. All she sees are the little details, which she uses to gradually build her understanding of the world.

She uses other objects to learn about nooks and crannies too: Alex loves jamming pencils and pens into openings—electrical outlets need extra protection these days. Toys that involve the insertion of pegs or differently shaped objects into various openings are a great alternative.

Alex is always on the lookout for new objects to research. One morning, John and Julia notice a funny smell while making toast. After much guesswork, they find evidence of Alex's latest discovery: The toaster slot is just the right size for a ballpoint pen!

She still loves stacking blocks, and her towers keep growing, now reaching up to six or eight blocks. She has started arranging blocks in rows too. She lines up all sorts of things. Can she line up all her stuffies and all her toy cars? Trains are a particular favorite: Not only do they fulfill her desire to line them up, they also *move*. How amazing is that?

This year, Alex will move from the vertical to the horizontal plane. Almost all her peers follow the same internal blueprint: First build up, then out. She ultimately combines the two, starting to fashion stair-like stacks and her first three-dimensional structures. But the structures are random; if a grown-up joined her and said, "Wow, a house!" she would think, "Oh yeah? That's a house? If you say so." Alex isn't picky when it comes to these interpretations. For all she cares, it's a house—she doesn't have any set goals for her building yet. She builds for the sake of building.

Being "Me"

Alex begins to develop real preferences for certain games. She's working on forming her personality, because something fantastic has happened in recent months: She's come to realize she's her very own "me"! She exists and operates independently of other people. This year, she simply must explore what that means.

At the moment, independence and saying no are one and the same to Alex. Figuring out free will remains a challenge. What does it mean to "want" something? What Alex wants can change every few minutes. Saying no makes her feel like an independent person. She can do things differently than other people. It's easier to express opposition at first.

It will take many months for her to make her own logical decisions, or to consider other variables in that process. Saying no is how Alex currently determines the outcome of a given situation. She's just getting started with figuring out her desires, feelings, and who she is.

Practicing Autonomy

Alex's parents wonder why her decisions are so wild and random sometimes, to which Alex would respond that her considerations are anything but deliberate. Her "decisions" are just spontaneous desires and impulses. A person can only make real decisions when they're able to foresee the outcome. Alex can do that in a few instances, such as when deciding what to eat or play, which color she likes best, whether she wants to sit on a grown-up's lap, or which book she wants to read—in other words, things that are happening *right now*. If her desire extends even a tiny bit into the future, she is unable to anticipate what will happen.

Nevertheless, Alex experiences many such desires, some of which can really throw a wrench in the works. Since she rarely knows what she actually wants and could really use some guardrails to steady her course, it's too much for Alex to handle when her family follows her lead and caters to her every desire. That isn't what she wants.

It's a real dilemma: Alex spends all her time trying to take the lead, then gets terribly upset when it works. She momentarily relishes the thrill of victory, then feels like someone who lands a leadership role without any of the qualifications required for the job. Though she's shortsighted, she has to make decisions and live with the consequences. She has to deal with her parents' bad moods, because they're annoyed that their routine is messed up. Alex had no idea her "decision" would cause such a stir. All she wanted to do was to try saying "no." How the heck did she wind up with so much responsibility?

John and Julia face their own dilemma. They've read about the autonomy phase, which is all about Alex's training of that new muscle, but they fail to realize how undeveloped Alex's intentions are. Her thought processes are not nearly as advanced as her parents may imagine. They assume that autonomy means the same to Alex as it does to them—namely, the making of self-directed decisions. As a result, they want to grant her as much freedom of choice as they can.

But now they start to wonder: Should their child be allowed to decide everything herself, or should they take the lead sometimes? What should they do when things dissolve into chaos? They become insecure and timid about the whole situation. They don't really know when to take the lead, and besides, Alex is so powerful in resisting that sometimes it's easier just to give in. John and Julia refer to their parenting style as "needs-based," overlooking the fact that security and a sense of bearings are fundamental human needs.

Alex, meanwhile, still doesn't understand autonomy. She wants to act independently: help out around the house, squeeze the toothpaste onto her toothbrush, grab her jacket, sweep the floors, set the table. She wants to be useful. She has no clue why her parents are constantly asking her to make decisions.

However, the overall vibe tells Alex that her parents are happy when she makes decisions. Without knowing what the words mean, she hears herself described as a "real character," "self-confident," and "self-directed," which her parents seem to appreciate. This teaches her how to make "decisions."

Like most people, Alex would love to get everything she wanted. Daily experience now reveals that her wants and needs are two different things: Needs are fundamental and must be fulfilled; wants are not. Eating is a need; having a third helping of ice cream is not.

It's helpful for Alex when her parents see the need behind the want. For instance, they might point out that she's actually tired and say no to what she's asking for. It will take months, even years, but this kind of feedback teaches Alex to gauge her wants and needs herself. She comes to understand what a reasonable wish looks like, when to express that wish, and how. She learns what kinds of wishes create chaos for her family. Her desire to know her bearings is central. During this period, she needs a strong external sense of security and orientation, since everything feels so jumbled inside her body.

"What's That?": The Questions Begin

Alex is starting to ask concrete questions about the world. Who, what, how—she wants to know everything, and soaks it all in. She gradually discovers the usefulness of language. Books help introduce her to new worlds.

Toward the end of this year, reading finally looks like what her parents imagined. Alex loves snuggling with Dad or Mom while they read to her. They have a shelf full of wonderful children's books, but Alex usually wants to read the same book they've read a hundred times before. And we're back to repetition. This ritual provides Alex with a tremendous sense of security. She's absorbing language and learning new words. Since written language is slightly different from spoken language, reading helps her to internalize new arrangements of words. It's so comforting to know the story already and not have to navigate through suspense.

Alex likes short books best, with simple storylines, lots of pictures, and mundane events. Her parents are desperate to *finally* read something else. Alex, meanwhile, delights in hearing the same story over and over. Everyday life is exciting enough as it is.

Drawing Her Own Conclusions

Alex's world has expanded a little beyond whatever is in front of her at this very moment. She discovers the weather, or how plants grow, and draws her own conclusions. For instance, she might think that sunshine always means it's warm. The fact that a sunny day can also be cold just doesn't make sense to her.

Whenever Alex puts two and two together, she loves telling people about it: "It's raining," she says, when Mom comes home in a wet jacket. Or she'll observe, "Paula spilled," when she sees a stain on her friend's T-shirt. Alex is proud of her discoveries and likes following the rules. Instead of imposing rules on others, she tries to show that she understands what's going on and that she wants to maintain order in her little world.

Alex can now remember conversations—or promises—from the day before. Blatantly guided by self-interest here, she is more likely to remember a promised trip to the toy store than a dentist appointment. She recognizes several colors now, so when asked to get the blue cup, she knows which is which and reliably returns with the blue one.

Her parents might think that she can count when she rattles off the numbers one to ten, but it's like a poem that she memorized. "Real" counting requires an understanding of quantity and amount. Any quantity beyond two is murky in Alex's head. She cannot count to three yet.

But she's working on it. To develop this understanding of quantity and amount, Alex starts by piling things, then scattering them about the room. (See Quick Reference—Play Schemas, page 86.) Relying on her senses for help, she learns that you can pile stuff, then split the pile up. She'll use this fundamental understanding of quantity and amount later on, when applying the theoretical notion in math class.

Alex makes piles of stuffies and piles of sand. She has to try all sorts of materials. One day, she moves all the books she can reach from the living room to her bedroom. It's quite a distance for her, and along the way she figures out how much strength she needs for this task: how heavy the books are, how many will fit in one hand, how slippery they can be, how many trips she has to make, and how long it takes to get to her room. Alex is acquiring a sense of time, transport, route, distance, and quantity. She makes a big pile of these books, then spreads them around the room; this is how she realizes that lots of things can be split up.

A few weeks later, Alex tries the same thing with all the baking ingredients she can find. During this particular experiment, she trails flour the entire way from the kitchen to the living room.

Her parents are not at all happy about her carefully crafted piles of flour, baking powder, and sugar in the living room. They scold her for making another mess, but she isn't aware of her greatest defense: "Listen, I am *never* making a mess. I'm learning! This is toddler math! All in service of the A I'll get in math class in a few years, which is something I'm sure you'll want."

As this year draws to a close, her many experiments will have taught her the difficult concept of "rows"—which means now she knows how to get in line for the slide at the playground. She never understood the logic behind this gathering of people, who all follow the same inscrutable rules and move forward way too slowly. At the supermarket too, lining up at the register was always such a bore, just another instance of constraint. The concept of waiting in line was a mystery to her.

Waiting is still extremely difficult. Like most people, Alex doesn't love to wait. At her age, she can wait for about thirty seconds. After that, she needs an activity or something to observe.

As ever, Alex wants nothing more than to help out around the house! What could be more exciting? It's a chance for her to learn so much, on so many different levels. In the kitchen, John and Julia still use the toddler tower, which allows Alex to stand beside them and watch what's happening. Soon, she's volunteering to help. It can be tricky for her parents to find appropriate tasks. They have, however, discovered that she learns very quickly when they break down tasks into small steps, explain them clearly, demonstrate, then allow her lots of practice. Sure enough, she can do small household tasks, like setting the table or sweeping the floor. And she loves being told what a good job she's doing!

She's getting better at routines. We take our shoes off inside. We wash our hands before eating. Though she occasionally remembers on her own, the moment something else grabs her attention, she forgets and needs to be reminded what to do.

The Concept of Time and Magical Thinking

Time is a real puzzle. Alex doesn't have much sense of the past or future, only the present. She doesn't understand when grown-ups say they'll do something "later" or "in a minute." For all she knows, that could mean next December. Saying it will happen "after lunch" is a little more concrete and sometimes makes sense to her. It's best when the grown-up uses a familiar image. For instance, they might say, "Your parents will be here soon. The traffic light is red. They have to wait." This visualization can help Alex develop a concept of time. Time that she can *see* is best, like an hourglass or a bright digital timer.

It's a challenge, though. Alex has no concept of the past, yet the grown-ups are always asking about it. After pickup from day care, she sits in her car seat with Mom or Dad in front and feels super relaxed. The scenery rolls by. That woman is wearing a red dress. That little doggy is sniffing a lamppost. The air smells like car. Her car seat is soft, and she can lean her head back. Then the questions start: "What games did you play at day care today?" or "What did you have for snack?"

This doesn't have anything to do with what's going on right now. Right now is car time. What's with all the questions about day care? Alex lacks the ability to rewind the images in her mind and deliver a structured account of the past. She might recall individual moments, but describing them for others is tricky. She tries—for her parents' sake—and goes along with the suggestions they make, or she might just say the first thing that pops into her head.

This year marks the start of Alex's magic phase. She has no interest in logic. She can't distinguish between what grown-ups call "reality" and the stories in her head. Sometimes she tells stories that she thinks are true, and she takes serious offense when the grown-ups say she's "lying." She's right to be offended too, because she isn't lying. In order to lie, a person needs to know what the truth is and intentionally misrepresent it. In Alex's mind, the truth is tied to her emotions, not to facts.

In a dispute with another child over a toy, Alex might insist that she had the toy first. Her desire to have had the toy first is so powerful, the feeling convinces her that she actually did. She can't see the big picture, rewind the situation in her head, or a step back to view herself from the outside. She lacks the distance from herself that's required to determine objective facts. To her, the truth is whatever she's thinking and feeling.

Role Play and Crafts

Alex loves re-creating scenes from everyday life when she plays. She'll put her dolls to bed, park her cars in the garage, go grocery shopping, feed her stuffies, and throw birthday parties. Naturally, these items now have feelings and needs: Her doll has an owie, or her teddy bear is hungry. Later on, Alex will look for playmates in these scenarios and give instructions, like "Now you're the baby" or "You're shopping at my store." John and Julia are buying a lot of groceries from her these days. Although Alex observes the process almost daily—first we make a list of what we need, then we go to the store, pick those items from the shelf, and head to checkout and pay—her play reveals that only certain details have stuck. A bunch of random stuff winds up in the cart. She doesn't understand yet why she's putting those things there.

Over the next few months, Alex begins to occupy herself for brief periods, maybe ten to fifteen minutes. Sometimes it goes on much longer, as she becomes fully engrossed in her play and appears to forget her surroundings. John and Julia know not to disturb her when this happens. Generally, her attention still jumps around. She'll want to check out this thing for a minute, then that thing, because her learning is still more incidental than intentional.

Alex is now starting to do arts and crafts. She learns how to hold scissors and make a few cuts. It's tricky business, moving her fingers in such coordinated fashion. She can't cut a straight line yet. The focus at this point is on the movement of cutting.

For the most part, she's still clenching the crayon or marker in her fist, but her drawings are starting to resemble actual images. When asked what she's drawing, the response is wildly imaginative, because here too, her mind is further along than her hands, which can't convey all her great ideas yet. Her descriptions can change suddenly: The circus tent she was drawing is now a shark.

Alex is still in the scribbling phase, primarily drawing circular or spiral forms or lines that she later stitches together to make a circle. She loves watercolors and lays them on thick. She doesn't mind the shade of brown that results from mixing every color in her paint set—to her, it's all about the process, not the outcome. She likes the sensory experience of using finger paints, thick paintbrushes, clay, or making things out of sand, and she adores peg puzzles. Soon, she'll learn how to thread beads on a string.

Alex's favorite activity is playing outside. Countless motor and sensory experiences await, whether she's playing with sand, dirt, rocks, water, leaves, grass, or twigs. Alex immediately calms down when she's outside. The ever-changing yet peaceful surroundings fulfill her wish for discovery.

Quick Reference—Soft Skills

Soft skills are personal attributes or abilities such as teamwork, empathy, initiative, creativity, self-management, ability to address conflict, self-esteem, motivation, passion, and problem-solving. Your child is practicing these things every day!

This is exactly what's happening while your child is at play: They're tapping into motivation and coming up with their own ideas for games. They're developing personal passions and getting to know themselves. For instance, trying to get a doll's crooked arm into the sleeve of its jacket—your child works and works at it until they get the arm into the sleeve. Now, with that figured out, what other games can they play with the doll? Later, your child will encounter conflict with other kids and learn how to reach an agreement on what (or how) to play.

Free play is critically important for your child. They will learn soft skills during free play that they cannot learn through organized activities. Give them a lot of space—create an environment in which they can try things out. You do not need to teach them anything; these games develop organically and at their own pace. Just make the occasional comment to acknowledge your child and their good ideas. Everything your child produces is wonderful—that's the message to convey, and it's a tremendous boost to their development.

Feelings and Relationships

Alex recently became her own "I" or "me" and is working on her sense of self. She is starting to experience feelings that only "I" can have: pride, guilt, envy, and shame. You can't feel ashamed if you don't know you're "you." Life is about to get more complicated in this respect. When Alex breaks the rules or encounters rejection, she experiences unpleasant feelings. She has to figure out how she's going to deal with this.

Alex also feels pride now, like when she accomplishes something all on her own. Praise and recognition are very important to her during this phase, and she will call direct attention to herself by saying "Look!" or "I did it!"

John and Julia gathered that it's better not to shower Alex in praise. They fight their own natural impulse to praise her, which irks her. Their body language tells her how happy they are, yet they put all this effort into finding "neutral" responses. All she wants is for someone to share her joy in what she's accomplished. She doesn't care what that looks like. Sharing her happiness is the main point. It's very important to her, so she tries to do it whenever possible.

Learning to Cope with Feelings

Until now, Alex relied entirely upon grown-ups to help regulate her emotions. That is very slowly starting to change. When she feels tired or sad, she sometimes knows what might help—she'll hug her stuffie or blankie, climb onto a lap and start snuggling, or find a quiet space.

This is not yet the case for bigger feelings, which are still very common for Alex. Every day has its frustrations, as she encounters one thing after another that doesn't work or that she isn't allowed to do. Feelings boil up inside her, causing the entire system to overheat. It's impossible for her to think clearly, let alone behave reasonably. She can stand there or lie down, cry or scream, but that's it. In these moments, she needs someone who will name the feeling and help to carry the weight of it, to ease the burden (see Feelings and Tantrums, page 182).

Playtime is a chance for Alex to practice handling various emotions: She might be gentle and caring toward her stuffie one day, then scold it for being naughty the next. This demonstrates that she can read and respond to others' emotions and intentions. Or maybe she rushes to nab her favorite toy when she sees her friend Paula headed for it. When Paula starts to cry, Alex remarks, "Paula's crying." She observes her friend with concern and offers comfort. Alex is beginning to experience empathy—though for her to give up the toy would be asking too much. She is just starting to realize that things can belong to her. It's difficult to share these newfound belongings. She has to see sharing in action many times; a grown-up needs to repeatedly demonstrate what it looks like to share. Occasionally, she'll hand something over, but her toys are as important to her as cars or cell phones are to her parents. That makes sharing a real challenge—one that requires much practice to overcome.

Fears emerge during the magic phase—a time in which toys can talk and a sock might intentionally be unkind. Alex's biggest fears are the dark and mean animals. She wants to be comforted when scared, but logical solutions still don't make much sense to her. A ritual to ward off scary animals—maybe a magic spell—is much more effective.

First Toddler Friends

Alex plays a lot with Paula these days. Their parents refer to them as friends, which is true, but they're *toddler* friends. Friendship in young children is less about the individuals themselves—rather, children are "friends" when they do the same activities. This can also change very quickly.

For the first several months of this year, Alex enjoyed playing with others, but when it comes down to it, the children aren't really playing *with* each other. They run or scoot around together. They watch one another, hand toys back and forth, or cook or build things side by side.

Cooperative play requires communication and a shared goal—skills that Alex and Paula will develop over the course of many months. They will learn what they want, and that their friend might want something different. They will learn to assert themselves and to ease off. They will learn to regulate their anger and develop solutions other than shoving or hitting.

Alex and Paula each have a plan in mind, but there's no plan B, and it's hard to accept someone else's plan. Sometimes it works, but usually not.

Alex can participate in about five minutes of "true" cooperative play. For that to happen, she and Paula each need to have their own ideas as well as be able to accept the other one's ideas, and on top of that, they need to discuss and agree on what they're going to do, all of which will take quite a long time to figure out.

Alex is starting to narrate what she's doing, like announcing, "I'm driving around the corner." This is a foundational skill for cooperative play. It's starting to pay off that her parents often narrated what she was doing with her toys while she played. Now, she's starting to do this herself.

Movement

Alex's world is speeding up—she can even run short distances now. She tries different ways to walk and run. She likes jumping and practices wherever she can. She's working on climbing stairs too. To start, she has to get both feet on the step to feel safe, before moving on to the next one.

When Alex throws a ball now, she can choose the direction—it doesn't just soar through the air willy-nilly. She mostly uses her forearm to throw, while the rest of her body doesn't move.

If someone gently tosses a big, soft ball to her, she can hold out her arms and use her belly to help catch it. The pitcher has to use good aim and toss it straight to her, because she will stand there motionless, hoping the ball lands in her arms. She still has a hard time gauging its trajectory.

Alex has also started to scoot around on her balance bike, opening a whole new world of movement. Using both legs to propel herself forward, she moves around fast—often much faster than her parents would like.

She has continued to practice getting dressed and can now put on simple items of clothing by herself. If she has trouble with a certain garment, her parents break down the process into smaller steps, showing her how it's done. They always let her complete the final step, which gives her a feeling of accomplishment.

Alex still likes to pour liquids from one container into another. This requires her to do different things with her hands at the same time, which is a fun skill to learn. Her parents read that it's good to introduce screw caps for Alex to practice wrist rotation—an important skill for learning how to write when she's older—so they find a few containers with screw tops and let her play with them.

Speech

Alex's first fifty words were a long time coming, but after crossing that threshold, her speech development suddenly takes off. Her vocabulary explodes, jumping from fifty to four hundred words in just a few months. She's easy to understand now, although sibilants like *s* or *sh* are still tricky, so "sing" might come out "thing."

Alex can ask questions and puts this skill to use—after all, she needs to discover all there is to know about the world. She asks "Where?" and "What?" and who did or didn't do this or that. Certain questions will come up so often, John and Julia are amazed that she doesn't know the answer yet, but as always, her brain requires lots of repetition.

Alex can't respond to "why" questions yet, as she is incapable of providing objective reasons. If someone asks her a "why" question, she might invent a reason—one that may or may not have any basis in reality.

At a Glance: 2-Year-Olds

Thinking and Play

Alex is still working on becoming an "I" or "me," diving into the details of the world around her. Autonomy is important to her. She is eager to help and wants to be an active, participating member of the family.

Alex is acquiring the basics of science and math, and her approach is definitely hands-on! She's in her magic phase, and she doesn't see the logic in situations.

During playtime, Alex re-creates scenes from everyday life, builds things, and loves crafting and scribbling.

> Alex and the ball: She understands the basic principle—balls roll because they're round. Things with corners don't roll—only round things can do that.

Feelings and Relationships

Now that Alex is aware of being "me," she's starting to experience the emotions that accompany this awareness, like shame, pride, envy, and guilt. She's getting to know her desires better and exploring her free will, working on handling frustration, and trying to cope with her tantrums.

For the most part, Alex still engages in "parallel play" with other children. She's figuring out what it means to have her own ideas, all while starting to consider other people's ideas, which she can only manage for a short while.

Movement

Alex can run short distances, and she practices climbing stairs and jumping. She loves her balance bike, which keeps her parents on their toes. She can dress and undress by herself with simple items of clothing.

Speech

Alex is asking lots of questions these days. She can understand a lot, and she can say quite a lot too. Sibilants like *s* or *sh* are still tricky, so for now she says "thing" for "sing." Her vocabulary is growing exponentially, jumping from around fifty to four hundred words in just a few months.

Quick Reference—Day Care

It Takes a Village

Day care is a controversial subject for children younger than three. Some parents believe children should spend the first three years at home. Others argue that day care offers their kids more resources and opportunities. Many parents don't have a choice, because they have to return to work.

Studying the effects of day care on babies and toddlers is extremely complicated. Countless factors are at play, including quality and duration of care, the child's personality, and what the child would be doing at home instead. This mix of variables means that scientific studies have reached positive, negative, and neutral conclusions. In other words, it's easy to find a study that supports your personal beliefs on the matter.

Biologically speaking, children are meant to be part of a group and cared for by various people. What we've come to see as normal is an anomaly in human history: this notion of children being tended by only one or two adults—leaving caregivers alone at home all day with the kids, *plus* expecting them to come up with all sorts of games and other forms of engagement. It's a dubious tradition in the Western world—one that understandably leads to burnout. Your partner and other people—like grandparents, aunts, uncles, friends, and babysitters—can both help you and show your child other lived realities. Who might be a welcome addition to your family's rotation—maybe Grandma, a nanny, regular sitter, or meetups with other families? The idea that a "child belongs with their mother" is still widely accepted and creates a lot of stress and worry. Of course children belong with their mom or dad, but that doesn't necessarily mean 24-7.

The idea that sending your child to day care amounts to "outsourcing" your duties as a parent, allowing strangers to raise your child, is an unfair misrepresentation of what really happens there. In many day cares today, children are given weeks to acclimate to the space, and parents are encouraged to stay until their child establishes a relationship with one of the caregivers there. Early childhood educators have developed comprehensive approaches for helping children to settle in. These approaches are tailored to each child's needs and discussed with parents in advance. At the end of the day, friends—not strangers—are looking after the children.

It's impossible to generalize as to which form of care is best for your child. You rarely have a choice, because you have to return to work. Please do so without any guilt, and open your child to new experiences at day care. A fun playground and long list of resources are of secondary concern—the teachers' attitudes toward children are what matters most. After many years of working with early childhood educators, my impression is that most of them are passionate about their profession. They are deeply committed to "their kids" and routinely go the extra mile for them.

Consider your child and living situation. What makes the most sense? What kind of personality does your child have? How do *you* feel? Is spending the day with your child generally fun and fulfilling? Or do you secretly think, "If I have to fill this bucket with sand one more time, I might scream"? Be honest with yourself and make the decision that is best for you and your child, if the option is available to you.

6

Development at Age 3

Thinking and Play

Development is still a major focus for Alex—he is on the move all day long. Sitting still is a missed opportunity for development. He's at work learning more about the world. Though he's grasped a lot of the basics, he is nowhere near done.

It's difficult to comprehend that an amount doesn't change when its appearance does. For instance, Alex is still trying to understand liquids.

One day, Julia divides what's left of the orange juice between Alex and his friend Paula. Alex checks to make sure they're both getting the same amount. Paula's glass is taller and narrower. Alex pitches a fit, because it looks like Paula is getting way more orange juice than he is. He refuses to believe that it's the same amount of juice, because he has learned to measure liquid based on how high the line appears. Volume is a foreign concept to him. Fairness and following rules are very important to Alex.

Quick Reference—Theory of Conservation

An Amount Doesn't Change Between Containers

Jean Piaget was a Swiss psychologist who specialized in child development. His models of cognitive development are still used today, though some aspects have been criticized or expanded upon. He is perhaps best known for "conservation tasks."

In a conservation task, a child is shown two glasses containing the same amount of liquid. The contents of one are poured into a narrower glass, resulting in a higher line. The child watches closely.

Although the child witnesses every step of the process, they will typically make the same logical error until age four or five: They are convinced that the narrower glass contains more liquid. They don't yet realize that an amount does not change when poured from one container to another.

Children make similar mistakes with other objects, like coins: "There are more coins because they're in a pile." You can show a child that this isn't the case, but they won't absorb the lesson; the next time it comes up, they'll reach the same conclusion.

To understand that an amount doesn't change simply because it's somewhere else requires a lot of experimentation and "work" with liquids and other objects first.

Alex is asking lots of questions: how, what, why—he wants to know it all! John and Julia can get tired of answering so many questions that seem so obvious to them. The thing is, Alex can't see what appears so clearly to his parents. He can only focus on one aspect of a situation at a time. He still needs to learn that multiple factors are at play when assessing a situation. His parents will have to continue answering the same questions, because he needs lots of repetition before the answers sink in.

Learning Math While Setting the Table

Alex has a good grip on personal hygiene and getting dressed, though from time to time he needs some help. For the past few months, John and Julia have tried to break down the process of getting dressed into small, manageable steps. At first, they helped him put socks on his feet, and he pulled them up his legs; later, he learned to pull them over his heels, which is much harder. He's got it down pat now. He's mastered zippers and buttons too, and only occasionally needs help. It's easiest for him to put on his shoes while standing. He can't always tell the difference between right and left, so sometimes his shoes end up on the wrong feet. But his sense of accomplishment in having put them on by himself is much more important.

Household chores are still the best way for Alex to learn. He loves to sweep, cook, do laundry, wipe up spills, and water the plants. These tasks teach him different series of movements, deepen his understanding of the world, and turn him into a real team player. He can tell the difference between different sizes of the same object and sort objects according to size. For instance, he knows that in the silverware drawer, big spoons and little spoons each have their own compartments in the silverware organizer. He especially loves setting the table—another great opportunity to practice his math skills. How many plates do they need today? Where do they go on the table? How do you make sure that there's a fork beside every plate? How do you determine what other items you need—and how are they related to what's for dinner? You don't need a fork to eat soup, but you do for vegetables; for pasta, Mom and Dad usually want both a fork and a spoon.

One day, Julia asks Alex to set the table for dinner. It's just after Christmas, and during the holidays, John and Julia always set up an extra table in the living room for guests, then continue to enjoy the setup themselves for a few days. It's time to put the table back in storage, but John has to rearrange the small garden shed to make room for it. The table waits on its side in the backyard.

Alex, meanwhile, knows his task—which he takes very seriously—and arrives in the living room, only to discover that the table is gone. Where is he supposed to put the plates now? It doesn't occur to him to swing back to the other table—the one in the kitchen—because for days, he's been eating at the Christmas table. He is quick to adapt to new rituals, and he assumed that he and his family were still going to eat at the Christmas table.

He is determined to accomplish his task. Where is that darn table? The back door is open, so he looks outside and finds the missing furniture. He doesn't think it's weird to find the table on its side in the grass; if there's one thing he knows, it's that the craziest stuff happens in this world, and this is just another example. His job is to set the table, so he very carefully balances the plates one by one on the edge of the table. He is very proud of completing this task, despite the many obstacles.

When John turns around, he is bewildered by the sight of plates balancing on the edge of the table; Julia is equally surprised to discover the kitchen table hasn't been set, while Alex proudly returns from the backyard.

The Great Misunderstanding

Alex loves helping in the kitchen. Unfortunately, a classic misunderstanding emerges between him and his parents: Based on their own interest in the matter, his parents assume that he is invested in the outcome. They want a beautiful, delicious cake. They try to accomplish this with as little effort as possible, because the steps are familiar to them—and they want to get it done in the most efficient way.

Alex, on the other hand, doesn't care as much about the outcome. Learning the process is what counts. He needs to understand and master the individual steps, which means trying all of them out—repeatedly. Sometimes he'll even make the steps harder for himself, just to learn a new variation. For instance, when rolling out the dough, he might draw the rolling pin all the way back, then launch it all the way forward. He loves big, strenuous movements. The sensory experience—smelling, touching, moving, mixing things together and watching them transform—is like a party to him. Sure, cake is yummy, but that's nothing compared to this learning experience.

John and Julia have a very hard time with all the learning and experimentation going on in the kitchen. Alex makes such a mess! Items are constantly falling or spilling, every surface is sticky, he has no sense of objective, and the process goes so slowly.

But they'd have greater success if they showed more faith in Alex, provided kid-size utensils, and broke down the process into smaller steps. Alex can sense that he's getting in the way and finds his peace with spending most of his time as a spectator. He tries to learn by watching and gobbles up the cake when it's done.

Paula's parents, however, report that they've given up on cooking and baking with her, because her behavior is completely unmanageable. She's always grabbing at what they're doing, and they can't turn their backs for a second for fear of the chaos she'll unleash.

Paula tries using speed to do more on her own. She ignores her parents when they say "no." She can't help it—they say it all the time. If she listened every time she heard "no," she would miss out on far too many learning experiences. For the benefit of her own development, she has to defy her parents' wishes occasionally. But ultimately, she wants to be a valued, helpful member of the family and to show her parents what she can do and what they're helping her learn every day.

A Sense of Time

Alex is beginning to understand time. When something great is happening, time passes way too quickly, but then time seems to stand still. He knows that events occur sequentially—for instance, breakfast comes before lunch. That said, sometimes he forgets and things get mixed up. He uses terms like "yesterday," "early," "late," "morning," and "night," but it's all a little muddy to him, so he might slip in a "day before tomorrow" or a "day after yesterday." He doesn't know what to make of it when his parents say they'll be "right" back, because what does "right" mean? It's helpful for him to visualize the passage of time using an hourglass or timer.

Alex also has a hard time reconstructing and talking about the past. He's in awe of the big kids who talk about their weekends during circle time at day care. They're able to give a structured account of what they did over the past two days—*and* in the order in which they did it! What a remarkable skill.

Alex can't do that yet. He shares random details as they occur to him. They don't fit together logically or build toward a conclusion. Identifying exactly *when* something happened in the past still gets mixed up in his mind.

He can't respond to a question like "How was day care today?" It's too abstract, plus the answer is found in the past. His parents ask specific questions, like "Did you play with Paula today?" And they always ask what was for lunch.

Alex remains in the phase of magical thinking. He can't see logic; he feels happily assured of knowing everything he needs to know, and he simply fills in the gaps with magical stories and ideas. He remains incapable of lying, because first he would need to know what the truth is and then deliberately distort it. His "truths" are situational and based on emotions—he doesn't understand objectivity. In his world, facts are highly subjective (see Quick Reference—Lying, page 196).

Magical thinking can be used to Alex's benefit too. For instance, he is comforted knowing that his stuffie protects him at night, that casting a magic spell gets rid of the monsters under the bed, or that the special rock in his pocket makes him invincible.

Fun with Language and Counting

With Alex's brain developing at top speed, he is getting better at telling stories. He's good at memorization and likes reciting rhymes and singing songs from day care. If he forgets what comes next, reminding him of a word or two is usually all it takes to get him back on track.

As Alex's knowledge of language grows, he's ready to investigate words that he isn't allowed to say. Alex discovers that certain words get a big response from the grown-ups, who call them "bad words." He can make grown-ups overreact—what an amazing feeling. If no one reacts, though, it gets boring quickly and he soon loses interest.

Alex thinks it's hilarious when people fall down or make weird faces or movements. He loves slapstick humor. Doing things "wrong" or making funny sounds is also a favorite. He laughs himself silly when grown-ups pretend to be in lots of pain while they play doctor. On the other hand, irony and sarcasm are lost on him; his language skills can't comprehend that yet.

He's beginning to understand the reasons behind certain behaviors and proudly shares his wisdom: "We need air to breathe." "Scissors are for cutting." "You can drink water or wash things with it."

John and Julia are proud of how well Alex can count, as he confidently rattles off numbers. They view it as a foundation for math skills, but Alex primarily learns math through action, like when setting the table. His "counting" has more to do with recitation than with an understanding of quantities. He is just beginning to understand that items can be assigned numbers. But this understanding can get wonky when he tries counting real objects; he might keep starting over or tapping the same objects as he counts up.

Soon enough, he can make sense of quantities up to four. He'll bring his parents three blocks when they ask, or he'll notice that four objects are grouped together. He can tell people how old he is now, proudly holding up three fingers. He'll pick up the rest in the coming months and years through play and problem-solving. His parents can also show him how to solve certain everyday problems (see Quick Reference—Thinking It Through, page 119).

Coloring and Making Connections

Alex can play with certain tabletop games, simple board games, and puzzles. He's much more serious about puzzles, and he'll sit there, turning the pieces this way and that, trying to get them to fit.

He's deeply invested in the "connecting" scheme these days (see Quick Reference—Play Schemas, page 86), figuring out how things fit together (or how to *make* them fit). He's learning all about connections and gaining experience in statics, stability, and construction.

Alex enjoys threading beads on a string, connecting one section of railroad track to another, and gluing items together. He also builds a lot with Legos or blocks. He's been trying to tie together string or ribbon, but knots are a challenge. Once he learns, there is no end to the knots he'll tie, as he has to practice them all. One morning, John discovers that his bathrobe belt is a tangle of knots.

Alex also loves connecting toys and building tunnels and paths in the sand. He can keep himself occupied for at least ten minutes now, sometimes much longer.

When coloring, Alex announces that he's writing and scribbles on the paper in an imitation of writing. His drawings are mostly scribbled too, though he can explain the image he's trying to make either as he's doing it or after it's done. "That's the mountain and that's the cave and there's the dog." He's been working on houses, trees, and cars too.

Alex can draw an image that resembles the sun: a roundish shape with lots of lines coming out of it. By the end of the year, he'll be able to draw humans. Like most of his peers, he initially makes drawings of people that resemble tadpoles or amoebas, with long lines for legs attached directly to a big head. Sometimes they have arms too, likewise tacked onto their head. He might add a few crooked lines or circles to represent mouth, nose, and eyes.

The best is going outside, where Alex can move freely, without fear of breaking anything, and play in the dirt, sandbox, grass, or gravel. The outdoor world stimulates all his senses; the changes in weather, the seasons, and the variety of plant life mean something new is always out there to discover. He might even encounter ducks, dogs, butterflies, earthworms, and other animals and insects.

Feelings and Relationships

Alex needs someone to help him understand and regulate his feelings. He continues to have spectacular meltdowns that he can't cope with on his own (see Feelings and Tantrums, page 182).

He's still figuring out his desires and free will as well. He often struggles to accept other people's boundaries and his own—a skill that needs to be modeled for him (see Autonomy and Boundaries, page 126).

Regulating Emotions with Empathy

As long as Alex's emotions aren't too big, he is better at regulating them. When he feels sad, he'll come up with his own ideas about what might help, whether that's climbing into Mom's or Dad's lap, cuddling with his blankie, or finding a quiet corner. Sadness is easier to cope with than anger. Anger is very difficult to get under control; it's a real struggle.

But honestly, Alex can't help noticing that his parents could improve the way they manage anger too. It seems that even grown-ups have to practice this, and they also slip up sometimes.

The frequency of Alex's tantrums tapers off toward the end of the year. He needs an understanding person to help shoulder the burden of big feelings as well as clear boundaries within which he can test his desires and free will.

Alex is making lots of major changes these days. He is trying hard to manage his frustration. He knows that it's better to solve conflict without hitting or shoving (provided this is modeled for him enough times), though sometimes he forgets. He'll repeat certain lines he's heard the grown-ups say, like "I need to take a break and calm down!" He's obtaining vocabulary for his emotions, and this helps him get them under control. He's trying to better understand the reasons behind various emotions, so he'll ask why another child is crying or venture a guess, like "That girl is sad because she dropped her ice cream."

Alex is starting to cooperate with others. He's learning that you can't always get what you want. This allows him to be part of a group.

Alex has developed empathy—true empathy! He can consider another person's perspective and use it to explain things, like "Mom and Dad don't like mud on the floor because it's so hard to clean." This huge step opens a wonderful new world to him: the world of other people.

What do other people feel? And how do you interact with them? "Mom, you're tired. You need to take a nap," Alex says, bringing Julia a blanket. It isn't quite as obvious to him that his mom needs more than two minutes to rest, because his sense of time remains a work in progress. Still, it's tremendously significant that he has developed a sense of empathy and can see that other people have different feelings and reasons for behaving.

Learning to Share

All this knowledge contributes to our three-year-old's learning how to share. Alex now realizes that a playmate might also like to play with his toy. Sharing is interesting, though . . . how do you do it? Alex needs to learn by example, observing concrete instances of sharing in his everyday life. He needs role models. Yet Alex is constantly hearing grown-ups say things like "Hey, that was my glass"; "You're always eating off my plate"; "I can't lend you my car"; "You can't borrow my sweater."

What is Alex supposed to make of all this? Is sharing good? Does it only apply to certain things? The whole concept is confusing.

Alex simply loves making other people happy. It's great when people ask him for help. He adores handing out presents. He won't make a fuss when his parents set a boundary he doesn't like, as long as he knows that it makes them happy. He'll readily demonstrate for others how something works, sharing his wisdom with the world.

Shame is a new emotion for Alex. He frequently feels embarrassed. John and Julia are surprised to find him embarrassed by things that hadn't bothered him before. For one, they are no longer allowed to talk openly about him to other people, because he feels exposed. He also feels self-conscious in new situations and around strangers.

Alex is encountering more fear these days. He's afraid of the dark, his doctor, animals, and supernatural creatures like monsters or ghosts. He's scared of bad people too, because he is starting to divide the world into good and evil.

Playing Alone and with Others

It's finally time to start playing with other kids! Alex has developed the skills required for true cooperative play. He starts with simple role-playing games. Alex can adopt roles like mommy, daddy, doctor, and salesperson. He'll stay in character and add certain details to flesh them out, reenacting scenes from everyday life: routines like grocery shopping or seeing the doctor. Sometimes he'll play pirate, knight, princess, or wizard. He moves from role to role, maybe starting as the daddy, then the mommy, then the baby, which introduces him to different perspectives. He can now use language to discuss and reach agreements with others. He can also move between make-believe objects, clearly imagining what they represent: For instance, a wooden block might first be a telephone, then a piece of cake. In the coming months, Alex will develop these roles even further, preparing for each by changing into different costumes.

Reaching agreements with other children can still be very difficult. Alex gets frustrated when his ideas are ignored, when he has to wait, and when others make him play *their* game. Playing with others comes with lots of disappointment. It's important for him to experience this frustration. Interacting with other children will get easier over time, provided he gets lots of practice.

The most common objections that Alex makes during this period are:

"You're not my friend anymore" and "You're not invited to my birthday party." These words can unleash an emotional meltdown in another child, which is overwhelming to Alex.

On one such occasion, Alex's parents and his friend's parents try to make peace between the children. They can't agree on who was in the right, and they end up in conflict themselves. The children don't hold grudges and go back to playing together the next day, but it takes weeks for the air to clear between the grown-ups.

> ### Quick Reference—Play
>
> **Harder Than It Looks**
>
> Your child needs four basic skills to be able to play with others.
>
> 1. They're capable of developing their own ideas for play. They can tell what they want to do next, then do it.
>
> 2. They can name an idea and explain what they're doing. For example, they might announce that they're a tiger or say, "My car is driving around the curve. Vrooom." Sometimes they'll use sounds to indicate their plan.
>
> 3. They can maintain eye contact with others and "read" faces. In other words, they notice and draw their own conclusions from others' facial expressions and body language. They can interpret signals such as "That person likes my idea," or "That person wants to do something else."
>
> 4. They can adapt their behavior according to what they read in others' faces. How do they do the "social dance," in which one leads while the other follows and then switches positions, thus allowing the game to develop?
>
> **When Does This Start Happening?**
>
> Cooperative play requires certain skills that take years to develop.
>
> Ideas for play might start occurring to children toward the

end of the first year, then keep developing. These are isolated, short-lived impulses, to start; it will be a while before your child can make real plans like "Now I'm going to build a house." Boredom is tremendously valuable, as it teaches children to perceive those quiet internal impulses.

From the basic level of language, your child can't name what they're doing until they're at least one-and-a-half (or more realistically, two-and-a-half) years old. Reading faces starts early, but interpreting the nuances found there and identifying other people's motivations are difficult skills for anyone under three.

The fourth skill is most challenging, as children learn to respond to other people and to adapt their behavior to fit the situation. This skill continues to develop and remains very limited until age three.

True cooperative play is harder than it looks, and every child builds these skills at a different rate. Expect to see cooperative play starting from age two and a half to three. Before then, your child will be happy playing alone, or alongside other kids in "parallel play."

How Can You "Teach" Your Child to Play?

If your child hasn't gotten the hang of playing with others after their third birthday, or if you work with children and would like to help some of them learn to play better, start with close observation. Which of the four skills does your child need to work on?

If they have trouble describing what they're doing, you can provide helpful prompts during moments of following. You might say, "Wow, that car is driving so fast," or "Your doll got a boo-boo," to teach your child how to name their own actions. Developing ideas for play requires time and space as well as someone to notice and value your child's impulses. Once they become immersed in play—that precious condition that adults sometimes refer to as a "flow state"—nothing more is required of you. Idling can be beneficial; finding a path out of boredom is a useful skill for children to develop.

Your child has learned to read faces by interacting so often with yours. They will have to study a whole lot of faces, with a whole lot of facial expressions, to learn to tell them apart. Cell phones can significantly impede this learning, as your facial expression becomes neutral and disturbingly unreadable for your child. The interaction comes to a screeching halt, which your child assumes must be their fault. After using your phone, make a deliberate effort to reestablish a connection with your child and give them a big smile.

Give your child a little help in reading other kids' behaviors: "Oh, look, those friends would like to use the sand pail too." You can narrate social situations for your child like a sports commentator, providing a play-by-play account. Describe exactly what's happening, so your child can anticipate what to do next. You can also make suggestions: "Sweetie, if you just take the other car, then you can both drive cars together." Over the long term, of course, it makes sense to teach your child how to assess social situations on their own.

Movement

Balancing is so much fun, and Alex will find any opportunity to practice, whether on the curb or the edge of a flower bed. He can even hop briefly on one foot.

Self-feeding is going great too. Alex isn't using a fork and knife at the same time yet, but he's working on it. He can carry a full cup to the table without spilling. It's no mean feat, walking and holding his cup steady and keeping an eye on where he's going all at the same time. He wants to do as much as possible on his own, eagerly scooping out peanut butter and jelly (just how much is too much?) and spreading it on his toast.

Alex can catch a big ball. He holds out his arms and actively tries to gauge the ball's trajectory, which isn't easy. He uses his whole arm to throw, winding up and trying to arc the ball. He's putting his body into the throw, instead of just his forearm. Alex can throw much farther now too. He loves riding his balance bike. His movements are well coordinated, and he moves fast.

Speech

Alex can speak in the past tense now, though he'll make occasional grammatical errors, like "Grandma goed to the store." He can tell the difference between commands such as "Put the scarf *on* the bench" and "Put your shoes *under* the bench." More complex statements remain difficult to process.

Alex's pronunciation is improving too. Sibilants like *s* or *sh* are still tricky, as are consonant clusters like *br* or *cl*, so he might call his shoes his "soos" or his broom his "bwoom." "Truck" might come out "duck," which eventually leads to the important discovery that sounds can change the meaning of words.

If Alex doesn't know the word for something, he'll make one up. The oven, for instance, becomes "bakercake," since that's basically (or at least most importantly) what it does.

He's also starting to apply the words that he's learned to new situations. One day, after reading a book about a farm, he sees John taking laundry off the line and asks, "Are you picking socks?"

Alex's friend Paula knows more words and talks more fluently than he does, whereas his friend David is taking his time and sounds like a two-year-old. Both are normal.

At a Glance: Three-Year-Olds

Thinking and Play
Alex is working on difficult tasks, like understanding liquids and performing small assignments correctly. The process is more interesting to him than the outcome. He's practicing structured storytelling and is firmly situated in the phase of magical thinking. He continues to engage in schematic play and ask lots of questions about the world around him.

Feelings and Relationships
Alex can regulate his feelings now, unless they're too big for him. He still has tantrums. He has developed a sense of empathy; he feels for others and responds to their feelings. Embarrassment is a relatively new and frequent emotion. He has a lot of fears too. He plays with other children and develops ideas for games together.

Movement
Alex loves riding his balance bike and doing other activities to practice balance. He can catch a big ball and throw it back using his whole arm. He can even carry a full glass from points A to B without any accidents.

> Alex and the ball: He can anticipate what will happen, though he still makes lots of mistakes. He can tell where the ball will roll when he pushes it.

Speech
Alex sings, recites rhymes, and initiates conversations with people. His pronunciation is good, with just a few sounds giving him trouble. His grammar is nearly flawless, though sometimes he'll mix up verb tenses.

What to Know About 2- and 3-Year-Olds

If you don't remember what defines moments of leading and moments of following, please reread the summary on page 18. There's really just one question you need to ask when it comes to raising children: "Does my child need me to lead or to follow in this situation?"

Moments of Leading in 2- and 3-Year-Olds

Your child continues to face three obstacles during this period.

1. They often bump up against boundaries or limitations: either their own—because they can't physically do something yet—or those imposed because they're not allowed to do something.
2. Though desire and free will continue to develop, these are unwieldy forces that pull your child back and forth.
3. Big feelings are difficult to regulate and sometimes get the better of your child.

These obstacles are a major concern at this age. Review Autonomy and Boundaries on page 126 for a deep dive into each obstacle along with practical solutions.

The moments in which you should lead involve getting dressed and undressed, maintaining hygiene, eating, changing diapers, buckling into the car seat, grocery shopping, cooking, and other tasks, big and small. Your child is now familiar with these situations and various related routines, but they tend to focus on random details rather than the overall objective. For instance, they might love to touch the soft towel or turn the faucet on and off, but they don't know how much soap to use.

How Can My Child Do Things On Their Own?

If you want your child to master a certain task, narrate exactly what's happening and what comes next: "Okay, we're going into the bathroom . . . that's right, first we go to the sink . . . here's the soap—careful, not too much . . . good, good . . . now turn on the faucet . . ."

Even if your child can do certain tasks perfectly, sometimes they'll get caught up in the details, and your voice is the one thing that keeps them on track. Say what your hands are doing. Be as concrete as possible. That's what leading looks like. In a clear and loving voice, inform your child of the next step. Coach them through the situation.

If your child is unable to perform the task or doesn't want to do it, consider how you might break down the steps even further. What is getting in their way?

When your child balks at something, what they'd usually prefer to say is, "Thanks for the suggestion, but there's no way. It's too many steps at once, so I'd rather not do it at all. It isn't fun to fail."

Listen carefully to what you're saying. Was it too much all at once? "Go to the bathroom and wash your hands, but don't splash on the mirror, then come over here." That's too much. Your child can't keep it all straight. It's better to give just one instruction.

Over the course of these two years, the number of steps your child can manage will grow. By the time your child reaches age three, you might not need to narrate every single step: "Please go wash your hands" is plenty, and in most cases, they'll know all the steps that entails. Unless, of course, there's some major distraction or they're tired or it's something they don't like doing— then it might require closer supervision.

How Do I Help with Transitions?

Transitions are always hard for your child, whether between indoors and outdoors, day care and home, or playtime and dinnertime. The moment after one activity ends and before another starts—this "nothing" time— is challenging. Your child loses their bearings, and it happens every day. What is just a short walk to the bathroom for you can be a difficult phase of reorientation and readjustment for your child: a situation in which they encounters different surroundings, smells, sounds, and impressions. They need your leadership more than ever during transitions. Don't just leave them standing by the door in a coat and hat while you search for your keys; give them a task, like "Look at this book until I come back." At age two or three, your child can't wait by themselves yet. They can be inactive for thirty seconds at most, but then, unless you've given them a task, they'll go looking for a distraction. Your child needs something to hold on to during transitions—and that "something" is usually a connection with you.

If your child is in the middle of an activity and you'd like to change the scene—let's say it's time for dinner—remember that, like anyone else, your child would like to finish what they're doing before getting on board with what you're doing. Their daily tasks might be even more important than yours, because as a toddler, every minute of the day is spent learning.

When you'd like your child to shift their focus, show respect as you enter their world. Observe what they're doing and comment on it: "Oh, you're building something. Wow, you're using blue *and* green Legos." Now wait and watch, then say, "It's almost time to eat." Smile before giving instructions, and there's a greater chance they'll do as you ask.

What Rules Can I Set?

Lucky for you, your child doesn't question the rules yet, though they notice when you do. They can immediately sense the wiggle room when you ask, "How about we brush our teeth?" This is open to negotiation. Even if you don't formulate the instruction as a question, your child can tell the difference between a loving but firm tone of voice and an uncertain or pleading one.

You need to pretend (convincingly) that your rules are set in stone. Eating dinner, brushing teeth, getting dressed, and going to bed are nonnegotiable. You can provide visual aids by hanging pictures of each step of these routines on the wall.

Your child will want to test the boundaries and practice saying no. At this age, they'll often try to take the lead, but the pleasure of any victory is short-lived as they find themselves facing a bunch of problems and consequences they hadn't foreseen. Although they got their wish, it came at the cost of their most basic and important need: a sense of bearings and security.

Pay attention to what's developmentally feasible for your child. If you leave the mailbox key within reach, there's a good chance it will disappear one day—a lesson John and Julia learned the hard way when Alex was two. Your child is obsessed with exploration and discovery these days. They can't help it. Their developmental drive is stronger than ever, and it pushes them to try everything.

As a good leader, you should try not to have expectations of your child that they can't meet yet. It's fine to establish a handful of rules, but keep the number limited, because your child can't keep track of that many (or at least not for very long). The rules shouldn't be arbitrary. Consider what rules make the most sense for you and your family members.

What Do I Do When We Get Stuck?

Humor is the quickest solution to any standoff with your child. Humor immediately reestablishes your connection and eases your child's resistance. It's fun for them when you slip your hand into a sock and make it talk, saying it's sad that they won't put it on. After a good laugh, they're likely to be more cooperative.

Slapstick humor is a big hit with your child these days. It's a hoot when people trip or fall on purpose. If you were taught to take conflict seriously, try lightening up—a little fun goes a long way in making things easier.

Your child often invents games to offer solutions for different problems (see Quick Reference—Attachment Play, page 207).

They're also in a magic phase. A sense of logic has not yet developed.

Their imagination is more powerful than reality during these early years. Whenever it's not a good time for something they want to do, try to create a story to persuade them otherwise. Let's say you're in the parking lot and need to get home, but your child wants to be carried. You could say, "You want me to carry you, but wouldn't it be amazing if we were both giant birds with big, powerful wings and we flew home together to our nest?" Your child is likely to flap their arms all the way back to the car.

Above all, creativity and fun help relieve stress and forge a wonderful connection between you and your little one.

The example that you set still has the greatest effect on your child. They copy the things they experience in everyday life: first and foremost, *you*. Take an honest look at yourself. Are you modeling behaviors that you'd like your child to follow? Like it or not, you can't expect them to do what you won't do yourself.

We all have bad days. And you can always say you're sorry. It's the best remedy, as it teaches your child an important lesson: sometimes people make mistakes, but they can apologize. Your child doesn't need perfect parents. If you slip up and behave in a way that you didn't intend, there's no need to blame yourself. The same applies to your child. Show them that it's okay to make mistakes and that it's possible to apologize for them afterward.

How Do I Make My Child Happy?

If you want a happy child, find lots of ways to grant them independence. Think long-term: Once you've weathered the learning phase, with its glacial pace and countless "uh-oh" moments, your child will feel pride in having acquired new skills.

It can help to create a "yes space": an area where they can explore freely, without your having to say no. Notice any task with which they might still ask for help, then find ways for them to do it themselves the next time. Maybe the whole stick of butter is too much for them to handle at the dinner table, and they end up hacking it to pieces. Instead, give them a pat of butter in a small dish, with a kid-size knife. You're setting boundaries. You're leading.

Let your child help, so they don't lose that impulse. The goal is for them to become an engaged, full-fledged member of the family—not a passive consumer of services.

Moments of Following in 2- and 3-Year-Olds

When your child is playing, discovering something new, or experiencing emotions, your job is to follow.

At age two or three, a child is at the mercy of their emotions, which are big and difficult to regulate. See "Feelings and Tantrums" on page 182 to learn more. Make a point of naming your emotions; your child first learns empathy and care by getting to know your feelings and boundaries. Share them. Your child won't necessarily take them into consideration to start, but the input is important. They will draw on this information for years to come.

Starting around age three, children begin to recognize other people's emotions and respond with empathy. You can help by saying things like, "That makes Henry sad. He just wants to play with you." Help your child learn to "read" social situations. Like a sports commentator, you simply describe what's happening on the field. Your child has to learn what to pay attention to and how to assess different situations. At the same time, they're figuring out how to manage their own feelings and to endure rejection and conflict. Acquiring these skills is key, as they represent the foundation for cooperative play and social behavior.

What's the Difference Between Wants and Needs?

Your child may be expressing very strong desires these days, so it makes sense to distinguish between wants and needs. A need must be addressed as soon as possible. If your child is looking for human closeness or attention—or if they're thirsty, tired, or need to move—it's up to you to fulfill those needs, or at least to acknowledge them and say when they'll be fulfilled.

Wants are different. Sometimes they can get what they want, and sometimes they can't. If they're hungry and *want* ice cream, you can satisfy the *need* for food by giving them something else to eat. But your child must learn the difference between wants and needs. To understand what reasonable desires look like, they require time and clear guidance.

If your child does something that annoys you, try to identify the underlying need or want. If they keep putting their feet on the table at dinner, what might they need or want? Maybe they can't follow the conversation and feel left out, so they try to get attention this way. It's much easier not to fight the behavior and to tackle the underlying need or want: "Oh, are you bored? I can see you're done eating. Here, you can sit on my lap while I finish my conversation." This is all it takes to avoid an argument about feet on the table, because it immediately addresses the cause of the behavior. If your child could, they might say, "Hey, you're ignoring me. Pay attention!" Their language skills aren't capable of that yet, so it comes out in their behavior. Look for the underlying need or want right away, otherwise your child might become frantic and go to more extreme lengths to get your attention. If "now is not a good time," it can be enough for you to simply acknowledge and name the need or want. Every child—scratch that—every human, regardless of age, just wants to be seen.

How Do I Follow My Child During Play?

During playtime, your child takes the lead. Enter their world and observe. Yours is a passive role during playtime, as you follow your child. They know best when it comes to their own development, and they'll do whatever makes sense to drive it forward. Allow them to solve the problems that arise along the way. Simply watch, narrate what they're doing occasionally, keep them company—that's plenty.

Should your child become fully immersed in play and enter that amazing condition known as "flow state," when the rest of the world seems to melt away, there's even less for you to do. Be quiet or slip out of the room, careful not to disturb them.

If your child assigns you a role to play in a game, you are free to accept—but they will be quite particular about how they envision the game unfolding. You might also lack the endurance to perform a basic task over and over again. It makes perfect sense for you to grow bored by a game that your two- or three-year-old loves—you're at totally different stages of brain development. Fortunately, your little one is so stinkin' cute, it helps you to survive the boredom.

If playtime is not fun for you and you quickly lose interest, you can make a game of doing chores together. Don't ask them to clean the whole house, but if you're folding laundry, invite them to join in the fun. Follow your child's lead as they transform this chore into a game.

Always wait for your child to demonstrate what they want to do, and once the impulse is satisfied, let them move on. Eventually they will learn to finish what they start, and that's important, but you can't expect it from them yet. Right now, completing a task takes a back seat to encouraging your child's enthusiasm for the process at hand. Whenever possible, let them complete the final step, so they can enjoy a sense of accomplishment.

Your child still needs far fewer toys than you might think. Everyday objects are far more interesting, and your child wants to master their uses. Lots of playthings can be found outdoors too. Create a rotation schedule for toys: If you notice certain toys collecting dust in the corner of the room, swap them out. Some of those toys might awaken your child's interest when they reappear after a few weeks in the attic or basement.

At this age, your little one is starting to play with other kids, but they still need lots of practice in social behavior. Maybe everything will be smooth sailing; maybe you'll need to separate your child from others or mediate occasionally. Don't assume that they know how to do it on their own, or that your only role is to prevent misbehavior—be a role model for your child, clearly demonstrating the behaviors that you'd like to see. They will watch and learn. You can remove them from a conflict if necessary, or explain what they're supposed to do in that social situation and then do it with them. As a role model, *you* can apologize to the other child: "I am sorry that happened." Demanding that your child apologize is usually pointless, because they lack the insight to understand what they're saying and why they're saying it.

If your child is the "victim," show them how to remove themselves from a situation or ask for help. Do *not* discipline the other child. Leave that to the parents.

These skills and habits will keep improving, and your child will get even better at resolving playtime conflicts by themselves. When your child turns three, you can reflect on these disagreements and talk about possible solutions together.

I'd like to make a brief comment here, as this chapter closes: Some adults are wary of toddlers. For centuries, there have unfortunately been many periods when children were viewed by some as "tyrants" who must be controlled with an iron fist. In medieval Europe, people sought to "cast the devil out" of children; the notion that adults have to be on their guard around kids has proven remarkably tenacious. With this idea in mind, I won't mince words: Even during the autonomy phase, your child is a wonderful, loving little person.

Your child wants everyone in the family to be happy and comfortable, but they don't know how to make it so and would like someone to show them. Tell your child what you and other family members need. At age two, their response might be limited. By age three, their understanding will improve. But to achieve this understanding, they need you to keep them safe as they put their free will, desires, and emotions to the test.

BONUS

Feelings and Tantrums

Feelings—and their most dramatic expression, tantrums—are a big topic for lots of parents of toddlers and preschoolers. Young children act fully on their feelings, because there's no voice inside their heads saying, "That's enough. You have to stop now." Your child can't tell the difference between what's appropriate and what isn't.

Luckily, the feeling and expressing of raw, unfiltered emotions usually passes. Very few toddlers cling to the past. Adults are usually the ones stressing out about the "unreasonable" outburst, while the kids go back to playing happily.

What You Feel

Our children can be role models for us. They intuit that emotions just want to be felt. In my experience, feelings are like clouds: They lack substance, so we can afford to take them a lot less seriously than we do. Emotions might appear one at a time like fluffy cumulus clouds, whereas sometimes a thick cloud cover fills the sky—every day the clouds are different, and they are constantly changing shape. Gathering storm clouds of emotion might feel threatening; they rumble loudly and unleash a torrent of tears—I mean, rain—then blow over. Soon the sky is blue again, no clouds in sight.

This could be the case for us adults too, if we stopped resisting our emotions and instead regarded them with a little distance—if we simply acknowledged what was happening inside us, then observed as our emotions inevitably shifted and cleared. Resistance causes emotions to harden, making it tough to break through the pileup that results from refusing to really *feel* what you're feeling.

We know what emotions we would *like* to have: "positive" feelings, like happiness or joy. We would rather not experience "negative" feelings, especially anger and grief. That's why it seems as though happiness is more fleeting than anger and grief. When something good happens, we feel happy or excited, then the feeling passes. The same would happen with negative feelings, only we're so busy fighting them, we get in their way.

We develop countless methods to avoid negative feelings. Usually we opt for distraction or some form of numbing. We scroll on our phones, watch TV, eat, drink, take drugs—most people devise their own, almost reflexive response. The first hint of an undesirable feeling triggers automatic resistance, an act of regulation that may be as basic as wanting a cup of coffee.

The result is that the suppressed feeling often returns, and it doesn't take much to be triggered. You might have been stunned by some people's responses to what seem like minor grievances: a comment on social media, a red light, a sold-out item at the supermarket, a rainy day, a weird look from the neighbor . . . and sure enough, there's that old feeling again, just waiting for an opportunity to express itself.

We rarely use such moments as an opportunity for deep feeling. Instead, we explain away the feeling. We talk to friends about it, sometimes getting extra fired up. "You see it that way too, right?" "This is completely ridiculous, isn't it?"

At a certain point, minor triggers can no longer be used to justify big emotional responses, so we search for "bigger" reasons. We'll point to the political situation, a disaster unfolding somewhere in the world, ongoing social discourse, our childhoods, or some other cause that provides solid justification for our emotions.

Our goal was to avoid negative feelings, but we tend to achieve the opposite. We're stuck with our negative feelings. Sometimes this negativity influences our general attitude toward life, which seems normal, since many people are in the same boat. That's just life, we keep telling ourselves—and one another.

But then along comes your toddler, serving up a piping hot dish of negative feelings, and in the middle of the bread aisle, no less.

In this classic supermarket scene, you aren't the only one caught up in your child's outburst. Other adults get sucked in. Be prepared to hear everything from reproachful tongue-clicking and accusations of bad parenting to lines like, "Just let your kid have the damn thing." What your fellow shoppers are trying to communicate is this: "Listen, a child's screaming triggers me. It actually scares me. I have been bottling up my feelings for so many years, I can't risk them coming out."

This context might help you understand why your toddler's extreme emotional outbursts are so hard to handle. In some unfortunate cases, you might have two little kids on your hands—your toddler and your own "inner child."

Coping with negative feelings is a lifelong process. We grown-ups have to keep working on it too. When we were kids, it was far less common for adults to help us shoulder the burden of our emotions; instead, we often learned to ignore or banish our feelings as quickly as possible.

This isn't your parents' fault. Sadly, it has been the case for ages, and your parents were just the latest in a long lineage of people who were raised the same way. The last couple of centuries gave rise to some strange ideas about how to behave toward children in general, but particularly regarding how to address their emotions and needs.

Outside of Buddhist monasteries, the notion that feelings just want to be felt is not too widespread. Learning to observe an emotion in your body from a distance—but with interest—is challenging. But it's the best way to make peace with your feelings.

Your Child's Feelings

In infancy, or stage one, feelings are shared between two people. While your baby can express emotions, they can't even begin to regulate them. You respond automatically: When your baby cries, you pick them up, rock them gently, and make comforting sounds. You're helping them learn how to regulate their feelings.

During stage two, between ages one and two, your child gradually becomes aware of their feelings. You support this awareness by naming those feelings, thus teaching your child to do the same. You simply tell your child what they're feeling: "Oh yeah, that makes you mad," or "Yay! You're happy now," or "Sure, that makes you sad." At this age, it isn't helpful to ask your child what they're feeling. They don't know the answer—they need you to identify it. Read your child's face to see what's going on. You might misjudge, but you can always try again next time. It's a good sign if your child contradicts you at some point and says, "No, I'm not mad. I'm sad." This is cause for celebration, because it means they're learning to recognize their feelings.

Remember that toddlers can only feel *one* emotion at a time. Internal inconsistency doesn't exist for them yet; they can't experience multiple feelings at the same time. They will be consumed with rage—then suddenly their anger vanishes. They'll swing between love and hate within seconds, one feeling replaced by another.

Your child is little, so there's only room for one thing at a time: one thought, one feeling. When a new one comes along, the old one has to go, because there isn't room for both in such a small space.

Many parents struggle with the fact that during this phase, their child will only respond to help from *one* person, either Mom or Dad. This is linked to the way toddlers experience emotions. Of course they love both parents, but they can't feel love for one at the same time as they feel love for the other. Some toddlers switch rapidly back and forth, whereas others ignore one parent entirely when both are present.

Stage three occurs around ages two or three. During this phase, your child has to learn how to cope with individual feelings. This is the start of a lifelong process. They're still incapable of experiencing multiple emotions at the same time, but they're working on managing emotions individually. Happiness is easy. Sadness is harder, but anger is usually the most difficult.

Remember that your child is maturing with every emotion they experience. They need to learn to accept that life is full of constraints and hardships that we can't change. That's a difficult lesson to learn. It shows progress when your child bursts into tears of distress after a tantrum—it means they're starting to accept the limitations of life and to find a way forward within them.

You continue to help your child by naming what they're feeling, then sticking it out together. They can't bear the weight of the emotion on their own yet. They simply need you to be there, making comforting sounds, offering soothing touch, and helping to shoulder the burden. But pay close attention to what your child needs right now; they might also need space—from you and the rest of the world.

If your child's feelings are too big for *you*, you can always step out of the room. Take care of yourself first. Recall the safety instructions in airplanes. They tell you to secure *your* oxygen mask first, before helping others, because it's no good if you pass out while busy helping someone else. And remember: Your child's anger is just a feeling, not a life-threatening emergency, even if that's what it sounds like.

Lots of parents wonder why their child is so well-behaved in the care of others but then breaks down as soon as Mom or Dad shows up, or "wreaks havoc" when they get home. It comes down to trust. Your child can let loose when you're around. It's like how you put on a good front at work and reserve your less attractive habits for the privacy of home.

In stage four, your child starts learning to respond to other people's feelings. They've been able to perceive your feelings since the age of one, but it takes years to build a sense of empathy: to understand what other people feel and react accordingly. They'll be three or four years old before they recognize what you're feeling *and* respond appropriately.

Your child won't start juggling multiple emotions until the final stage, at five to seven years old. They'll start differentiating and might say, "I am so mad at David, but I still want him to be my friend. Hmm . . . I have to decide how to act." When asked if they want something, they can now answer, "Maybe." Ambivalence is another new option—it is possible to be very happy and a little bit sad at the same time.

As always, when we're talking about childhood development, it's important to remember that every child is different: Some pick up these skills sooner and others take a little longer. Some days are better than others, and this has as much to do with you as it does with your little one.

We often demand emotional maturity from children at far too young an age. Getting a handle on emotions is a challenging and lifelong process.

Shared Feelings

One major misunderstanding is that parents often think their kids are antagonizing them intentionally. This misunderstanding is common because children's powerful emotions often emerge at the worst times for adults: situations in which we're already stressed. We think we've reached a breaking point, but then we have to deal with a meltdown on top of it all. But children are not doing this on purpose.

Emotions are contagious. If you watch a person or spend time in their presence, the atmosphere they create will have an influence on you. This exchange is even more pronounced between you and your child.

Your child does not function independently; on the contrary, they perceive your slightest emotional disturbance. When they sense your stress, they do exactly what you wish you could do (if not for your resistance): They throw themselves to the floor and start screaming.

This is neither your "fault" nor your child's. You're just two human beings who are a little overwhelmed. Show yourself kindness and understanding. Be your own best friend and give yourself as much love as you give to your child.

What Do I Do About Tantrums?

In Autonomy and Boundaries (page 126), we established that your child really has their hands full during the toddler years. They're pulled this way and that by free will and unwieldy desires. They're constrained by their lack of skills and by boundaries established through external forces. And they're at the mercy of big feelings, as their prefrontal cortex isn't developed enough to keep emotions in check.

These first few years can feel bewildering as a result. Tantrums are par for the course, and many children experience multiple tantrums per day. Your child's personality largely determines the intensity of their tantrums, so not much can be done to change it. However, you can take certain preventive measures to decrease the frequency.

Once a tantrum begins, intervention makes far less sense than people might think. In my opinion, there's too much talk about all the things parents should do during a tantrum, when in reality, there is very little you *can* do. It just has to run its course.

It's as if your car went off the road and hit a tree. You're stuck, so what are you going to do? Sit tight, make a few calls, and wait for the tow truck.

The metaphor could be applied to tantrums: Okay, seems we just collided with the tree. This is happening now. Let's see what can be done. First, assess the situation. It gets a little more complicated now, as multiple factors are at play: Either your child can still cooperate or they've blown past that point, and you're either at home or out in the world. Let's take a look at four different scenarios.

Scenario A: Safe Space and Cooperative Child

If you're in a safe space—at home, for example—meet your child where they're at. Support them with short sentences like "Oh, that was tough," "I can see why you're upset," "Something like that makes you want to scream"; you are (succinctly) naming what your child is feeling and what happened. Or simply make sympathetic, calming sounds. If your child responds and calms down quickly, that's wonderful. That means they can cooperate, and maybe you can offer them something that they need or want. But first, they need to be seen and understood.

A tantrum isn't usually sparked by whatever your child just wanted, but by an underlying need. Is it a need for closeness, quiet, sleep, food, water, attention, or something along those lines? Try to satisfy that need. If "now isn't a good time," at least communicate that you see and understand the need.

Scenario B: Safe Space and Uncooperative Child

Here too, you might be at home or in some other safe space. After naming your child's feelings and what happened, it's clear to you: Nothing to do here. The car crashed into the tree. Wait patiently for the tow truck—I mean, for your child to unleash all their emotions. The duration varies widely among children: Some need just five minutes, while others rage for an hour straight. Know this: It *will* pass.

Now and then you can offer closeness, touch, a comforting sound, or a few words. You can stay nearby or leave the room, depending on what feels most appropriate.

What matters is that your child makes the first move toward reconnecting. Their crying will subside or their body language will change, signaling to you that they are capable of some level of cooperation. Try approaching them then, and decide together what they need. They will usually settle down now, because the feeling ran its course. As far as your child is concerned—and in contrast to how you might experience some of your own emotions—that means the tantrum is over and done.

Scenario C: Public Meltdown and Cooperative Child

If your child has a tantrum in public, it means they are too stressed. Check in with them to see if anything can be done. Lean in close and name what your child wants as well as the feeling that goes along with it: "That toy looks great, all shiny and red. I understand that you really want it." This often suffices, truly, because your child was only looking for understanding. Now there's a chance that they can cooperate, and maybe the two of you can come to an agreement: "What do you say we take a picture or make a note of it? Then we'll remember it, and you can ask for it for your birthday."

Scenario D: Public Meltdown and Uncooperative Child

This is what I like to call a "firefighter's helmet scenario," because it's best to put on your imaginary firefighter's helmet. When firefighters encounter a child in a burning building, they don't lean over and say, "Hey there, do you want to come with me? No? Maybe you want to bring your teddy bear with you? Want to try climbing down this cool ladder all by yourself?" No. They grab the child and run, because now is not the time or place for lengthy discussion. The same could be said in the grocery store, when your child is lying in the middle of the aisle, screaming, and every passing adult has something to say about it. If your child is being abundantly clear that their capacity for cooperation has bottomed out, you don't have many options available. What might work? Can you pick them up and remove them from the situation, while being loving and levelheaded and describing exactly what your hands are doing? Can you get them in the grocery cart seat and clear out? Or leave your cart there, go outside, and come back later? Ask a fellow shopper for help? Or simply tough it out, finish your shopping quickly, then skedaddle? Whatever you decide, you *must* act, because you and your child are far too vulnerable in this public setting, which is not suited for your handling of powerful emotions.

Remember: If you feel angry too, then avoid picking up your child against their will. In that moment, your movements are usually too rough, which scares them. You need to calm down first, maybe taking several deep breaths. And never pick up someone else's child against their will.

Tantrums are one of the most challenging aspects of parenting. Feelings just want to be felt. This might be one of the best things we can teach our children.

The fewer rules, the better—and that means for everyone. Life simply has too many variables to cram into a strict framework of rules.

PART 4

From Preschooler to Kindergartener to First-Grader

Please do not compare your child too closely with our "average" child, Alex. Development does not follow the law of averages. Your child is probably slower in one area and quicker in another. They might not display certain traits or behaviors, whereas others are highly pronounced—all of that is normal. Your child is unique.

7

Development at Age 4

Thinking and Play

Alex has wrapped up the better part of her early development. Now the pace of development slows down somewhat, since much of the foundation has been laid. She can use her body with some control, speak clearly and understand what's said to her, and draw on a decent store of basic knowledge of the world around her.

Alex spends a lot of time thinking and wants to understand everything. She still gathers information by touching and trying things, but she's added more thinking to the mix. One rainy day, Alex and Julia are in the car. The windshield wipers move steadily back and forth. Alex watches them intently, then asks, "Do they know it's raining?"

Perhaps the most important thing Alex will discover this year is her ability to comprehend the thoughts and beliefs of other people. She will realize that other people might see things differently than she does. This opens her to a true understanding of other people's behavior.

Alex can now see: David is crying because he wants to be part of the group, but the other kids aren't letting him play. What can she do? Well, she could play with him, or she could ask the others if it's okay for him to join them. This skill allows her to shape situations for a totally different kind of togetherness.

Another simple fact that she will soon understand: If a person isn't in the room, they can't know what's happening there. Alex didn't really get that before—she figured everyone was aware of exactly the same things. When she was younger and grown-ups told her that Santa could always see her and knew if she had been bad or good, she was good (for goodness' sake!) because she believed it. Now, doubt starts creeping in, because she's been thinking about it. . . . How on Earth did Santa pull *that* off?

Quick Reference—Lying

Acquiring the Capacity to Fib

Grasping "theory of mind" is key to interacting with other people. One needs to be capable of adopting others' perspectives. This skill tends to develop around ages four or five, but as always, some children will develop it sooner and others later.

The classic "false belief task" was developed by Heinz Wimmer and Josef Perner in 1983, with the study of Maxi and the chocolate. Children of different ages watched this scene unfold: Maxi puts his chocolate bar in Box 1 before leaving the room. While he's gone, his mother removes the candy from Box 1 and puts it in Box 2. The researchers then asked the children where Maxi would look for the chocolate when he returned. The younger children assumed that Maxi knew what they knew, and they all guessed Box 2. Only the children ages four and older could reason, "He wasn't there, so he didn't see what happened. He's going to look in Box 1." They knew that people can act based on false or incomplete information.

Children can gauge other people's emotions and preferences from a much younger age. Even one-year-olds can read people's faces and recognize what they're feeling. It's much trickier to discern what is going on inside their heads.

The realization that people can believe false information and base their actions on that belief has major implications. With this newfound knowledge, your child can start adapting to the people around them, taking others' motivations and beliefs into account. Your child is now taking on complex lines of reasoning, like "Grandma thinks that everyone loves her meatloaf, which is why she always cooks it. But that's not true."

And with this kind of reasoning, your child has also acquired the ability to lie. Though an unpopular skill, it's a huge step forward in terms of cognitive development. Your child is not only being fake convincingly, they're creating a false belief in another person. This is an extremely advanced skill.

In the years between infancy and age four, your child is incapable of intentionally lying. They act solely on impulse. They're unable to anticipate the consequences of their actions and how other people will respond, and they use trial and error to find out. Right now, they want a cookie. Can they reach the cookie jar? There's only one way to find out.

Generally, when a child under the age of four is caught with their hand in the cookie jar, they don't realize it wasn't such a good idea until they see an angry adult approaching. Then, because of the adult's angry response, the child tries to escape the situation with a quick and rather helpless "It wasn't me," or "A monster took the cookie." Given that they're in the magic phase, they might try to come up with a fantastical explanation, then defend it wholeheartedly. In those early years, whatever your child believes represents the truth.

Your child's capacity to lie also allows them to adopt another person's perspective and to "walk in their shoes." They can

> shape situations by taking other people's interests into account. Lying is just a side effect of this important social skill; it can be very difficult to get along with people if you don't understand them.

Perception of Time and a Sense of Beauty

Alex is gradually acquiring a sense of time. Past, present, and future exist for her—and events seem to happen one after another. She recalls details from long-past occurrences that her parents completely forgot. Though she can't name the time or place, she remembers very clearly what kind of juice she drank at her friend's birthday party last summer.

Time still has to be kept concretely, though; the more abstract it becomes, the more difficult for her to grasp. When asked what day it is, she might respond, "Spring!"

It is now possible to ask Alex "What happened?" with greater likelihood of receiving a realistic response. Her responses used to be reflections of whatever she felt or believed—in other words, of what she wanted. Now Alex is gaining some distance from her own wants and needs. That said, this skill goes out the window temporarily if she's worked up.

This skill allows Alex to make minor decisions, provided they don't extend too far into the future. She now understands that before bedtime, she can either read a book or draw one more picture. Planning further into the future is tricky: After a sleepover at her friend Paula's house, Alex declares that she wants to do it every week; by the next week, she loses interest entirely. Her big declaration only applied to that one time.

Alex is also starting to appreciate beauty, though this doesn't necessarily apply yet to sunsets, nature, art, cars, or architecture. Her sense of beauty is different. For instance, she loves bright colors and might insist on wearing one color exclusively. Bright clothes are awesome, and who cares if they match or not. She loves painting her fingernails with her friend David. Wearing sparkly shoes or pouring glitter all over her drawings—amazing! Alex loves glitter—John and Julia, not so much, since it seems to find its way into every corner of their home.

Alex is still in her magic phase and spends a lot of time in an imaginary world populated by sorcerers, witches, and other enchanted creatures. She dresses up as a superhero or princess and is utterly absorbed by tales of magic. These things might scare her too, because magic is so real to her. Rituals can help chase off the monster under the bed or the ghost in the closet: Magical interventions calm Alex's fears far more reliably than citing the laws of physics or probability.

From Tadpole People to Schematic Scenes

Alex loves arts and crafts. She can cut a straight line now, provided she has been allowed to practice using scissors. If shown how, she can also tear strips of paper—she has to move her hands in different directions, which requires some practice. She's even using the tripod grasp: holding pencils and crayons with her middle finger, thumb, and index finger, just like a grown-up. But figuring out how much pressure to apply and how to use her wrist to guide the writing implement isn't easy.

Alex has fun mimicking writing. She says, "Let me jot that down," then fills a sheet of paper with zigzags and "reads" aloud what she's "written." She can now busy herself with play or crafts for about half an hour.

At the beginning of this year, Alex is still drawing her tadpole people: a circle with very long, skinny legs extending downward and a couple of skinny arms out to the sides. These circles with "rays" are also used to represent animals.

As Alex's observational skills develop over the course of this year, her depictions of humans become more nuanced. At some point, she gives them bellies, eventually followed by hands, faces, and hair. New figures arrive on the scene. Alex begins to draw squares and even diagonal lines, leading to the possibility of drawing houses, cars, and trees.

Soon she starts arranging the figures to create a particular scene. Alex has the mental maturity and motor skills to plan her pictures. The result is usually a schematic, stacked landscape: At the bottom of the page, she draws a strip of green to represent grass, followed by a strip of blue at the top for the sky, then fills the space between with buildings, trees, clouds, the sun, people, and other figures. Alex depicts what she knows more than what she sees; for instance, cars have four wheels, so when drawing a car from the side, she'll give it four wheels, all lined up in a row. Whatever she deems most important, she tends to draw the largest.

Alex uses lots of color too, to express mood. At one point, for several days in a row at day care, she draws all of her pictures in black. John and Julia are immediately concerned, as are her teachers—the grown-ups jump to all sorts of conclusions about what this could mean. Is Alex struggling? Did she have a traumatic experience? Should the adults intervene? How? Fortunately, one of her teachers has the presence of mind to ask the artist directly about her choice of color. Alex chirps, "I don't like the black, but the other markers were all dried up."

Alex can recite numbers, but actually counting is another matter altogether. She knows that when counting, each item gets its own number, but it doesn't always work out that way. She'll say numbers in the right order but sometimes skip over items while counting. She'll choose any big number to express large quantities: "I could eat a thousand fish sticks!" or "I want to invite a hundred people to my birthday party." Alex doesn't understand why her parents object—after all, "a hundred" just means "a lot."

Jokes and Swear Words

Alex loves telling long-winded stories about her day or whatever else comes to mind. When you have only recently learned to talk, there's no time like the present to put your new skill to use.

She's developing a real sense of humor now too, and can't get enough of hearing and telling jokes. Sadly, Alex's jokes aren't particularly funny to adults, because she usually loses the punchline along the way. How do you tell a joke so that other people think it's funny? She'll have lots of false starts as she tries different setups to the same joke, or she'll crack up in the middle, forget the punchline, or deliver the punchline first—but she's having a great time while doing it.

Alex can recite poems or nursery rhymes but will sometimes get embarrassed, because the prospect of messing up while lots of people are watching is pretty horrifying. It can be difficult to come up with new rhymes, but she loves repeating what she hears the big kids say and will laugh herself silly over rhymes like "banana fofana" or "nana-nana-boo-boo, stick your head in doo-doo." Trying to rhyme names is fun; she just loves the sound of "Jenny the penny" or "Kyle the crocodile." She still delights in slapstick. What's funnier than people falling down?

And speaking of fun with language: Swear words are awesome! They're a no-no, and Alex knows all about no-nos. She swears because of the big response it gets; if the grown-ups don't seem to care, swearing loses its appeal much more quickly.

An Eye for Detail

Helping out around the house is still a great way to encourage Alex's development; pairing socks, folding laundry, and cooking all stimulate learning on multiple levels. She's getting much handier in the kitchen and is starting to strategize in a meaningful way. One day, her parents can't find the kitchen scale to measure the flour for their sourdough starter and she yelps, "I have an idea!" She disappears, then returns with the scale from the bathroom—brilliant, as far as she's concerned.

Alex is starting to solve problems on her own, because her parents modeled that for her (see Quick Reference—Thinking It Through, page 119).

Tidying up is still tricky, as Alex's parents continue to overestimate her capacity for foresight: Alex takes in the details with little regard for the big picture. What does a picked-up room look like? Well, it always looks different—sometimes a sweater stays draped over the back of a chair or a pile of books remains on the table; sometimes her building projects can stay out on the rug but sometimes she has to take them apart. She still needs someone to break down this process into short, clear steps that lead to the desired result: "First, put away your blocks. Great! Now, pick up all your doll things."

Telling Alex to "Clean up your room!" is comparable to someone telling her parents to "Clean up your neighborhood!" How could they possibly respond to an order like that? Where would they start?

One day, Alex is in her room, her parents' order to clean up ringing in her ears. Faced with this daunting task, she tries to set her own goal. Cleaned-up rooms usually don't have any items on the rugs, so she carefully arranges all her belongings along the wall and off the rug. She is pleased with this genius idea.

Alex's focus on details has many benefits. Her visual perception has never been keener. She beats everyone at the card game Concentration; with a little practice, she finds it easy to remember where each card is located and which details go together. John and Julia are amazed at how often they lose the game to Alex.

Sometimes the grown-ups will notice just how carefully Alex listens and observes. While getting dressed one morning, John asks, "Is it raining out?" Alex gazes through the window, then responds, "No, Dad, it's raining down."

Grown-ups often privilege the ability to see the big picture over the beauty found in the details. Alex derives tremendous pleasure from the little ladybug she discovers between two leaves. She is delighted by the beetle's tiny legs and wishes she could stay there all day—but that would make her parents late, yet again. For Alex, being able to take her time is the best treat ever.

A Shift in Perspective

Alex loves role-play. She could play dress-up all day. She creates games based on the costume she's wearing, which allows her to try out different roles. What does it feel like to play a doctor, or a dog? She's been exploring the "orientation" scheme lately (see Quick Reference—Play Schemas, page 86), part of which includes adopting lots of different perspectives. She climbs onto tall furniture to see what the room looks like from up high, or she crawls under chairs or behind the couch. One day, she even rides on the bottom rack of the grocery cart. She is practicing with her body what's happening in her mind—namely seeing from different angles and adopting unfamiliar points of view.

Alex is now in the habit of saying "please" and "thank you," as her language skills continue to improve. Social niceties like these make life more pleasant, since people typically respond more positively. If you've modeled that it's polite to say "thank you" after someone gives something to you, Alex will do so reliably—and with pride.

However, she might forget to say "thank you" if she's too wound up. She gets so excited about a gift from Aunt Toni that she forgets to thank her, then feels embarrassed when Toni asks, "And what do you say?"

Alex is easily embarrassed these days. John and Julia prefer to redirect her in these moments by asking, "Do you like it? Would you like to say 'thank you'?" Or they take the opportunity to model the behavior once more, thanking Aunt Toni themselves and saying, in Alex's presence, that she appears to be happy about the gift.

It's important to be as concrete as possible in these situations, because Alex still takes language literally. When this happens again, John and Julia ask, "What's the magic word?" Alex looks confused, then sheepishly ventures a guess: "Abracadabra?"

Feelings and Relationships

Alex can manage her feelings now, and she can talk about them too. She still has tantrums from time to time—and needs help regulating these big feelings. She needs lots of recognition and regard; she wants to be proud of all the things she can do well. The family came up with a nice ritual to boost Alex's self-esteem: At bedtime, John and Julia tell Alex's stuffies about all the great things she experienced and accomplished that day. She loves when they do this and smiles from ear to ear.

Alex can resolve conflicts verbally, because she understands social situations so much better now. She demonstrates empathy and can make sense of what led to certain disagreements: "Paula made me mad. I wanted to play with the car, but she did too, and she just took it. That made me mad." This complex processing requires Alex to understand and gauge her own feelings and motivations—not to mention, those of her friend! Parental support goes a long way in helping her hone this skill. She is happy to have social situations explained to her. Soon she will understand that people do things "on purpose" or "by accident."

Alex has also started developing a moral code, classifying situations as right/wrong or good/bad. "That boy laughed when his friend got hurt. That's mean," she concludes. Or, "It was nice of them to let David play too."

Her First Real Friend

Paula is Alex's true friend now. Their friendship has moved beyond simply doing the same activities together and is now based on their connection as individuals. Alex experiences more frequent disappointment in her interactions with friends, as what they think is gaining importance. She has a lot of work to do on how to navigate conflict, reach compromise, or even downplay certain emotions.

Role-play is the most important type of play this year. Alex loves re-creating concrete, detailed scenes from everyday life with playmates. She might cook an elaborate dinner when playing house, have a doctor's appointment, throw a birthday party, or go grocery shopping. Other tasks prove more abstract; for instance, when she "goes to work," she simply slings a bag over her shoulder, leaves the room, then comes right back. She also plays lots of fantastical games with friends, featuring pirates, sorcerers, kings, and princesses.

Every Child Is Different

John and Julia have made friends with some of the other parents at day care. It's fascinating to discover the differences in their kids' development and how their skills emerge at different speeds. Almost more amazing is how clearly their personalities differ from the get-go; a lot seems innate. All the parents are starting to see how much their kids' personalities determine the ways that they parent. They realize that they don't actually have much say over how they raise their child.

Paula's parents, for instance, are similar to John and Julia. They want to raise Paula in a tranquil, loving, needs-based manner, but it isn't easy. Paula has a powerful developmental drive and, given the opportunity—however small—takes the lead in the family. She loves being in charge. On top of that, she is sensitive and prone to tantrums. She finds her own solutions to problems (see The Great Misunderstanding, page 160).

At this point, Paula prefers to take control in most situations—often against her parents' wishes. Her parents felt so helpless once, they even tried to punish her (see Quick Reference—No Punishment, page 222). For the most part, however, they try to avoid conflict and to "keep her happy" by meeting her demands whenever possible. Unfortunately, this doesn't keep Paula happy; on the contrary, it keeps her asking for more, which ultimately makes her less happy.

Paula takes the reins the moment she feels her parents aren't fulfilling their role in leading. Sensing her parents' uncertainty gives her the impression that they don't know what to do. That's a scary feeling, so she tries to do it herself. Paula needs her parents to be confident and to draw a clear line while also seeing and addressing her needs. It's a difficult balancing act for the grown-ups. For Paula, it would be best for her parents to anticipate (and address) her needs, so she feels their care. She needs the nonverbal assurance: "We know what's going on, don't worry. You're safe here. We see your needs, so you don't need to fight for them. We will take care of everything. We've got the situation under control."

Paula's parents need to exude confidence, keep their cool, and set clear boundaries without being gruff. Security and a sense of bearings are such fundamental human needs that Paula has been trying to achieve them on her own.

Exuding confidence is a challenge for Paula's peace-loving parents, who don't want their firm stance to come across as authoritarian. They're better suited to the loving approach; they loathe being dominant, which they equate with authoritarian parenting. They would much rather give in and let Paula lead the way. They shower her with attention. It's difficult for them to grasp (and even more difficult to put into practice) that love is not always soft and gentle; sometimes it's expressed through leadership and a firm (but still loving) stance. They've also realized that Paula is very active and needs a lot of opportunities for physical movement.

On the other hand, Alex's friend David is very sensitive to everything around him. He gets scared easily and worries about the world. If he passes a dog tied outside a store, he might burst into tears, because he thinks the dog looks sad. David's sensitivity expresses itself in all sorts of ways: The tag in his T-shirt bothers him, and for a long time, he refused to wear a raincoat. It took some sleuthing for his parents to figure out that David disliked the clammy feeling of the sleeves on his skin. They cut the tags off his T-shirts and gave him a long-sleeve shirt to wear under the raincoat, and problem solved.

David can easily get overwhelmed and doesn't do well with multiple activities in the same day. The world, with all it has to offer, is too much to take sometimes.

David's parents have had to adapt their parenting style to David's needs and wants. They can't overload him with appointments and activities. He needs a lot of space and time to play by himself. Playing gives him a chance to process impressions at his own speed. He often becomes fully immersed in play and loves playing outdoors: He could happily spend hours moving rocks in a stream.

David needs a lot of leading from his parents, especially when it comes to big emotional outbursts. He needs to feel their understanding.

He needs to know that they are here for him *and* that they will set him on the right course. He needs his sense of security regularly reaffirmed; like Paula and Alex, he feels lost when his parents give in to his impulses and let him decide. For instance, if he gets scared in the foyer at day care, he'll immediately want to go home. In that moment, he wants to be understood and comforted; he doesn't want this fleeting feeling to change his entire day. A loss of bearings is worse than being sad for a spell. Occasionally, the prospect of day care is legitimately too much for David to handle, and he needs a day off. Ideally, his parents will be able to plan for those days.

Generally, David needs his parents to shield him from overstimulation, which requires lots of planning on their part. They are loving, cheerful, and (most importantly) firm in helping him navigate his world. They are by his side when big feelings arise and give him lots of time to "digest" his experiences.

Quick Reference—Attachment Play

How Your Child Solves Problems

Adults tend to think that serious conversation is the only way to resolve conflict. This isn't the case for children: Play is a more relaxed and effective way to work through problems.

Your child takes the lead during playtime. If you simply follow—by placing a few items in the room, such as dolls, stuffies, modeling clay, or dress-up clothes—your child will typically "play through" whatever is currently bothering them. You can watch and name the actions and feelings that you observe.

If there is a specific issue you wish to resolve—let's say your child is scared of dogs—you can re-create the scene, then demonstrate the solution. How does Teddy respond when a dog approaches it? This is much better than having an abstract conversation to teach your child how to process fear.

Your child probably loves contingency or power reversal games, which turn the tables and help build their sense of security, trust, and authority as they provide the commands. For instance, they might intentionally drop their doll on the floor, and every time, you say the same: "Ouch!" This makes your child feel like they're controlling the situation. You might also pretend to be clumsy, scared, or confused—responses that invite your child to solve the issue for *you*.

Your child will often launch into nonsense games too, intentionally doing something wrong, like putting a shoe on their head. By doing this, they're inviting you to correct the wrong, and you are very welcome to engage if it works for you in the moment. Sometimes your child will turn to nonsense games if they're nervous about doing something wrong or feeling a lot of pressure. It's a playful way to diminish fear of failure and to reduce stress—it might work for you too.

Separation games like peekaboo, hide-and-seek, and tag teach your child how to manage being apart from you; play more of these games leading up to a period of separation.

Adults often have a hard time understanding regression games. If a situation causes your child to feel emotional strain or distress, they might briefly revert to baby behavior. A classic trigger is the arrival of a sibling. It's okay, and you can play along if they want to be a baby again, wrapped up in a blanket, babbling and cooing while you rock or feed them. This will help them overcome such a challenging situation.

Cooperative games, in which no one wins or loses—like role-playing or building together—are a great way to reestablish a good connection with your child.

Watch your child—they will offer the solutions you're looking for. And play with them. Together, you can transform troublesome feelings into laughter.

Movement

Alex can run now—and does she ever! She runs and runs until she's completely out of breath and declares, "I'm all tuckered out!" She is testing her physical limits. Just like her parents' trainer at the gym always says, "Push yourself to the limit, then push a little more. That's the only way to build muscle."

Alex can jump sideways, take a standing jump, and balance for about five seconds on one leg. She can climb now too—her hands and feet are well coordinated.

Toward the end of this year, she learns to ride a bike. Her parents read that it's best to avoid training wheels, because they mess with a child's sense of balance. Balance bikes provide better preparation for bicycles than training wheels do.

Alex's friend Paula learns to ride a bike quickly, within only a few days. Her parents have to find safe places for their little speed demon to ride, because at four years old, Paula has no sense of how traffic works.

Alex's fine motor skills have improved vastly, and with a little practice, she can tie knots and thread a needle. She can even make her hands perform different movements at the same time, which is extra challenging.

She can use a fork and knife on her own, since she was given enough time to practice. Household tasks such as chopping fruits and vegetables, kneading and rolling out dough, and washing dishes or unloading the dishwasher continue to benefit her development.

Speech

Alex has an active vocabulary of around 1,500 words. She's a great conversationalist, and she has internalized her routines to the point where she can respond to multiple instructions at once; for instance, "Take off your shoes, hang up your jacket, and wash your hands, please." In fact, she often remembers to do these tasks without being asked, unless she's distracted or tired. But that happens to grown-ups too.

She can recount her own experiences in chronological order as well as remember short stories. She knows the difference between the prepositions "on," "behind," "in front of," and "in." An instruction like, "Put the umbrella behind the bench and your shoes in front of it" is no longer the prepositional puzzle it once was. She also understands complicated sentences connected by the conjunctions "or," "so that," "after," "because," and so on.

Alex has brief conversations on the telephone with Grandma. Unlike when she was younger, she now understands that she's either listening or speaking when she's on the phone. She puts the appropriate emphasis on words and sprinkles her speech with expressions that she's heard grown-up use. Once, when the family had to get on the road, she wrapped up her call with Grandma by saying, "Great to hear from you, but I've got to run."

Alex continues to ask lots of questions. She loves telling long stories, using complex sentences—and the occasional creative verb conjugation or plural, like "mouses." Her parents jokingly call her "motor mouth"; she's just excited to share everything she knows about the world.

There's another trick that Alex might pick up this year: clapping out syllables. She can clap out two-syllable words like "apple." She figures out what words mean and comes up with her own explanations: "A catfish is a fish that looks like it has whiskers, but it lives in the water and doesn't chase mouses or have fur."

Language has become a tool for Alex: She uses it to assert her viewpoint and to persuade others. She has moved beyond "But I want to" and can now make arguments that strike her as entirely logical. At the same time, her ability to empathize keeps improving, so she starts negotiating with John and Julia.

At a Glance: 4-Year-Olds

Thinking and Play

The most important skill Alex picks up this year is the ability to empathize with others and adopt their perspective. Her drawings are more legible. She is the household champion of the card game Concentration, given her tremendous capacity for noticing and recognizing details. Meanwhile, big-picture thinking remains a challenge.

Feelings and Relationships

Alex loves role-playing games. She's good at playing with others, as her understanding of their feelings, motivations, and intentions improves. She still needs help regulating big emotional outbursts or tantrums.

Movement

Alex can run, jump, climb, balance briefly on one leg, and might even be learning to ride a bike.

Speech

Alex understands everything she's told, and she loves telling long stories. She can explain what words mean and actively use language to negotiate.

> Alex and the ball: She is familiar with the characteristics of a ball, and she has a much better sense of quantity. If three balls are on the floor and five are on the couch, she can immediately tell that more are on the couch.

8

Development at Ages 5 and 6

Thinking and Play

Done. Alex has laid nearly all the foundations that he'll need in life. He has a handle on movement, dexterity, speech, thought, and interpersonal relationships. Now he needs to hone the skills that are specific to his culture and to generally expand upon the basics.

Alex's capacity for logic is a work-in-progress. Logic will start to click at age seven or so. In the years leading up to grade school, he swings between logical and magical thinking. He still believes in magical creatures and solutions, but he's less certain these days. Santa Claus has lost his magic, and Alex adopts an air of superiority when he states that Santa doesn't exist. His reasoning is razor-sharp when it comes to the Easter

Bunny too: Rabbits and eggs have nothing to do with each other, he explains, so the whole thing is dubious. None of this diminishes his love of the stories, festivities, gifts, and secrets of the holidays. And he just wants to keep believing in certain things.

Alex has developed a decent sense of time. He knows what a regular day looks like and can more or less gauge what it means when Mom or Dad says "in a minute," though he's not a fan of waiting. Long-range planning is still tough. He wants to try out new hobbies, and he wants to do it *now*.

For example, Alex was intent on starting judo because his friend David was doing it. John and Julia found a good club and bought him the uniform. Alex was thrilled. And judo was a blast—for a while. But now he wants to try swimming and doesn't understand why his parents want him to stick with judo. Don't they know that hobbies are fun and you do them by choice? It makes no sense to Alex that his decision should hold indefinitely. It's almost like waiting for Christmas, which always takes forever!

At Alex's age, switching between sports is great for building different muscle groups and diverse skills, so John and Julia accept the fact that it's only a matter of time before Alex wants to try something new—yet again. For the next new hobby that rolls around, they might just borrow or rent the necessary gear rather than buying the stuff.

Alex's Relationship with Rules and Responsibility

Alex understands rules, which is not to say he can always follow them. He's still impulsive. As a toddler, Alex might have responded to rules by saying no, but he never questioned the rule itself. These days, he often wants to know the reason for a rule. John and Julia have a lot to justify and discuss—and it's exhausting.

Alex can read his parents very well. When they visit friends, he usually doesn't want to go home when they do, so he'll ask pretty please, with sugar on top, if they can stay. If they respond firmly, "Nope, sorry kiddo, we're already running late," he'll usually accept. However, the slightest indecision—maybe they check the time or say, "Hmm, we'll see"—signals that there's wiggle room. Sometimes, as soon as they look at their phone, he'll zoom off and yell "Awesome, thanks!" while John and Julia are left to wonder what, exactly, Alex just took as a yes.

Having to discuss every single detail with Alex is exhausting, but John and Julia learn a lot about which rules make sense from his point of view. He can make many decisions on his own now. The family has to keep adapting to these changes, but generally, the fewer rules, the better for everybody.

Alex is starting to understand the rules of the road. He knows what traffic lights and certain road signs mean. He is good at telling the difference between right and left, but only from his position; when someone comes toward him, he doesn't realize that his right is their left. Riding his bike on the road is still tricky, but walking is great. He knows to wait at crosswalks until the light changes; look left, right, and left again before crossing; then check one more time when he reaches the middle before crossing the second lane. Alex and his parents have practiced this many times.

Alex becomes eager to take on more responsibilities. He wants to be an important, active member of the family. It's best to assign an entire range of duties to him. A task like "Sweetie, can you grab a new bottle of apple juice from the pantry?" is no fun, because who wants to be just a gofer? Besides, Alex already knows how to do that, so there's nothing new to be learned.

A better role would be that of "Apple Juice Manager." It's up to the AJM to keep track of how much apple juice is in the pantry, to let Mom and Dad know when inventory is running low, and to make sure they pick some up the next time they're at the store. Exploring the relationship between supply (apple juice in the pantry) and demand (thirsty drinkers) is an interesting challenge. It teaches Alex new skills, such as organization and planning. He needs some help to start, as with any new skill.

Alex still loves scientific experimentation, which is becoming more and more involved. When he's sitting at the dinner table with his parents but all they want to do is have a boring conversation, he takes the opportunity to investigate something more interesting, like the relationship between weight, length, and gravity: He positions a spoon at the edge of the table and sees how far he can push it until it falls. How does the tipping point change when something is in the spoon—like spaghetti sauce, for instance? Now, as ever, he is a researcher and scientist.

What's more, rule-breaking is a surefire way to get the attention he so desperately needs. When his spoon falls, splattering the floor with tomato sauce, his parents' exasperation means he's finally got their attention again. These are rather extreme measures, but negative attention *is* better than none at all. It's difficult (and kind of embarrassing) to recognize and articulate the sentiment, "I wish you would just notice me!" Sometimes he'll ask, "Can I sit on your lap?" though he also feels too big for that. In an invitation to attachment play (see Quick Reference—Attachment Play, page 207), he'll routinely ask, "Will you play with me?" but more often than not, his parents encourage him to play on his own because he's so good at it now. How else is he supposed to reconnect with Mom and Dad after a long day, without seeming like a baby? Alex is at a bit of a loss.

He loves group activities that everyone enjoys. He is always on the lookout for new challenges. After years of training in Lego construction, he is thrilled to help assemble the new furniture. Whereas John and Julia are annoyed by the number of screws involved, Alex can't get enough. There is so much for him to learn, and he's doing a lot of independent thinking too. All those times when his parents thought out loud while working through problems (see Quick Reference—Thinking It Through, page 119) are paying off. He wants to do as many things as he can on his own!

Alex is in preschool. His skills are solid in counting and "subitizing," which means he can, for instance, tell how many dots are on the side of a die without counting. His understanding of quantity and amount has vastly improved.

Quick Reference—Math

Laying the Groundwork in Everyday Situations

Written in collaboration with Janna Spannagel, math teacher and founder of "Die Matheflüsterin" (The Math Whisperer), an online math course in Germany

After spending their toddler years acquiring lots of math skills through play (see Quick Reference—Play Schemas, page 86), your child is ready to move on to preschool math. School math requires preexisting knowledge, so it will be a lot easier for your child if they come equipped with "pre-numeric" skills.

Everything is easier to learn when built upon a foundation of knowledge, including elementary math. Either your child will pick it up easily, make connections with what they already know, and have a sense of what the concepts could mean; or it will all be a big question mark. To prevent the latter, here are simple ways to build this base of knowledge into your family's everyday routine.

GAME 1

In certain processes, the order of operations is important, and in others, it doesn't matter. For example:

- "Do we need to pour the bubble bath into the tub before or after the tub is full? Why?"
- "Does it make a difference if you put your left shoe on first, then your right, or can you do it the other way around too?"
- "Should we put the potato chips in the grocery bag first, then the canned tomatoes, or the other way around?"
- "When making hard-boiled eggs, is it better to put the eggs in first, then the water, or the other way around? What about when cooking noodles?"
- "Have you ever tried putting your undershirt on after your sweatshirt? Is that even possible?"

These questions will prompt new lines of thinking and set the stage for argumentation, which is a key skill in mathematics. But how do these "swapping" scenarios relate to math? Try applying the basic understanding gained through these questions: When does the numerical order of an equation not matter? Addition. When *does* the order matter? Subtraction. These are common errors in school that can be avoided by building preexisting knowledge. You will soon discover lots of everyday situations to practice this skill.

GAME 2

Collect some used packaging like a cereal box, toilet paper roll, or a Toblerone box—otherwise known as a rectangular prism, cylinder, and triangular prism, respectively. When you cut along the edges or at the corners, you and your child are in for some amazing discoveries. How often do the same shapes appear? How does the round toilet paper roll suddenly turn into a square? (This is the lateral surface of a cylinder . . . but we'll save that for later!) Can these shapes be used to build something new?

Lots of fun discoveries can be made here, while your child develops a greater perception of shapes, patterns, and forms.

GAME 3

Create classification systems around the house, maybe starting with the bookcase. Arrange the books according to size. Then, every time your child puts a book back, they'll encounter the challenge of placing it within the system you've created together.

This game requires practice. Involve your child in the process as you model it for them. How do you know where this book goes? What's your strategy? The same applies for games and puzzles in the closet or silverware in the drawer. You can also sort plates, coins, or crayons according to size. Your child can learn a lot from existing classification systems, which create a

> basis for understanding mathematical systems like the order of numerical series or the structure of ranges.
>
> Being well-prepared to enter school doesn't mean that your child knows how to crunch numbers perfectly. It's more important that they acquire the basic skills they'll need for *learning* to crunch numbers. Fortunately, this can be done in everyday play!

Alex recognizes letters and will start learning to write his name. Lots of kids at preschool are doing the same. When it comes to learning how to read, it's better to focus on literacy than on the concrete skill of writing. When does reading occur in everyday life? John and Julia read through the grocery list with him and let him help check the recipe for dinner or follow along during bedtime stories. Alex benefits from lived experiences of reading in everyday life. That way, learning the alphabet at school won't bore him.

The final months of preschool before beginning kindergarten are tough for Alex. He can sense the impending transition, and it's exciting. He's impatient.

Artist and Collector

Alex's drawings and paintings have become very detailed, but these days he'd rather build three-dimensional structures. Drawing and painting aren't really his thing—but he can draw human figures with heads and bodies, arms, legs, and other details. He can also draw (and name) geometric forms. The size and arrangement of these figures reflect his inner reality: More important things are made larger. "X-ray" pictures are fun too—images that depict multiple layers at the same time. For instance, he'll draw the outside of a house as well as the rooms and furniture inside.

Alex loves collecting—and collecting from nature is best. He still loves playing outdoors—especially building dams and small shelters in the woods. Every time he goes out, he simply *must* bring home an extra-special stick or stone that he's found—but ideally, lots of them. He tends to keep items from his collections in his pants pockets, so John and Julia make sure to check before doing laundry.

His parents are also perplexed by Alex's long-standing fascination with dinosaurs. He knows their names and always makes sure Mom and Dad are pronouncing them correctly. How much longer do they have to trip over prehistoric reptiles every time they walk through the living room?

Moral Development and Punishment

Beyond the rules that apply at home, Alex is learning about rules in society. It's strange and confusing to him: What can and what can't you do?

You have to be polite, for one thing, and Alex knows those rules. You say "please" and "thank you." His parents do that all the time too, so he follows their cue.

Cutting in line isn't allowed—unless Mom or Dad is in a real hurry, in which case it seems to be okay. Hmm. Sometimes they drive too fast in the car—this seems to be allowed under certain conditions that Alex cannot comprehend, but he knows about the speed limit. Recently, his parents were pulled over for speeding, which made them mad. So, it's unfair to get a ticket for breaking the rules. Huh.

Alex has learned to tell a grown-up whenever something breaks, but when they were on vacation, his parents broke a drinking glass at their rental and didn't tell the owner. Is that right or wrong?

Alex has gained the capacity to lie. A big jump in brain development allows him to lie and cheat because he has learned to see from other people's perspectives—a very important skill (see Quick Reference—Lying, page 196). He's trying to tell the difference between polite, socially acceptable lies and their less desirable counterparts.

Maybe lying is a little like keeping a secret: Mom and Dad taught Alex that some secrets are good and some are bad. Bad secrets make his tummy hurt. Good secrets are like not telling Grandma about her birthday present, so it will be a surprise—that gives him more of a funny, fidgety feeling.

Is it the same with lying? If a lie makes everyone feel better, is it okay? Aunt Toni gave him a present, and his response, "Thank you for the present," seemed preferable to what he really wanted to say, which was, "Are you serious?! What kind of baby junk is this? I'm never going to play with this."

You aren't allowed to take items from a store without paying, but Alex can't help noticing that Mom stops by the free samples multiple times for another treat. It must be okay to do that, then, if you really like something.

At a toy store one day, Alex sees a figurine that his friend David has too. Alex is thrilled, because he has wanted this toy for a long time. It's so awesome that he found the exact same one here—now he and David can play with them together! He happily pockets the toy without any grown-ups noticing.

Back at home, Alex plays with the toy in his room. He realizes that they didn't pay for the figurine, nor did he even ask to take it. He feels bad and doesn't know what to do. He's never faced a problem like this before. Playing with the cool toy certainly isn't fun anymore. He shoves it under his bed and tries not to think about it anymore. This is usually what he does when feeling overwhelmed: He ignores the problem. It's like when he was a toddler and thought closing his eyes would make him disappear.

The next day, Julia finds the toy under Alex's bed and asks him where it came from. Feeling guilty, Alex tells her that he took it from the toy store. Julia is appalled. She stands there, completely frozen. Alex stole? A whole narrative immediately plays out in her head, in which this episode is the start of a dark phase. Is there no keeping Alex on the straight and narrow? All she can see is the deed, without considering her child's age.

Alex feels even worse when he sees his mother's face. He has never seen her like that; this must be more serious than he realized. He feels utterly helpless and does not want to be the cause of this response. What can he do?

Julia doesn't know what to do, either, and she leaves Alex's room without a word, toy in hand. She needs to calm down first. She calls John and they discuss their options, because one thing is certain: They must impose consequences, but what should those look like? They don't have any strategies for action, because they never saw this coming.

John and Julia agree that Alex should lose screen time privileges for the next several weeks and stay in his room for now.

Alex is in time-out. For the last few hours, he had a guilty conscience and a terrible tummy ache, almost like he was going to throw up. This punishment is changing his mind. But he isn't sitting there, thinking about what he did, like his parents told him to.

Quite the contrary: Alex thinks the punishment is totally unfair. He has a keen sense of fairness and can't tell how taking the toy and losing his screen time are related. He gets angry, which feels a lot better and more powerful than feeling guilty.

His parents took something from him that he loves. They specifically chose something that would hurt him. They took advantage of the power they have over his life.

Alex senses an unexpected feeling, one with which he's familiar from conflicts with other kids at day care. For the first time, he views his parents as adversaries. He wants to take something from them that *they* love. He can't articulate it, but he feels the desire for revenge mixed with fear and guilt.

John and Julia aren't happy about this punishment. They wish they hadn't imposed it, but what were they supposed to do? They're mad, and there have to be consequences for Alex's behavior. Right?

A couple of days later, Paula's and David's parents come over for dinner. The kids love playing together, and their parents are friends too. David's parents don't have much to contribute to the conversation, as

David is always very careful—too careful, in fact. He would rather not do a thing at all, rather than risk doing it wrong.

Paula's parents, on the other hand, have lots to say on the matter. Just the other day, Paula was playing on the hood of their car and put a big scratch in it. She couldn't explain herself, so her parents took away her tablet. They have had to do that a lot lately, because Paula has been talking back, throwing tantrums, and playing rough with other kids. Last week, they picked her up from a neighbor's house and found her using a tablet, which led to another fight. The other day, Paula beheaded a bunch of her mom's favorite flowers in the garden! Paula's mother is at her wit's end. She doesn't want to be in a power struggle; she wants to treat her child like an equal. Paula feels the same way, and it's taking a toll on their relationship.

Paula's parents wonder what they should do. They're responsible for their child's learning about right and wrong. They can't just ignore such (mis)behavior. Right?

Quick Reference—No Punishment

Teach Your Child How to Find Solutions

It is widely assumed that punishment helps to improve a child's future behavior or leads them toward true insight. For hundreds of years, we believed that mistakes must be punished. Punishment usually makes children feel humiliated, mistreated, scared, angry, helpless, sad, and even indifferent or vengeful.

A lot of people talk about "logical consequences" instead of discipline, though they usually amount to the same thing: nice new approach, same old attitude.

Generally, people who feel good will behave well. Behaviors tend to mirror how we feel about life and what we secretly think about ourselves. When children receive negative messaging such as "You're so bad that you deserve to be punished," they will probably tend toward bad behavior in the future.

Wouldn't it be better for your child to learn how to respond constructively when mistakes happen? Wouldn't it be better for you if your child continued to come to you for advice and didn't feel they had to hide mistakes for fear of punishment?

Skip the Punishment and Head Straight for the Solution

Problems typically break down into two phases.

- Phase 1: Feelings—You probably get angry, sad, or disappointed when your child makes a big mistake. These are legitimate feelings, because you are human and you worry about their behavior. Whatever you usually do to get a grip on your feelings, do it now: whether it's sleeping on it for a night, taking a walk around the block, calling someone, crying, or whatever else. Your emotions are your business. Your child is not responsible. But if you find that you aren't truly angry or sad and can move straight into finding the solution, that's even better!

- Phase 2: Solution—What do you do once the feelings pass? Assess the damage. Do you need money for repairs? Was someone hurt, and reconciliation is needed? Can you and your child fix it together? What can your child do on their own? You want to teach your child, not punish them. Encourage them to come up with their own ideas. In rare cases, no solution is needed, because you can live with the outcome of the mistake, and all you need to contend with are the feelings. Don't search for a "consequence" if it isn't necessary. Look for a constructive way to sort out the problem, involving your child as much as possible. This will help to build problem-solving skills and teach them not to fear making mistakes.

After talking it through with their friends, John and Julia decide they don't want to punish Alex. For them, it's most important to have a good relationship with him, and they want him to learn how to deal with problems. They lift all punishments the next day, apologize to Alex, and decide with him what they should do next. They explain that a store is like a person, in that you can't just take things from it. The conversation is uncomfortable for Alex, but he's starting to feel like part of a team.

John and Julia explain that they have to bring the toy back to the store and pay for it. They want Alex to be there too, but they promise to do all the talking; he can stay in the background and watch. They realize that Alex learns best through modeling.

After working up the courage, Alex announces that he's ready a few days later. He holds his parents' hands tight and hides behind them at the store. John and Julia do not humiliate him in front of the staff by insisting that he say sorry. They do the apologizing for him, using "we" throughout, and they settle the matter with as little drama as possible. They pay for the toy and the store owner thanks them. The grown-ups acknowledge the courage required of Alex to do this, and he feels proud of himself. Afterward, the three of them go out for a special meal. He is cheerful and relieved, because this whole ordeal weighed heavily on him. It is truly resolved—and unlikely to happen again. Everyone in the family will remember this experience. They learned a lot.

Feelings and Relationships

Alex is better at managing his feelings. Anger is still a tough one, but that's the case for grown-ups too. When his feelings get too big, he needs external help (see Feelings and Tantrums, page 182). Luckily, even he is embarrassed by screaming in the supermarket now, as he's starting to care more about his image.

He can comfort others and anticipate emotional responses to certain situations: "No, we can't do that, or David will be sad." He can wait, allow others to finish speaking, and contribute to solving conflicts. He apologizes of his own accord and cultivates real friendships, because he understands and knows how to engage with social rules.

Alex is developing a very important skill at the moment: He can feel more than one emotion at a time. He can be angry at David while knowing what a good friend he is, and he can weigh these two feelings—anger and affection—against each other. It doesn't always work, but the dramatic exclusivity of emotions begins to ease over the next few years.

Alex's feelings are shifting inward, where they often play out. This can make it harder for his parents to read him.

John and Julia also wonder why Alex doesn't want to help out around the house the way he used to. His natural impulse to help is diminished. Alex doesn't need these tasks to develop skills anymore, and he's lost interest in a lot of them.

For a few years now, Alex has been hearing remarks like, "This place is a pigsty!" and "Ugh, now I have to tidy this mess up!" and "Please don't open that. I'm too tired to pick up after you." This leads him to conclude that cleaning is a huge pain and should be avoided. Clearly, the main goal in life is to have as little to do as possible. Sitting on the couch seems to be the most desirable situation. Although Alex doesn't yet distinguish between "work" and "play," he observes enough to know that it's best to avoid what his parents refer to as "work."

Competition

Alex loves playing with others, even in big groups. When playing with lots of kids, he tries to find where he fits in the group. He senses dynamics like competition and peer pressure. What do you need to do to gain others' approval? It isn't always clear, plus it changes according to the group. In judo, his friends respected his agility; at day care, he did best by sharing and being kind; with the neighborhood kids, roughhousing is the ticket.

Alex enjoys board games and can happily sit at the table long enough to play until the end. It's usually lots of fun—unless Alex loses! Winning and losing are major topics this year. He's becoming better acquainted with what he can do well . . . and not so well. The latter is hard to accept. He wants to be the best! These days, he would do anything to win. The desire is so powerful that he'll even draw on his newfound capacity to cheat.

Alex and his friends come up with all sorts of competitions for comparing themselves. Though these situations can be difficult at times, they also teach him a lot about himself. He wants to learn more about his own limits and areas for improvement. Boasting and preening are normal behavior for him and his friends at this age. They like exaggerating and overestimating their skills. Grown-ups can help Alex learn how to realistically gauge his abilities, deal with defeat, and recognize that losing should have no bearing on self-worth.

Taking a break from competition, Alex also has fun with role-playing games and staging theatrical performances with his friends. Everyone dresses up and puts on a show.

But he and his troupe have not yet mastered that sort of structure; they wear elaborate costumes and take great care in preparing the stage, seats, and ticket sales. The parameters are clear; they just don't understand the inner workings yet. The play might open with one of the children making an announcement, then everyone running back and forth a few times, fully costumed, and laughing themselves silly. The end. This scene can be performed numerous times in different costumes. John and Julia watch, more than a little bemused, and peek surreptitiously at the time, but at the end of the day, it's sweet to see the kids having so much fun.

Movement

Alex has such great control over his body that he can balance like a tightrope walker and even take a few steps backward. He's faster than ever and can run almost a hundred feet in about ten seconds, which he's very proud of. He can do about ten standing jumps forward, balance on one leg for ten seconds, and hop forward maybe five times on one foot.

He loves cruising around on his bike and has the stamina for short rides with a grown-up. The rules of the road are still over his head, though, and riding in a city or town is too much for him alone.

Alex's hands can do everything he wants them to do; he can even hold a full deck of cards and draw or place individual cards. This was very hard to learn, and at first, he would always drop them. He learned that he has to loosen his grip just enough to draw the card, but not so much that they all scatter.

Alex also locks in his motor skills. Walking, running, hopping, jumping, climbing, swinging, and other types of movement all come naturally. When running around, he can make himself stop, to avoid crashing into his playmates.

If John and Julia want to teach him a new form of movement, it's better to give him a goal than to focus on the movement itself. For instance, if they want to teach him how to throw, they can demonstrate the motion, then say to him, "Look at me and throw the ball into my arms." He will need to find the best way for his body to do that.

Speech

Alex's language development is largely complete. He doesn't encounter any difficulties with speaking or comprehension in everyday life. He can register multiple instructions at once, then perform these tasks in the correct order, provided he isn't distracted along the way. He's become a great participant in conversation too: First, he'll listen to what people are talking about, then he'll consider a response before chiming in with his own ideas.

His vocabulary continues to grow. He asks what unfamiliar words mean and usually remembers their definition.

Alex can come up with rhymes now, like "house" and "mouse." He can also break down polysyllabic words, like "chocolate," to name one of his favorites.

He's interested in written language. He tries to write words, leading to new discoveries. For instance, he tells John, "Your name and Mom's name both begin with 'J.'" Alex even catches on to simple irony, now that he feels so confident in speaking.

At a Glance: 5- and 6-Year-Olds

Thinking and Play

Alex can adopt other people's point of view, make sense of their thoughts and feelings, and respond to them. He likes taking on responsibility and begins grappling with moral issues. What can and what can't you do in society?

Feelings and Relationships

Alex does a good job of finding his bearings and his role in groups. Competition and winning are important to him; losing gracefully is not one of his strengths yet. He can feel multiple emotions at once, which lessens some of the drama of years past, when he could only feel one big thing at a time.

Movement

Alex's body has internalized all basic motor skills and performs them automatically. He can also learn the new

> Alex and the ball: If he has four balls and someone takes one away, Alex can use counting to figure out that he still has one . . . two . . . three balls. He practices writing the word "ball." He likes how the letters look.

movements required for certain sports. He can walk backward, run, do standing jumps, and hop on one foot.

Speech

Alex talks like a grown-up, only he'll need to work on expanding his vocabulary in the coming years. He develops an interest in writing.

What to Know About 4- to 6-Year-Olds

If you don't remember what defines moments of leading and moments of following, please reread the summary on page 18. There's really just one question you need to ask when it comes to raising children: "Does my child need me to lead or to follow in this situation?"

Moments of Leading in 4- to 6-Year-Olds

Moments of leading occur in any situation with a goal. At this age, that includes morning and evening routines, cooking, shopping, cleaning, household chores, doctor's appointments, hobbies, and some arts and crafts, board games, or projects. Circle time and other structured activities at day care and/or preschool fall into this category as well. A major task at hand is streamlining family routines, bringing individual obligations and needs into line—at times, an impossible tangle that requires good management skills.

Everyday life is starting to become fairly stressful for your child, and they're only four, five, six years old. Their developmental drive is still very strong, which makes sitting a big challenge. Add up all the time they spends sitting—from the breakfast table and drive to day care/preschool to circle time, arts and crafts and other table-based activities, lunchtime, then back into the car, then the dinner table—you'll find they tend to get far less movement than they need.

This presents a problem for your child. They're facing one moment of leading after the other these days, almost as many as adults face. If you're wondering why your child can be so uncooperative, it's because they're running on fumes.

How do I create moments of leading?

For the first few years of your child's life, you broke down processes into small steps and described them: "Okay, now we take the soap . . . that's right, we're washing our hands again . . . here's the towel."

Your child probably doesn't need that anymore, unless they're very stressed. They do, however, need your help with all the transitions over the course of a day. After putting on their socks, what can you do to prevent them from getting distracted and forgetting about their pants? What can you do to help them remember that next step? Your child needs frequent redirecting to put them back on track, but given how distractible they are at this age, that redirection can be difficult to secure. As soon as they spot a toy or have a sudden idea, whoops—there goes the plan (in this case, getting dressed).

Using the morning routine as our example, how might your child best manage this? Can you prepare anything the night before? Can you take pictures of the routine and hang them on the wall? Would an hourglass help with showing the passage of time? Can your child get dressed in the kitchen while you're preparing breakfast? You can look over and say, "Great! Socks are on. Now come pants."

Before every moment of leading, you need to establish a connection with your child. Look at them, make eye contact, and smile if you can. An impatient instruction hollered from across the room won't get you far. It can be overwhelming, how many steps go into the morning routine, and they need your ability to focus for support.

Which rules does my child need, and which are unnecessary?

Rules are a double-edged sword. On the one hand, they provide a sense of security and help your child find their bearings. Rules lend structure to everyday life, and kids feel pride in learning and understanding them. On the other hand, if the rules are overly rigid, they can create conflict between you and your child. If already contending with a day full of moments of leading, your child will be overwhelmed by too many rules and unable to follow them. Everybody needs a certain amount of time in their day when they can just release.

Let's break down rules into three categories.

1. Safety rules: It makes sense to prohibit and regulate dangerous things. Your child then learns to trust you and follow these rules, because they know: "This must be really important!" Safety rules are always enforced. We do not lick the knife. Period. We do not play with the bottles under the kitchen sink. Period. We only cross the street together. Period. We do not play alone by the lake or pool. Period. Safety rules are not up for discussion.

2. Social rules and laws: These rules are abstract and often difficult for your child to understand. Fortunately, they have learned a lot through observation and trying out. These rules involve having good manners and generally knowing what's socially acceptable in groups of peers. Your child accepts rules like, "You don't litter because the police say so." (Among other reasons!)

3. Organizational rules: Organizational rules make everyday life easier. For instance, it's better to hang your coat in the hall closet than to throw it into a huge pile on the floor and have to

search for it when you're rushing out the door in the morning. Even though your child might prefer the latter, they learn that the house rule is "We hang our coats in the hall closet."

Your child will probably question the rules at some point. Take their questioning seriously. It can be helpful to look at these rules as if for the first time, just like your child is doing. What if they want to do it differently, and you give their idea a try for a while? You can still lead by saying, "You know what? That's a great idea. I've changed my mind. Let's do it the way you suggest." This also gives your child the feeling that they're a valuable member of the team with good ideas.

Your child has probably learned to respond with greater flexibility to situations. How many rules do they really need? Every child is different. Do rules help to ground them and make them feel safe? In that case, keep the rule in place, as a sense of security is a basic need.

Or does your child "rebel" against the rules? Why? Is a basic need being neglected? Or is the rule no longer necessary? Be honest with yourself. Does your child need this rule, or does it have more to do with your need for control and structure?

A lot of what we do in our families is done just because "it's always been that way." And if we turn those traditions into rules, we may end up overly restricted.

Your child can sense that every day is different. There isn't a single moment that's identical to the one before or to the one that happened yesterday. Maybe the messy living room doesn't bother you one day, then the next you have friends coming over and want the house looking nice. Fine, that's a reason with a purpose—"Mom wants us to pick up"—and not some arbitrary rule.

What if, to reframe, you referred to organizational rules as "habits"? As soon as parents try enforcing a rule, their tone of voice changes. They stiffen a little and say things like "you're supposed to" or "you have to." Kids don't tend to respond well. Ask yourself if the rule is pushing your child away. Are you losing sight of the current moment, because you insist on upholding the rule?

If instead we learn to watch out for one another as a family, most conflicts can be worked out. Why does your child always jump on the couch, even though it's not allowed? Are you engaged in a power struggle, and they're breaking the rule to make you mad? Or—and this is a likely reason—do they just need to move their body to burn some energy off? If you can tolerate the behavior, a child engaging in a power struggle will soon abandon it, because it was just about being "bad" and your response to it. Meanwhile, a child who's desperate to move their body will hop happily away until this fundamental need is fulfilled.

Rules are dynamic. They are part of a process constantly reshaped by your child's rapid development and changing needs. Stay flexible, and keep checking in on your rules and habits to see if they are still serving you and your family.

Should I Punish My Child?

Your child has learned how to lie—though I prefer the term "fib," because dishonesty is less harmful during this phase than you might think. They might start fibbing a lot, trying it on for size (see Quick Reference—Lying, page 196). It's just another developmental phase, one they'll probably grow out of by age eight. Be a role model, impressing upon your child that nothing bad will happen if they tell the truth. Try not to dwell on it, otherwise your child might self-identify as a "liar" and potentially keep up the habit after the phase passes. Simply move on to the next topic and forget the fib.

When it comes to discipline, you might want to follow Alex's parents' example (see Quick Reference—No Punishment, page 222).

For hundreds of years, people have been subject to harsh punishment for their misdeeds. History has conditioned us to believe that people deserve to be punished for their mistakes. The urge to seek revenge, blame, and atonement has deep cultural or religious roots for many people.

I am a big fan of a solution-oriented approach. What if you skipped punishment altogether and put your energy into finding the solution? These are the "logical consequences" that so many parents want to work toward. It makes life far easier for you and your child.

Generally, punishment does not serve in leading a child—if anything, it causes the situation to get out of hand. Your child is hard to lead when engaged in a power struggle, because unlike you, they don't have scruples that stop them from certain behaviors. They might not have any boundaries in trying to retaliate. It's better not to go down this road at all, but if you're already there, try to change course. Luckily, every day is a new day for your child, and their drive to cooperate with you is powerful.

Your child is a quick learner and learns best by watching you. They absorb what you do more than what you say. For years, they've been watching you like a hawk. If you apologize when you mess up, they'll probably do the same. If you say "please" and "thank you," they will too. Accepting your own mistakes leads your child to accept theirs.

Perfection isn't humanly possible. Modeling your imperfection teaches your child that people make mistakes or that situations can go awry if you're tired or something gets in the way. But we have the power to change and do things differently next time. Sometimes it works; sometimes it doesn't. Discovering this is a huge relief for your child.

Keep a close eye on your own behavior—yours is the only behavior you can control, after all, with greater long-term effects for your child.

When it comes to leading, the best tool in your toolbox is FUN! Nothing is more effective at easing a tense situation than introducing an element of levity. Your child is often one step ahead of you, and all you have to do is join in the fun. Playing a game is always preferable to having a serious talk (see Quick Reference—Attachment Play, page 207).

Imagination is one of our superpowers as humans. If your child is doing something totally out of line or wants something they can't have, meet them where they're at: "Oh yeah, that's a great idea. That would be awesome, wouldn't it? Imagine if we could all make a wish and get what we wanted. I would ask for wings so I could fly." Exaggeration and wild, make-believe solutions are absolutely allowed. Your child will probably jump right in, then the two of you can go back and forth with your flights of fancy while taking care of the task at hand. Incorporating fun allows you to lead much more easily and effectively.

Moments of Following in 4- to 6-Year-Olds

Moments of following mainly occur when your child is playing or experiencing emotion. They lead and you follow until it's time for you to lead again.

How do I respond to tantrums?

Your child is much better at regulating emotions now. Unless, of course, those emotions are too powerful. It's still normal for your child to struggle with emotional outbursts and need your help. Just being there is enough—they can articulate what they need from you. If you are not in a position to give them what they need right now, say so. You can be honest with each other about where you're at. To learn more about your child's emotional landscape, see "Feelings and Tantrums" on page 182.

Do I always have to play?

Your child wants to play with you now as they would with their friends, as real playmates. You are finally "allowed" to come up with your own characters, help build things, or play board games and cards. Even so, playtime is their "thing," so follow their lead. This isn't a pedagogical scenario in which your child has to learn something. It's about spending time together and having fun.

See Quick Reference—Soft Skills (page 149) for a reminder of how much your child gains from being given the time and space to play freely. Boredom is an important experience for your child, as it can give rise to valuable new ideas. They need as much unstructured time as they can get—it is critical for their development.

And if you don't feel like playing, that's normal too; after all, you already have the skills that these games are helping your child to develop. If they're always asking you to play, shared activities like cooking, baking, crafts, or another hobby amount to the same thing—these are all fabulous "games" for them. The main point is spending leisure time together every now and then.

How do I avoid merely managing my child's everyday life?

When your child reaches this age, it's a good time for you to reflect on your bond. With younger children, bonding occurs almost automatically: Just *try* being around a baby or toddler without immediately smiling or lifting the pitch of your voice or showing physical affection—it's practically impossible. Younger children are programmed to exude this inviting quality. They might as well be screaming: Take care of me! Form a bond!

With preschool-age kids, however, it's all too easy to neglect your bond. Entire days can pass where all you're doing is managing aspects of your kid's life. After all, you're busy too. Everyday stress often takes precedence and besides, your child can do a lot on their own now.

Track how much undivided attention your child receives from you on a given day. Do you still smile at them multiple times a day, like when they were a baby? Or are you starting to look at them like you would at an adult coworker, just another person in the room trying to make it through the day? If the latter is the case, make a deliberate effort to reestablish and build your bond every day. All it takes is a smile and kind word here and there.

Occasionally, you need to "read" and address needs that your child can't articulate. If they're grouchy or wound up after a long day, they might not be able to say, "I'm exhausted. I need to take a break and could really use a hug." If they're in a bad mood, give them a big hug, commiserate with them about how difficult everything is, wrap them up in a blanket, and do something cozy. Maybe listen to an audiobook together, or chat in the kitchen together while you prepare dinner. This replenishes their reserves, allowing for greater cooperation.

Even helping your child when they ask you to put on their shoes is an opportunity to have a nice moment together, make physical contact, and reestablish your bond. Don't view this as extra work, but as a chance to respond to your child's request for bonding. All they want is connection. Giving that to them now makes for less stress later, and they'll be far more cooperative.

How do I show my child that they matter?

We often fail to recognize children's profound need to be a valuable part of a group. It is such a shame that we divide the world of children from that of adults to such an extent that we now scramble to find mutually meaningful activities. Though your child isn't using a computer yet, they have access to all sorts of practical activities.

We take time for our children, often in the form of involved excursions. Zoos, amusement parks, and museums are wonderful places, but it is equally wonderful and enjoyable for both parties to clean out the basement together, repair something in the home, prepare a living-room picnic, or bake a special cake. It may come as a surprise that doing one amazing activity after another can actually leave kids feeling unhappy. If being entertained is your child's only "job," over the long run, it's unfulfilling. They want to be useful and important.

Before your child enters school, help them discover that they are a mover and creator in their own right. I hope you have lots of tasks on your to-do list that your child can help with—ones that would be truly helpful for you. They are eager to take on responsibility and pick up new skills along the way.

It's becoming more important for your child to talk things out. Their language has developed to the point that they can have a true exchange with you. But they still have a different way of speaking, especially about problems. At this age, they mostly want to clear up misunderstandings. They might be cuddling or playing when suddenly, some thought or feeling pops up. Your child addresses the thought or feeling directly, without any lead-up, almost in passing and using very few words. This can be disconcerting as a parent, because adults open conversations with some background or exposition, linger on certain details, and provide a transition into the end. In your child's case, when they're done, they're done.

> ### Quick Reference—Listening
>
> **Understanding from the Inside Out**
>
> Listening is your greatest tool in the coming years, and yes, that includes during puberty. All any person wants is to be heard and understood.
>
> In the book *Momo* by Michael Ende, listening is the main character's superpower. Because of how well Momo can listen, she makes everyone around her feel intelligent, important, and valuable.
>
> Anyone can be a good listener. There are lots of ways to do it, and it doesn't really matter what you say. You can simply repeat or summarize what your child said in a friendly tone of voice, or identify the feeling that you see your child is experiencing. Another option is not saying anything at all. That's what Momo does. She just listens with rapt attention, projecting herself into the internal world of the person speaking.
>
> What matters is that you listen honestly and with all your attention. Forget your opinions. Forget your goals. Forget your responsibilities and the notion that you have to change your child's behavior. Try to understand your child from the inside

out. There's no better practical expression of love. If your child stops listening to you, it's time you started listening to your child.

You're not trying to change anything—you're just trying to understand. Amazingly, listening has the power to bring about more change than any labored attempt to improve a behavior.

A Bowl of Positive Moments

Back when I was still making house calls, I met a family struggling through lots of problems with their sons. They devised various strategies to overcome this difficult situation, one of which was collecting rocks. The rocks were placed in a bowl on the coffee table, each one representing the boys' "misconduct." Whenever one of the boys was disobedient or disrespectful or broke a rule, another rock was added to the bowl.

Every evening, the family came together to count the rocks. I clearly recall how one of the boys would start slinking about the living room in the afternoon, eyeing the bowl fearfully. Each rock was tangible evidence of everything he'd done wrong that day.

The moment I saw that, I tossed out all the plans I'd prepared and said, "I would do it the other way around: From now on, these rocks represent positive moments. Starting every morning, add a rock to the bowl for every positive moment you have."

Disappointment clouded the parents' faces. They expected me to come in with comprehensive measures to regulate their sons' behavior. And now I wanted them to collect rocks representing positive moments? Did they even have any, when all they did was fight? At first, the parents were wary and the boys uncertain, but then they got into the idea.

For the first few days, Mom and Dad had a hard time identifying positive moments. The kids had to help, drawing their parents' attention directly to everything that went well. It was amazing, in fact, how many positive moments they had each day, and the number kept growing.

Weeks later, I returned for a follow-up visit. Mom couldn't contain her happiness and relief as she described how important the positive moments became and how much had changed in their family life. In the evening, as they counted the rocks, they recalled everything good that had happened that day. The boys were constantly on the lookout for positive moments, and wouldn't you know it, more and more of them started occurring.

As time passed, the boys' problematic behaviors diminished, and after the family did away with punishment altogether, those behaviors vanished. No greater intervention was required, and I don't think they're a unique case. All any family needs is a bowl full of positive moments that they just keep refilling.

What to Look Forward To

Your child has acquired the major skills they'll need in life. You successfully made it through the most challenging years.

If your own learning inspires you to do things differently going forward, don't worry: Your child is not stuck in their ways, and they're still developing so fast, you'll have many opportunities for change. Starting over is always possible.

Why is this my concluding point? Because you don't need anyone "translating" your child's behavior anymore.

Your child can express themselves; they have a sense of self and they're starting to think logically. You can really talk to each other now. Your most important role is that of listener.

Listen carefully. What is your child trying to communicate? They're old enough for you to be able to tap into memories of yourself at that age. Try seeing from the perspective of your child. What would you have wanted?

Remember *Momo* by Michael Ende and try to be a good listener, just like the story's protagonist. Forget your opinions and goals and step fully into your child's shoes.

You will coach your child as they continue to grow. Standing on the sidelines, you call out suggestions to help lead them through life.

Work together to decide how best to handle certain situations. You can now talk about strategies that you used to manage nonverbally. How should we do this? What works for our family? Revisit your rules every so often. Do they still reflect what's best for your child?

When it comes to what's "not allowed," only create rules that your child can follow effectively; everything else should be allowed. Peer pressure is often far too great. If "following the rules" makes your child a target for bullying, it might force them to decide between being obedient to you and not getting bullied—more often than not, they'll opt for the latter. The number of secrets they feel they have to keep will grow. To avoid that, try to be on your child's side and offer advice from personal experience, so they don't feel alone. They need to be able to trust that you will always act in their best interest.

It's wisest to bend your own rules if it means your child isn't forced to choose between you and external pressures. Don't allow the rule to drive a wedge between you. Responding with flexibility also preserves your influence over your teen, so they'll ask you for advice the next time too.

Write your own story with your children. Make sure you're maintaining a good bond. Smile at your teen the way you did when they were little; even if they refuse to show it, they still really need you.

It's not easy for you, because you're always reevaluating your own rules and boundaries. The guiding question should be: What is the best for my child? Do I need to rein in my need for security, control, or orderliness, because my child's need for friendship and new experiences takes precedence?

When one of my sons was thirteen or fourteen years old, he was invited to a party, and something was weighing on him. He told me, "Leon [aka the coolest kid in class] is going to be there tonight. You and Dad always say, 'No drinking, no drugs, and no R-rated movies.' I don't even want to drink, and definitely don't want any drugs, but if I tell them I'm not allowed to watch R-rated movies, everyone will laugh at me and think I'm a loser." I listened intently, then responded, "In that case, I suggest you break our rules."

Huh? Strange thing for a mom to say, but Leon appeared before my eyes, and I saw how easily he and his clique could make life very hard for my son. It was impossible for my son to follow our family rules without paying consequences outside our home.

Now, it makes me very happy to hear my sons, who are young adults, refer to my husband and me as their "safe space." We're allowed to keep coaching them. We're part of their real lives.

My husband and I were least successful with those lessons we were most insistent on teaching them—lessons that seemed so important at the time. We can't help but roll our eyes and laugh when we remember how badly we wanted them to learn to play musical instruments. We went all-out, and it was all for nothing, because our boys had zero interest in this particular pursuit. We had lots of lovely plans like this one—things we thought we "should" do—that failed spectacularly. Our boys were much quicker to pick up the practices that we modeled. If my husband and I had been passionate musicians, maybe our grand plan would have worked.

At the end of the day, your child decides what they're interested in. You can present them with options, but they have the final say. Your child will come up with their own ideas too, about what they want to do in life.

My Hope for the Future

I would like to close with an anecdote on children's development from 1912 by the great educator Maria Montessori:

... Once in our public park in Rome, the Pincian Gardens, I saw a baby of about a year and a half, a beautiful smiling child, who was working away trying to fill a little pail by shoveling gravel into it. Beside him was a smartly dressed nurse evidently very fond of him, the sort of nurse who would consider that she gave the child the most affectionate and intelligent care. It was time to go home and the nurse was patiently exhorting the baby to leave his work and let her put him into the baby carriage. Seeing that her exhortations made no impression on the little fellow's firmness, she herself filled the pail with gravel and set pail and baby into the carriage with the fixed conviction that she had given him what he wanted.

I was struck by the loud cries of the child and by the expression of protest against violence and injustice which wrote itself on his little face. What an accumulation of wrongs weighed down that nascent intelligence! The little boy did not wish to have the pail full of gravel; he wished to go through the motions necessary to fill it, thus satisfying a need of his vigorous organism. . . . As a matter of fact, if he had filled his pail he would probably have emptied it out again in order to keep on filling it up until his inner self was satisfied. . . .

[Children] are not understood, because the adult judges them by his own measure: he thinks that the child's wish is to obtain some tangible object, and lovingly helps him to do this: whereas the child as a rule has for his unconscious desire, his own self-development. . . .

That beautiful baby in the Pincian Gardens is the symbol of this: he wished to coordinate his voluntary actions; to exercise his muscles by lifting; to train his eye to estimate distances; to exercise his intelligence in the reasoning connected with his undertaking; to stimulate his willpower by deciding his own actions; whilst she who loved him, believing that his aim was to possess some pebbles, made him wretched.

Montessori's observation is more than a hundred years old. In the century-plus since she published this text, many different people have reported similar findings in various ways. Maybe in this century, we will finally learn to understand children's objectives and take their real, profound needs seriously, allowing us to live together in peace and to avoid major misunderstandings. I wish that with all my heart. Remember: You need to do far less than you might think. Just keep on loving. The rest will take care of itself.

My very, very best to you and your family.

Acknowledgments

Gratitude is the queen of feelings. It's impossible to be tremendously grateful and unhappy at the same time. Deep gratitude produces a sense of love, steady joy, peace, attentiveness, and connectedness with your life. Gratitude is really all we need to focus on to be happy. Like so many things, however, it can get lost in the shuffle of everyday life, and sometimes we need reminding.

I feel lucky to feel as much gratitude as I do, for as many wonderful people as I do.

Thanks to the team at Fischer Verlag, who were so kind and deeply invested in this project. Special thanks to Martina Seith-Karow for her support and outstanding editorial work.

Thanks to Kira Brück, an amazing journalist, who guided me in writing with such aplomb—and at one point boosted my own flagging powers by sending a photo of her son dressed up as a superhero, with *super*powers to spare.

Thanks to my followers on social media, who show such incredible support and were generous enough to share delightful tales of their own kiddos' exploits. I couldn't use them all, unfortunately, but special thanks to Bianca, Isabelle, Mendy Charlin Steenbock, Michaela Sezgin, Maendy Böhm, Lisa-Maria Hauge, and Sandra Brandenburg.

Thanks to Noemi Gügel (@einbauchgefuehl) for your kindness and competence in helping run my online courses and lending your expertise to participants as an educator and sleep coach—thank you for proofreading the chapter on sleep.

Thanks to Ina Orlovious, my favorite physiotherapist, for proofreading all the sections on movement—and even acting out the various stages of a baby's development. It was a hoot!

Thanks to Regine Gresens, a midwife and lactation consultant who taught me so much about nursing and with whom I took so many long walks, talking business.

Thanks to Sabina Köhler, my favorite speech pathologist, who made so many important corrections in all the sections on speech, and did so with such kindness. She points out that language development cannot actually be broken down by year. She's right!

Thanks to Frauke Ludwig, who had so many great suggestions for the section on carrying babies.

Thanks to "math whisperer" Janna Lisa Spannagel for all her insights into childhood math.

Thanks to my dear friend Kathrin Rath, who stood by me for decades now, come what may. You read every last word in this book without flagging. Your feedback was on point and crystal clear (read: "No, no, no, that doesn't make sense . . .") and helped me through every crisis.

Thanks to my parents—it would seem there's no stopping you from being amazing parents! You gave me so much, then showed my children the same care. I am so grateful for having grown up with you. It's unbelievable that you proofread this entire book with your usual dedication. You are parents driven by passion.

Thanks to my two marvelous sons—this book wouldn't exist without you. First, in addition to all the love you've shown me, there is no end to all you've taught me. Second, without you, no one would know my name, let alone ask me to write a book for their publishing house. I need your honest feedback and advice: "Sorry Mom, but honestly, your videos aren't good enough for YouTube. Post on TikTok instead. You can do stuff like that there." Listening paid off, yet again. I am unspeakably grateful for the wonderful young men you became. Thank you for sharing your lives so openly with us.

Thanks to my husband! For going on thirty years, you have been the wind beneath my wings. You always believe in me, even when I'm feeling shaky. For this book, you once again endured neglect without complaint, picking up my slack on household chores and money matters, and providing invaluable feedback. It is wonderful to share life and so much love with you.

References

Beller, Simone. *Kuno Bellers Entwicklungstabelle 0–9*. Berlin: Forschung und Fortbildung in der Kleinkindpädagogik, 2016.

Berger, Renate. *Grenzsteine der Entwicklung nach Michaelis: Entwicklungsbeobachtung und -einschätzung von Kindern im Alter von 0–6 Jahren*. Freiburg im Breisgau: Herder, 2023.

Bünder, Peter, Annegret Sirringhaus-Bündner, and Angela Helfer. *Lehrbuch der Marte Meo Methode: Entwicklungsförderung mit Videounterstützung*. Paderborn: Vandenhoeck & Ruprecht Verlag, 2022.

Cierpka, Manfred. *Frühe Kindheit 0–3 Jahre*. Berlin: Springer Medizin Verlag, 2014.

Die Praxismappe: Kindliche Spielschemata. Freiburg im Breisgau: Herder, 2019.

Görisch, Olaf. *KurzCHECK: Sprachliche Entwicklung von Kindern*. Hamburg: Verlag Handwerk und Technik, 2017.

Harms, Thomas. *Emotionelle Erste Hilfe*. Gießen: Psychosozial-Verlag, 2016.

Holodynski, Manfred, and Wolfgang Friedlmeier. *Emotionen: Entwicklung und Regulation*. Berlin: Springer Medizin Verlag, 2006.

Jenni, Oskar. *Die kindliche Entwicklung verstehen*. Berlin: Springer Verlag, 2021.

Kasten, Hartmut. *Entwicklungspsychologie: Lehrbuch für pädagogische Fachkräfte*. Haan: Verlag Europa-Lehrmittel, 2014.

Largo, Remo H. *Babyjahre*. Munich: Piper Verlag, 2015.

———. *Kinderjahre*. Munich: Piper Verlag, 2022.

Metzinger, Adalbert. *Entwicklungspsychologie Kompakt: 0–11 Jahre für sozialpädagogische Berufe*. Cologne: Bildungsverlag EINS GmbH, 2021.

Mock-Eibeck, Anja. *KurzCHECK: Kognitive Entwicklung von Kindern*. Hamburg: Verlag Handwerk und Technik, 2018.

———. *KurzCHECK: Motorische Entwicklung von Kindern*. Hamburg: Verlag Handwerk und Technik, 2018.

———. *KurzCHECK: Sozio-Emotionale Entwicklung von Kindern*. Hamburg: Verlag Handwerk und Technik, 2020.

Montessori, Maria. *Kinder sind anders*. Edited by Jürgen Overhoff. Translated by Percy Eckstein and Ulrich Weber. Stuttgart: Klett-Cotta, 2022.

———. *Praxishandbuch der Montessori-Methode*. Edited by Harald Ludwig. Freiburg im Breisgau: Herder, 2010.

Neubronner, Dagmar. *Der Neufeld-Ansatz für unsere Kinder*. Bremen: Genius Verlag, 2015.

Petermann, Franz, and Angelika Kullik. *Emotionsregulation im Kindesalter*. Göttingen: Hogrefe Verlag, 2012.

Petermann, Ulrike, Franz Petermann, and Ute Koglin. *Entwicklungsbeobachtung und -dokumentation EBD 3–48 Monate*. Mülheim an der Ruhr: Verlag an der Ruhr, 2021.

———. *Entwicklungsbeobachtung und -dokumentation EBD 48–72 Monate*. Berlin: Cornelsen Verlag, 2017.

Saumweber, Katja. *Schemas im Early Excellence Ansatz*. Berlin: Heinz und Heide Dürr Stiftung, 2014.

Schneider, Wolfgang. *Entwicklungspsychologie*. Edited by Ulmen Lindenberger. Weinheim: Beltz Verlag, 2012.

Siegler, Robert, Nancy Eisenberg, Judy De Loache, and Jenny Saffran. *Entwicklungspsychologie im Kindes-und Jugendalter*. Berlin: Springer Verlag, 2016.

Further Reading

Davies, Simone, and Junnifa Uzodike. *The Montessori Child: A Parent's Guide to Raising Capable Children with Creative Minds and Compassionate Hearts.* New York: Workman, 2024.

Doucleff, Michaeleen. *Hunt, Gather, Parent: What Ancient Cultures Can Teach Us About the Lost Art of Raising Happy, Helpful Little Humans.* New York: Avid Reader Press, 2021.

Gonzalez, Carlos. *My Child Won't Eat!: How to Enjoy Mealtimes Without Worry.* London: Pinter & Martin, 2012.

MacNamara, Deborah. *Rest, Play, Grow: Making Sense of Preschoolers (Or Anyone Who Acts Like One).* Vancouver: Aona Books, 2016.

Montessori, Maria. *The Montessori Method: Scientific Pedagogy as Applied to Child Education in "The Children's Houses" with Additions and Revisions by the Author.* Translated by Anne E. George. Second Edition. New York: Frederick A. Stokes Company, 1912.

Moralis, Shonda. *Breathe, Mama, Breathe: 5-Minute Mindfulness for Busy Moms.* New York: The Experiment, 2017.

Solter, Aletha. *Attachment Play: How to Solve Children's Behavior Problems with Play, Laughter, and Connection.* Goleta, CA: Shining Star Press, 2013.

———. *Tears and Tantrums: What to Do When Babies and Children Cry.* Goleta, CA: Shining Star Press, 1998.

Tsabary, Shefali. *The Conscious Parent: Transforming Ourselves, Empowering Our Children.* Vancouver: Namaste Publishing, 2010.

Index

A

Alex (case study)
    average vs. normal child development, 3–4, 80, 138, 194
    ball and progression of learning, 46, 63, 112, 154, 172, 211, 228
    phases of childhood development explained via, 2
anger and frustration. *See also* tantrums
    frustration tolerance, 122
    "no," 56–57, 115, 128–29
    of older children, 224–25
    of parents, 71–72, 191
    of toddlers, 84, 92–93
antisocial behavior, pre-social behavior vs., 109–10, 123–24
apologizing, 124, 181
arts and crafts. *See also* drawing
    2-year-olds, 147–48
    3-year-olds, 164–65
    5- and 6-year-olds, 218–19
attention
    attention span of toddlers, 15, 122
    object permanence and, 51–52
    overstimulation and, 27, 31–32, 34, 45, 61, 66
autonomy, 126–34
    age-appropriate tasks and, 104–5
    emotions and impulsiveness, 132–34
    feeding and, 96
    free will and, 100–102, 129–32
    learning independence with, 126
    Montessori on, 243–45
    natural limitations and setting boundaries, 127–29
    for planning and doing things, 83–85
    practicing, by 2-year-olds, 141–43
average vs. normal child development, 3–4, 80, 138, 194

B

babies, development of. *See also* development at 0–6 months; development at 6–12 months
    basic and developmental needs, defined, 67–68
    feelings at different developmental stages, 185
    Leading and Following for, 64–73
    6–12 months, 48–73
    12–18 months, 81–98
    sleep and, 74–77
babywearing consultants, 59–60
"bad words," using, 163, 200–201
balance
    balance bikes for, 152, 154, 171
    learning to walk and, 95–96
    practicing, 170
balls
    catching, 152, 170–71
    kicking, 110
    progression of learning with (Alex case study), 46, 63, 112, 154, 172, 211, 228
    throwing, 110, 227
basic needs of babies, defined, 67
beauty, sense of, 198–99
bedside sleepers, 45
bicycles
    balance bikes, 152, 154, 171
    riding, 209
blocks, stacking and arranging, 11–12, 87, 89, 105–6, 140
body language
    assessing danger and, 55
    eye contact, 34, 55, 91, 168–70, 230
    facial expression, reading, 55–56, 91–92, 150–51, 168–70
bonding
    baby's time apart from parent, 69

bonding (continued)
　bedtime and, 74
　following baby for, 70–71
　"over bonding," 70
　with 5- to 6-year-olds, 236–37
books, pre-reading activities with, 90–91, 108, 143–44
boredom
　overstimulation vs., in babies, 31
　of parents, 118, 123, 180
　of 3-year olds, 169–70
boundaries
　autonomy phase of toddlers and, 127–29
　creating "yes space," 115–17, 128–29, 177–78
　parent's safety rules, 56, 97, 100
　toddler's setting of, 107–8
brain. *See* cognitive development; thinking and play
breakable household items, 118–19

C

café example, 1
car and tow truck example, 189
carrying by toddlers (transporting play scheme), 86, 87, 106
carrying of babies, 36–38, 59–60, 67
categorical thinking, 103–4
cause and effect, baby's understanding of, 27, 35
cell phones, 55–56
change, understanding readiness for, 69–70
child behavior. *See also* childhood development; manipulation by young children
　interpreting, 2–3
　negative reinforcement of, 215
　positive reinforcement and, 239–40
　starting over, 5- and 6-year-olds and older children, 241
　translating (*see* narrating by parent)
childhood development. *See also individual developmental stages*
　average vs. normal, 3–4, 80, 138, 194
　early development and pace of, 9, 81, 132, 195
　reinforcement of, 11–12
　worldview of children vs. adults, 1–3
child proofing, 51, 59, 115–17
clapping, of syllables, 210
classification systems (math game), 217–18
climbing, 84, 104, 110, 117
cloud example, 182–83
cognitive development. *See also* thinking and play
　memory, 28, 144
　metacognitive dialogues, 120
　nursing for, 42
　prefrontal cortex and, 132

sleep and, 44
symbolic play by toddlers, 105–6
colic, 33
coloring. *See* drawing
communication. *See* body language; feelings and relationships; language and speech development; narrating by parent
communication, physical contact as, 0–6 months, 34–35, 36–38
competition, ages 5 and 6, 225–26
confidence, of child, 237–38
confidence, of parents, 10, 13–14
conflict
　fighting by 1-year-olds, 109–10, 124–25
　resolving, age 3, 167–68
　resolving, age 4, 204
connecting play scheme, 87, 164–65
conservation tasks, 157, 158
consultants
　babywearing, 59–60
　lactation, 40–42
　physical therapists, 33, 37
　sleep coaches, 75
containers
　conservation tasks, 157, 158
　filling and transferring, 88, 118–19, 153
　object permanence and, 51–52
cooperative play. *See* friends
co-sleeping, 74–77
crankiness. *See* tantrums
crawling, 58–59
crying
　causes of, in babies, 31–34
　comforting babies and, 67
　frustration of toddlers, 92–93
cups, 96

D

day care, as support system, 125
day care, for 2- and 3-year-olds, 155–56
decision making. *See* autonomy
desire
　free will and, 100–102, 129–32
　perceiving, 107–8
development at 0–6 months, 25–47
　at a glance, 46–47
　feelings and relationships, 29–35
　Leading and Following, 64–73
　movement, 35–38
　nursing, 39–42
　Quick Reference—Nursing, 41–42
　sleep, 43–45
　speech, 39
　thinking and play, 25–29
development at 6–12 months, 48–73
　at a glance, 63–64
　feelings and relationships, 53–58
　Leading and Following, 64–73
　movement, 58–59

Quick Reference—Carrying, 59–60
sleep, 62
speech, 61–62
thinking and play, 48–53
development at 12–18 months, 81–98
  at a glance, 98
  feeding oneself, 96
  feelings and relationships, 91–95
  learning by doing, 85–90
  movement, 95–96
  Quick Reference—Play Schemas, 86–89
  speech, 97
  thinking and play, 81–85
development at 18–24 months, 99–125
  at a glance, 112–13
  feelings and relationships, 106–10
  movement, 110–11
  Quick Reference—Thinking It Through, 119–20
  speech, 111–12
  thinking and play, 99–106
development at age 2, 139–56
  at a glance, 154–55
  feelings and relationships, 149–52
  feelings and tantrums, 182–91
  movement, 152–53
  Quick Reference—Day Care, 155–56
  Quick Reference—Soft Skills, 149
  speech, 153
  thinking and play, 139–48
development at age 3
  at a glance, 172
  feelings and relationships, 165–70
  feelings and tantrums, 182–91
  movement, 170–71
  Quick Reference—Play, 168–70
  Quick Reference—Theory of Conservation, 158
  speech, 171
  thinking and play, 157–65
development at age 4, 195–211
  at a glance, 211
  feelings and relationships, 203–8
  movement, 209
  Quick Reference—Attachment Play, 207–8
  Quick Reference—Lying, 196–98
  speech, 209–10
  thinking and play, 195–203
development at ages 5 and 6, 212–40
  at a glance, 228–29
  competition, 225–26
  feelings and relationships, 224–25
  movement, 226–27
  Quick Reference—Listening, 238–39
  Quick Reference—Math, 216–18
  Quick Reference—No Punishment, 222–23
  speech, 227–28

thinking and play, 212–24
diaper changing, toddlers and, 85
Die Matheflüsterin (*The Math Whisperer*, online course), 216
distance, managing, 54–56
distraction, repositioning and, 31–32
dividing and scattering play scheme, 87–88
Does My Child Need Me to Lead or to Follow? (Schwarzlmüller), 4–6
Doucleff, Michaeleen, 76–77
Doucleff, Rosy, 76–77
drawers, 50, 56, 89–90, 93–94, 104, 159
drawing
  coloring, age 3, 164–65
  schematic scenes, 199–200
  scribbling and, 91, 103, 148, 164
  of "tadpole people," 164, 199
dressing and undressing, 15–16, 110–11, 127–28, 153, 159

E

eating
  dexterity and, 111
  independence in, 118
  self-feeding, 96, 170
"either/or" choices, 101
embarrassment (self-consciousness, shame), 167, 203
empathy
  as undeveloped, 91–92, 109, 124
  in 3-year-olds, 165–66, 173, 187
  in 4-year-olds, 195–96
Ende, Michael, 238, 241
enveloping play scheme, 87
equipment
  bedside sleepers, 45
  carriers/slings, 59–60
  noise-canceling headphones for parents, 72
  strollers, 36–37
  toddler towers, 104, 117
experimentation. *See* thinking and play
eye contact, 34, 55, 91, 168–70, 230

F

facial expression, reading, 55–56, 91–92, 150–51, 168–70
false belief task experiment, 196–98
fear, 151, 167, 206–7
feelings and relationships. *See also* friends
  in babies, 29–35, 53–58
  in toddlers, 91–95, 106–10, 120–22, 132–34
  in 2-year-olds, 149–52
  in 3-year-olds, 165–70
  in 4-year-olds, 203–8
  in 5- and 6-year-olds, 224–25
  one thought/feeling at a time (2- and 3-year-olds), 136, 185–86

feelings and relationships (*continued*)
    regulation of emotion, 30, 44, 91, 165–66, 173, 187
    tantrums and, 182–91
    unpleasant feelings of parents, 71–72
fibbing (lying), 196–98, 219–20, 223–35
fighting. *See* conflict
filling and transferring play scheme, 88
flow state, 169
free will, desire and, 100–102, 129–32
friends
    babies and, 57–58
    competition with, 225–26
    cooperative play, 151–52, 167–70, 180–81
    friendship, in 4-year-olds, 204
    sharing and, 109, 151, 166–67
    toddlers and, 94–95, 108–9
frustration. *See* anger and frustration; tantrums

G

gender-neutral advice, 3, 6
Gresens, Regine, 41–42
grocery shopping examples, 9, 13–14, 66

H

habits, organizational rules as, 232–33
hands
    dexterity, of toddlers, 110–11
    discovery of, by babies, 27–28
    grasping of items, by babies, 49
    handedness, right vs. left, 96
    pincer grasp, 59, 96
happiness
    having fun with your child, 78
    independence and, for 2- and 3-year-olds, 177–78
    Interaction = Parenting + Fun, 7–10
    Quick Reference—Moments of Happiness, 19–20
    valuing, 71
head banging, 62
hip health, in babies, 36–38
hobbies, 5- and 6-year olds, 213
household tasks, age-appropriate
    for toddlers, 90, 104, 118
    for 2-year-olds, 145–46
    for 3-year-olds, 159–60
    for 4-year-olds, 201–2, 209
    for 5- and 6-year-olds, 215
humor, 120, 163, 176, 200–201
Hunt, Gather, Parent (Doucleff), 76–77

I

"I"/"me" concept, 52, 99, 106–8, 141, 149–52
immune system, nursing and, 41–42
impulsiveness, 56–57
    of toddlers, 82–83, 93–94, 116, 132–34
    of 5- and 6-year olds, 213

independence, supporting, 117–19, 126
Indigenous peoples, parenting by, 76–77
infancy. *See* babies
interaction between children and parents, 2–3, 7–10

L

lactation consultants, 40–42
language and speech development
    babies and, 39, 61–62
    toddlers and, 97, 111–12, 121–22, 153
    in 2-year-olds, 143–44, 153
    in 3-year-olds, 158, 162–63, 171
    in 4-year-olds, 200–201, 203, 209–10, 219
    in 5- and 6-year-olds, 227–28, 238
    listening and, 238–39
    metacognitive dialogues, 120
    "no," 56–57, 115, 128–29
    "okay" signals, 15
    "please" and "thank you," 203, 219
    reinforcement needed for, 12
Leading and Following, 7–20. *See also* narrating by parent
    about, 5
    excessive Leading by child, 16
    in babies, Following, 70–73
    in babies, Leading, 64–70
    in toddlers, autonomy phase, 131–32
    in toddlers, Following, 120–25
    in toddlers, Leading, 114–20, 142
    in toddlers, for work–life balance, 17
    in 2- and 3-year-olds, Following, 178–81
    in 2- and 3-year-olds, Leading, 178–81
    in 4- and 6-year-olds, Following, 235–40
    in 4- and 6-year-olds, Leading, 229–35
    interaction with children as, 2, 7–10
    moments of, defined, 11–12, 13–16, 18–19
    for moments of happiness, 19–20
liquids, conservation tasks, 157, 158
liquids, water play, 83
listening, 238–39
"logical consequences" (punishment vs. solutions), 222–24, 234–35
logical thinking, expectations for, 212
Ludwig, Frauke, 59–60
lying (fibbing), 196–98, 219–20, 223–35

M

magical thinking, 146–47, 151, 162, 176–77, 212–13
manipulation by young children
    history of misunderstanding of, 181
    incapability of, 69, 187–88
    smiling misunderstood as, 94, 133
Marte Meo method, 10
math skills
    in 2-year-olds, 144
    in 3-year-olds, 159–60, 162–63
    in 5- and 6-year-olds, 216–18

Maxi and the chocolate experiment, 196–98
memory, 28, 144
metacognitive dialogues, 120
Mishmash Method example, 8
modeling, by parents, 13–14, 181, 234
Momo (Ende), 238, 241
Montessori, Maria, 243–45
Montessori method, 116, 128
moral development
    lying (fibbing) and, 196–98, 219–20, 223–35
    moral code of 4-year-olds, 204
    "please" and "thank you," 203, 219
    punishment vs. solutions, 222–24, 234–35
    stealing and, 220–21
Moro reflex, 36, 65
motor development. *See also* hands; movement
    nursing for, 42
    positional relationships, 50
    stopping activity as, 95–96, 227
    in toddlers, 100
    wrist rotation, 153
mouth, putting items in, 49
movement
    in babies, 35–38, 58–59, 68
    in toddlers, 95–96, 108, 110–11
    in 2-year-olds, 152–53
    in 3-year-olds, 170–71
    in 4-year-olds, 209
    in 5- and 6-year-olds, 226–27

N

name recognition, 61
name writing, 218
narrating by parent
    babies, explaining what is happening, 17
    babies and shared moments, 72–73
    for feelings and tantrums, 186–87
    routines, 5- and 6-year-olds, 230–31
    saying what hands are doing, 15, 18, 22, 65, 114
    slowing down directions, 65–66
    vocabulary and, 2- and 3-year-olds, 174, 179
    vocabulary and, toddlers, 97
"naughty smile," 94, 133
nearness, managing, 54–56
needs
    basic, 67
    developmental, 67–68
    wants and, 142–43
negative attention, 215
"new city" example, 131
"no," 56–57, 115, 128–29
noise-canceling headphones for parents, 72
nursery rhymes, 39–40, 57–58
nursing, 39–42

O

object permanence, 27–28, 51–52
"okay" signals, 15
order of operations (math game), 216–17
organizational rules, for 5- and 6-year-olds, 231–33
orientation play scheme, 88
outdoor play, 148, 164–65
overstimulation, in babies, 27, 31–32, 34, 45, 61, 66
oxygen mask example, 71, 186–87

P

parallel play, 108–9
parenting concept, interaction vs., 7–8
parents. *See also* narrating by parent
    acknowledgment of child's task completion, 15–16
    anger of, 191
    baby's crying and stress of, 32–34
    boredom of, 118, 123, 180
    cell phone use by, 55–56
    confidence and, 10
    interaction between children and, 2–3, 7–10
    modeling by, 13–14, 181, 234
    parenting style and uniqueness of child, 205–7
    play schemas and role of, 88–89
    response to tantrums by (*see* tantrums)
    sleep of, 45
    stress of, 75–76
    support needed by, 68–69, 124–25
    unpleasant feelings of, 71–72
Perner, Josef, 196–98
physical therapists, 33, 37
Piaget, Jean, 158
pincer grasp, 59, 96
play and perception. *See also* friends; toys
    attachment play, 207–8, 215
    babies and, 27–28
    cooperative play development, age 3, 167–70
    free play and soft skills, 149, 235–36
    outdoor play, 148, 164–65
    parent's following of play, 2- and 3-year-olds, 179–81
    play vs. work, 5- and 6-year-olds, 225
    Quick Reference—Play Schemas, 12–18 months, 86–89
    role-playing, 147–48, 179–81, 202-2–203, 204, 207–8, 214
    supporting play, by toddlers, 122–24
    symbolic play, by toddlers, 105–6
"please," 203, 219
positional relationships, 50
positioning play scheme, 87
positive reinforcement, 239–40
postpartum recovery, nursing for, 42

preschoolers to kindergartners to first graders, 193–240. *See also* development at age 4; development at ages 5 and 6
   age 4, 195–211
   ages 5 and 6, 212–40
   Leading and Following for, 229–40
   looking forward to following stages, 241–45
pre-social vs. antisocial behavior, 109–10, 123–24
prisms (math game), 217
public tantrums, 184, 190–91

Q

questions. *See* language and speech development
Quick Reference
   Attachment Play, 207–8
   Carrying, 59–60
   Day Care, 155–56
   Listening, 238–39
   Lying, 196–98
   Math, 216–18
   Moments of Happiness, 19–20
   No Punishment, 222–23
   Nursing, 41–42
   Play, 168–70
   Play Schemas, 86–89
   Soft Skills, 149
   Theory of Conservation, 158
   Thinking It Through, 119–20

R

reading and writing
   books, pre-reading activities, 90–91, 108, 143–44
   name writing, 218
reflexes, of babies, 35–38, 60
regulation of emotion. *See also* feelings and relationships
   empathy and, age 3, 165–66, 173, 187
   expressing emotion vs., toddlers, 91
   falling asleep and self-soothing, babies, 44
   help needed for, babies, 30
reinforcement, negative, 215
reinforcement, positive, 239–40
repetition, 65–66, 90
responsibility, naming roles for, 214
rhymes, nursery, 39–40, 57–58
rhyming, 228
rocking, as calming, 31–32
role-playing. *See also* play and perception
   by 2-year-olds, 147–48, 179–81
   by 3-year-olds, 179–81
   by 4-year-olds, 202–3, 204, 207–8
   for responsibility, 214
rooting reflex, 35–36
rotation play scheme, 89

"rouge test," 99
routines
   for babies, 53, 62
   for 3-year-olds, 160
   for 4-year-olds, 204
   for 5- and 6-year-olds, 230–31
rows, concept of, 145
rules
   for toddlers, 82–83, 93–94, 109–10, 123–25, 129
   for 2- and 3-year-olds, 175–76
   for 5- and 6-year olds, 213–18, 231–33
   helping older children with external pressure, 241–45
   pre-social vs. antisocial behavior, 109–10, 123–24
running, by toddlers, 152

S

safety
   boundary setting for, 56, 97, 100
   child proofing spaces for, 51, 59, 115–17
   child's feeling of, 16
   climbing by toddlers and, 104, 110, 117
   rules of, for 5- and 6-year-olds, 231–33
   "yes space" and, 115–17, 128–29, 177–78
sand pie example, 102–3
Schwarzlmüller, Claudia, 4–6
security, creating by Leading, 64–65
self, sense of. *See* "I"/"me" concept
self-awareness of child, reinforcement needed for, 12
self-consciousness (embarrassment, shame), 167, 203
senses, of babies, 26–27, 28, 39–40
separation anxiety, 55, 74, 93
shame (self-consciousness, embarrassment), 167, 203
sharing, 109, 151, 166–67
shoes, 159
sight, of babies, 26–27, 49
silverware, 96, 118, 159–60, 209
sitting, 58
sleep
   by babies, 43–45, 62, 68, 74–77
   sleep coaches, 75
   by toddlers, 74–77, 119–20
smell, sense of, 27
smiling, after breaking rules, 94, 133
smiling, first instance of, 25
social behavior. *See* feelings and relationships; friends
socks, 127–28, 159
soft skills, free play and, 149, 235–36
songs, 39–40, 57–58
sorting by 2-year-olds, 139–40, 145
sorting play scheme, 88
Spannagel, Janna, 216–18
spoons, 96, 118

sports, 5- and 6-year olds, 213
standing and pulling up, 58–59
startling reflex, 36, 65
stem cells, maternal, 42
step-to pattern, by toddlers, 110, 152
stomach pain, from crying, 33
stopping, ability of, 95–96, 227
"stranger danger," 54–56
strangers, self-consciousness and, 167
strollers, 36–37
structure, created by parent, 16, 115–17
sustained shared thinking, 119–20
symbolic play, 105–6

T

tantrums, 182–91
    car and tow truck example, 189
    cloud example for, 182–83
    feelings, at different developmental stages, 185–86
    feelings, identifying, 186–87
    feelings, shared, 187–88
    negative feelings leading to, 182–85
    in public places, 184, 190–91
    responding to, 188–91, 235
taste, sense of, 28
temperature sensitivity, 27
"terrible twos"/"toddler defiance," 126. *See also* autonomy
"thank you," 203, 219
theory of mind, lying and, 196–98
thinking and play. *See also* magical thinking; play and perception
    drawers used for play, 50, 56, 89–90, 93–94, 104, 159
    in babies, 25–29, 48–53, 99–106
    in toddlers, 81–85
    in 2-year-olds, 139–48
    in 3-year-olds, 157–65
    in 4-year-olds, 195–203
    in 5- and 6-year olds, 212–24
    logical thinking, expectations for, 212
throwing of items, by babies, 46, 57–58
time, experience of, 146–47
    in babies, 28–29
    in 2-year-olds, 146–47
    in 3-year-olds, 146–47, 161–62
    in 4-year-olds, 199–200
    in 5- and 6-year olds, 213
toddlers, 79–134. *See also* development at 12–18 months; development at 18–24 months
    12–18 months, 81–98
    18–24 months, 99–125
    average vs. normal development in, 80, 139
    feelings at different developmental stages, 185–86
    sleep and, 74–77

toddler to preschooler development. *See also* development at age 2; development at age 3
    feelings and tantrums, 182–91
    Leading and Following, 173–81
    2-year-olds, 139–56
    3-year-olds, 157–81
toddler towers, 104, 117
tools, use of, 84
touch (tactile system), carrying and, 59–60. *See also* hands
toys. *See also* balls
    blocks, 11–12, 87, 89, 105–6
    containers as, 51–52, 88, 118–19, 153, 157, 158
    experimentation in babies with, 52–53
    household items as, 51–52, 72–73, 83, 88, 98, 106
    household items as, breakable, 118–19
    rotation of, 123, 180
transforming play scheme, 87
transitioning between activities, 174–75
transporting play scheme, 86, 87, 106
tummy time, 38, 58

U

uniqueness of individual children
    average vs. normal child development, 3–4, 80, 138, 194
    parenting style and, 205–7
    personality of babies, 66–67

V

vocabulary. *See* language and speech development

W

walking, 85–90, 95–96, 110
wants vs. needs, 178–79
water, playing with, 83
waving, 61–62
Wimmer, Heinz, 196–98
work–life balance for toddlers, 17
World Health Organization (WHO), 41–42

Y

"yes space," creating, 115–17, 128–29, 177–78

About the Author

CLAUDIA SCHWARZLMÜLLER is one of Germany's leading parenting experts and a child psychologist who has been working with parents for over twenty years.

kinderdolmetscher.com | ⬚ **kinderdolmetscher**